THE UNFOLDING STORY

Resources for reflective worship on the Old Testament

NICK FAWCETT

Kevin
Mayhew

First published in 2000 by
KEVIN MAYHEW LTD
Buxhall, Stowmarket, Suffolk IP14 3BW

0 1 2 3 4 5 6 7 8 9

ISBN 1 84003 604 4
Catalogue No 1500376

Cover design by Jonathan Stroulger
Edited by Katherine Laidler
Typesetting by Louise Selfe

*To the members and congregation
of Belle Vue Baptist Church, Southend-on-Sea,
who offered so much friendship, support and encouragement
to me during my formative years*

ABOUT THE AUTHOR

Nick Fawcett was born in 1957. He studied Theology at Bristol University and Regent's Park College, Oxford. His early years of ministry were spent in Somerset and Lancashire, and from 1989 to 1996 he was Minister of Gas Green Baptist Church, Cheltenham. From November 1996 to June 1999 he served as Toc H Chaplain and Development Officer for Wales and the West of England.

He is now concentrating full time on his career as a writer, proof-reader and indexer. His books to date are *No Ordinary Man* (1997), *Prayers For All Seasons* (1998), *Are You Listening?* (1998) and *Getting It Across* (1999), all published by Kevin Mayhew. He has also written the texts for the *Best Loved Choral Melodies Choral Collection* (1999) and had four hymns chosen for inclusion in the Churches Together Millennium Hymn Book *New Start Hymns and Songs* (1999), both also published by Kevin Mayhew.

He lives with his wife, Deborah, and their two young children, Samuel and Katie, in Wellington, Somerset.

CONTENTS

INTRODUCTION

The meditations, readings and prayers in this book were originally published in *Grappling with God,* a series of four books written as a tool to help individuals and small groups wrestle with some of the complex issues thrown up by the Old Testament and, at the same time, to discover some of its inexhaustible riches. *The Unfolding Story* aims to broaden the scope of the material, recognising that, for all too many, the Old Testament represents a closed book. Not only do the majority rarely if ever take time to read it; the truth is that they see little reason for doing so.

This book, therefore, follows a format specifically designed for use in public worship and/or quiet days. The majority of the 80 meditations have been woven into themed orders of service ready, as it were, for off-the-shelf use. An introduction has been added to each service, together with opening and closing prayers related to the subject of the service. The introductions for the meditations in *Grappling with God* have been rewritten here, where necessary, to serve as links in the service, once again tailored to the overall theme. Appropriate hymns are also suggested. All that needs to be added are prayers of intercession and space for an offering if the latter is required. Those using the material for a quiet day may like to observe a time of silence in place of the hymns. The few meditations not included in the service outlines can be used as stand-alone reflections during other times of worship.

The book is divided into four parts, representing the four main traditions within the Old Testament: Law, History, Wisdom and the Prophets. 'Law and promise' focuses chiefly on Genesis and Exodus while also dipping briefly into the books of Judges and Joshua. It moves from Creation to the founding fathers of the Jewish nation, from the Great Flood to the giving of the Law, from the promise given to Abraham to the first tentative steps into the Promised Land. 'Conquest and kingdom' takes us to the conquest of Palestine and on to the time of Esther and her courageous stand on behalf of her people. It covers such celebrated characters as Samson, Samuel, David and Solomon, some of the legendary names of the Bible. The third section explores three strands within the Old Testament: 'Wisdom, songs and stories'. It explores the books of Job, Proverbs and Ecclesiastes, the Psalms and the Song of Solomon, and, finally, the book of Daniel. We find here some of the most distinctive and startling books in the Old Testament, at times almost breathtaking in the frankness with which they tackle some of the great mysteries of life. To the unsuspecting reader they may come as something of a shock, yet many gain enormous encouragement through finding some of the questions they want to ask, but dare not, echoed in the pages of Scripture. Finally, in 'The Word of the Lord' we explore the message of the prophets and also the work of Ezra and Nehemiah, although the latter do not strictly fit into that category. Some will be familiar, not least the prophet Isaiah whose often unforgettable words have come to be seen as an integral part of the gospel itself. Others are less well known: Haggai, Zephaniah, Habakkuk, Malachi to name but a few. How many are familiar with these books? How many have even read them? Yet each is a part of Scripture and each has a message for us today.

It has to be admitted that there is much in the Old Testament which is difficult to come to terms with – a multitude of passages which can seem either dull and primitive or downright barbaric by Christian standards. To reconcile the God we find there with the God revealed in Jesus Christ is sometimes not easy. Yet to abandon the Old Testament because of such difficulties is to miss out on untold riches. Imagine Christmas or Holy Week without the great words of the prophet Isaiah: 'The people who walked in darkness have seen a great light'; 'He was wounded for our transgressions, crushed for our iniquities; upon him was the punishment that made us whole'. Imagine Good Friday without the unforgettable cry of the Psalmist: 'My God, my God, why have you forsaken me?' Imagine Pentecost without the wonderful vision of Joel: 'Your sons and daughters shall prophesy, your old men shall dream dreams, and your young men shall see visions.' Like it or not, the Christian faith has its roots firmly in the Old Testament, and it is in the light of its pages that, at least in part, the testimony of the New must be interpreted.

It is not just in the Christian seasons that the Old Testament comes into its own. Within its pages are some of the most unforgettable stories ever told: Noah and the Great Flood, Esau and Jacob, Moses crossing the Red Sea, Samson and Delilah, David and Goliath, Daniel in the lions' den, Shadrach, Meshach and Abednego, Jonah and the whale – and so we could go on. Here are tales which have captured the imagination of people across the centuries, and rightly so, for as well as communicating deep theological truths, they also speak directly to our human condition. Time and again we can identify with the characters in question, seeing something of ourselves in each one. It is, perhaps, in the raw human emotions so often displayed and the almost brutal honesty before God that the Old Testament's greatest strength lies. So much of what we see there mirrors what we feel and experience ourselves.

Every individual will approach the complexities thrown up by the Old Testament in their own way. For me they reflect a nation's grappling with God across the centuries. From a crude awareness of his nature way back in the mists of time, we move inexorably forward to an ever-deepening understanding of his greatness, love and mercy, all brought together in the anticipation of the promised Messiah. Not that the coming of Jesus means our picture of God is complete, for we must wrestle in our turn if we are to move forward in our journey of faith. God may be fully revealed in Christ but, as the Apostle Paul reminds us, as yet we see only in part. Like those who have gone before us, we must press on towards the kingdom he holds in store. In short, we too must grapple with God.

NICK FAWCETT

PART ONE

MEDITATIONS

LAW AND PROMISE

1
DON'T BLAME ME, IT WASN'T MY FAULT!

Adam

Reading – Genesis 3:1-13

Now the serpent was more crafty than any other wild animal that the Lord God had made. He said to the woman, 'Did God say, "You shall not eat from any tree in the garden"?' The woman said to the serpent, 'We may eat of the fruit of the trees in the garden; but God said, "You shall not eat of the fruit of the tree that is in the middle of the garden, nor shall you touch it, or you shall die".' But the serpent said to the woman, 'You will not die; for God knows that when you eat of it your eyes will be opened, and you will be like God knowing good and evil.' So when the woman saw that the tree was good for food, and that it was a delight to the eyes, and that the tree was to be desired to make one wise, she took of its fruit and ate; and she also gave some to her husband, who was with her, and he ate. Then the eyes of both were opened, and they knew that they were naked; and they sewed fig leaves together and made loincloths for themselves.

They heard the sound of the Lord God walking in the garden at the time of the evening breeze, and the man and his wife hid themselves from the presence of the Lord God among the trees of the garden. But the Lord God called to the man, and said to him, 'Where are you?' He said, 'I heard the sound of you in the garden, and I was afraid, because I was naked; and I hid myself.' He said, 'Who told you that you were naked? Have you eaten from the tree of which I commanded you not to eat?' The man said, 'The woman whom you gave to be with me, she gave me fruit from the tree, and I ate.' Then the Lord God said to the woman, 'What is this that you have done?' The woman said, 'The serpent tricked me, and I ate.'

Meditation

Don't blame me, it wasn't my fault!
All right, I did wrong –
 I can see that now, looking back –

but at the time there seemed no harm in it,
   certainly nothing to get steamed up about.
Just one tiny fruit, that's all it was,
   so why the fuss?
It wasn't *my* idea either, that's what makes it worse –
   it was that wretched woman,
   the one God supposedly gave me for company.
Some help she turned out to be!
'Go on,' she said, 'just one bite. It won't hurt.'
I tried to refuse, honestly,
   but she wouldn't take no for an answer,
   teasing,
   tempting,
   sulking,
   pleading,
   until at last, against my better judgement, I gave in,
   anything for a bit of peace.
Yes, I should have been stronger,
   I can't quibble with that.
I should have listened to the voice of conscience
   and done what I knew to be right.
But I didn't, and it's too late now for regrets,
   hard done by though I've been.
I was pushed into it,
   a victim of circumstance,
   caught up in a web outside my own making.
Not that it was all down to Eve –
   no, it's God I ultimately blame.
What was he thinking of,
   putting that tree there in the first place?
There was no need, surely?
We had enough and more than enough,
   so why put temptation in our way?
He must have known the risks –
   probably even saw our fall coming –
   so what chance did we have,
   what hope of sticking to the straight and narrow?
If you ask me, we got a raw deal,
   almost, you might say, a miscarriage of justice.
But give me credit,
   however wronged I may have been,
   however unfairly treated,

there's one thing I can promise you:
you won't catch me making excuses –
not likely!

Prayer

Lord,
    we don't like being wrong.
It hurts our pride and goes against the grain
    to admit we've made a mistake.
Far easier to blame somebody else,
    to look for a reason which excuses our actions.
'We were forced into it', we tell ourselves,
    'our hands tied . . . ',
    but deep down we know
    that the responsibility to choose is ours,
    no one else's,
    each of us answerable for our own actions.
Forgive us, Lord,
    for those times we have shifted the blame
    on to others.
Forgive us
    for hiding behind falsehoods and half-truths
    rather than being honest with ourselves.
And forgive us
    for letting such excuses become so much part of us
    we no longer realise we are making them.
Teach us to make our own decisions
    wisely and with integrity;
    and when we go wrong,
    give us courage to admit it,
    and humility to accept our dependence
    on your unfailing grace.
Amen.

2

WHAT HAVE I DONE?

God

Reading – Genesis 3:14-19, 22-24

The Lord God said to the serpent, 'Because you have done this, cursed are you among all animals and among all wild creatures; upon your belly you shall go, and dust you shall eat all the days of your life. I will put enmity between you and the woman, and between your offspring and hers; he will strike your head, and you will strike his heel.'

To the woman he said, 'I will greatly increase your pangs in childbearing; in pain you shall bring forth children, yet your desire shall be for your husband, and he shall rule over you.'

And to the man he said, 'Because you have listened to the voice of your wife, and have eaten of the tree about which I commanded you, "You shall not eat of it," cursed is the ground because of you; in toil you shall eat of it all the days of your life; thorns and thistles it shall bring forth for you; and you shall eat the plants of the field. By the sweat of your face you shall eat bread until you return to the ground, for out of it you were taken; you are dust, and to dust you shall return.'

Then the Lord God said, 'See, the man has become like one of us, knowing good and evil; and now, he might reach out his hand and take also from the tree of life, and eat, and live for ever' – therefore the Lord God sent him forth from the garden of Eden, to till the ground from which he was taken. He drove out the man; and at the east of the garden of Eden he placed the cherubim, and a sword flaming and turning to guard the way to the tree of life.

Meditation

What have I done?
What *have* I done?
Day after day I look at the world I've made,
   intended to be so beautiful,
   so special,
   and I see hatred,

violence,
greed,
corruption –
so much that maims and mutilates,
destroying hope,
denying life.
Can you imagine what it feels like,
living with the awfulness of ultimate responsibility,
and bearing that burden not just for a fleeting span
but for all eternity?
I don't think you can.
But, believe me, whatever pain you've endured,
whatever sorrow,
whatever heartbreak,
it can never touch the agony
of watching your creation slowly tearing itself apart.
Was it all a mistake?
Some will say so, and I can't blame them.
Yet I had love to give and life to share –
would it have been any more moral to keep that to myself?
I could, of course, have made you like puppets,
every thought controlled,
every action directed,
but is that what you'd have wanted? –
unable to think or feel,
deprived of joy for lack of sorrow,
of love for lack of hate,
of hope for lack of fear,
of pleasure for lack of pain.
Don't tell me I'm not to blame,
for it just won't do.
I made you, didn't I? –
mine the hand that brought you into being,
so though the mistakes may be yours
the fault surely is mine?
Yet don't think I've given up on you,
for, perfect or imperfect,
I love you just the same,
and I'm going to go on loving you for as long as it takes,
giving my all for you,
my very life,
until the broken threads of creation

are woven together into a glorious new tapestry,
and we are one, you and I,
united in paradise,
now and for ever.

Prayer

God of all,
    we look at our world sometimes –
    at its suffering and sorrow,
    its hurt and heartbreak –
    and we don't understand why you let it happen.
We see hatred and evil,
    greed and corruption,
    so much that frustrates your will
    and denies your purpose,
    and we cannot help but ask,
    where are you in the face of it?
Our minds struggle
    to take in the great mysteries of life
    for we ourselves are a part of your fallen creation.
Yet though we cannot always make sense of your will,
    we believe that your nature is love
    and that the time will come
    when our questions will be answered
    and your purpose revealed.
Until then, help us to live with paradox
    and trust in your eternal promises,
    knowing that every moment of every day
    you are at work,
    striving to bring creation to perfection.
Amen.

3

IF ONLY I'D LISTENED

Cain

Reading – Genesis 4:2b-10

Now Abel was a keeper of sheep, and Cain a tiller of the ground. In the course of time Cain brought to the Lord an offering of the fruit of the ground, and Abel for his part brought of the firstlings of his flock, their fat portions. And the Lord had regard for Abel and his offering, but for Cain and his offering he had no regard. So Cain was very angry, and his countenance fell. The Lord said to Cain, 'Why are you angry, and why has your countenance fallen? If you do well, will you not be accepted? And if you do not do well, sin is lurking at the door; its desire is for you, but you must master it.'

Cain said to his brother Abel, 'Let us go out to the field.' And when they were in the field, Cain rose up against his brother Abel, and killed him. Then the Lord said to Cain, 'Where is your brother Abel?' He said, 'I do not know; am I my brother's keeper?' And the Lord said, 'What have you done? Listen; your brother's blood is crying out to me from the ground!'

Meditation

If only I'd listened,
    allowed time for my temper to cool,
    how different it might have been.
He tried to warn me,
    but I wouldn't listen,
    too piqued at my gift being snubbed,
    too full of resentment to listen to reason.
It seemed so unfair, that was the trouble,
    for I'd made my offering in good faith –
    the best of my crop,
    specially selected,
    fit for a prince –
    so when God turned it down I was furious,
    more hurt than I can tell you.
What was wrong with it, I wanted to know?

Why was Abel's gift accepted
and mine turned down?
It was one law for him and another for me,
that's how it seemed.
And somehow, the more I thought about it,
the more it got to me,
nagging away like a festering wound.
Was he gloating, I wondered,
sniggering slyly behind my back?
Or worse, was he feeling sorry for me,
striving to keep the look of pity from his eyes?
It was quite unfounded, of course,
all a phantom of my fevered imagination,
but once the seed was sown
there was no controlling it,
suspicion growing out of all proportion
until I could think of nothing else.
And as the sense of injustice mounted within me,
so too did the anger,
a dark and ugly cloud, full of menace.
I wanted revenge,
to vent my spleen,
so I lured him out into the fields,
determined to confront him.
Did I mean to kill him?
I like to think not.
I was going to knock him about a bit,
that's what I tell myself,
teach him a lesson,
show him who was boss,
but when rage was let loose it ran amok –
blind to reason,
blind to everything.
He had no idea what was coming,
that's what haunts me.
As we walked out together,
my hand on his shoulder,
there was no hint of mistrust,
not even the slightest hesitation;
just a look of innocent enquiry –
but it served only to fan the flames,
and with one blow I struck him down.

I thought the sentence harsh afterwards,
    even presumed to complain, would you believe?
As though I deserved better,
    sympathy,
    understanding.
Little did I realise the punishment yet to come,
    for I've had to live since then,
    day after day,
    with the knowledge of my foul crime,
    and that memory will stay with me,
    torturing my soul,
    until the day I die.
Lord, have mercy upon me.

Prayer

Gracious God,
    you are slow to anger,
    swift to bless,
    full of mercy,
    abounding in love.
Forgive us that we are so different,
    easily roused,
    reluctant to let go of a grievance,
    unwilling to forgive,
    grudging in showing affection.
Forgive us all those times
    we have nursed bitterness in our hearts,
    resentful of the success or good fortune of others.
Forgive us those many occasions
    we have acted foolishly,
    living to regret mistakes made in haste.
Help us to recognise
    that envy has no place in our lives,
    serving only to poison and destroy.
And help us to recognise equally
    that, though anger may sometimes be justified,
    we must learn also to control it
    before *it* controls *us*.
Amen.

4
'A RIGHT ONE WE'VE GOT HERE!'

Noah

Reading – Genesis 6:11-22

Now the earth was corrupt in God's sight and the earth was filled with violence. And God saw that the earth was corrupt; for all flesh had corrupted its ways upon the earth. And God said to Noah, 'I have determined to make an end of all flesh, for the earth is filled with violence because of them; now I am going to destroy them along with the earth. Make yourself an ark of cypress wood; make rooms in the ark, and cover it inside and out with pitch. This is how you are to make it: the length of the ark three hundred cubits, its width fifty cubits, and its height thirty cubits. Make a roof for the ark, and finish it to a cubit above; and put the door of the ark in its side; make it with lower, second, and third decks. For my part, I am going to bring a flood of waters on the earth, to destroy from under heaven all flesh in which is the breath of life; everything that is on the earth shall die. But I will establish my covenant with you; and you shall come into the ark, you, your sons, your wife, and your sons' wives with you. And of every living thing, of all flesh, you shall bring two of every kind into the ark, to keep them alive with you; they shall be male and female. Of the birds according to their kinds, and of the animals according to their kinds, of every creeping thing of the ground according to its kind, two of every kind shall come in to you, to keep them alive. Also take with you every kind of food that is eaten, and store it up; and it shall serve as food for you and for them.' Noah did this; he did all that God commanded him.

Meditation

'A right one we've got here!'
That's what they were thinking,
   and, quite frankly, I could hardly blame them.
Let's face it, building a boat in the middle of the desert,
   it's not something you see every day, is it? –
   an unusual hobby to put it mildly.

So it wasn't long before a crowd gathered
    and the laughter started,
    playful at first,
    good-natured banter mostly,
    but before long turning ugly.
They realised I was serious, I suppose,
    that I actually expected to use the thing,
    and that's when everything changed –
    first the sarcasm,
    then the insults,
    then the downright abuse.
'Who do you think you are?' they shouted.
'Get off your high horse you smug-faced hypocrite!'
I can repeat that bit – not the rest –
    but when I tell you
    we had to keep watch through the night,
    maybe that gives some idea of what I faced.
It was hard, believe me,
    and there were times, many times,
    when I felt like giving up,
    abandoning the whole thing
    and taking my chance with the rest.
What if I was wrong, I asked myself.
What if I'd dreamt the whole thing up?
A right fool I'd look then.
It may sound heroic looking back,
    but, believe me, there's nothing pleasant
    about being the odd one out –
    when you're the one on the spot
    I can assure you it's no joke.
Yet I believed God had spoken,
    that he'd called me to respond in faith,
    and when I looked around me –
    at the state of society,
    evil and injustice everywhere –
    there was only one option,
    only one response I could possibly make.
Not that I took any pleasure in what happened next –
    when the wind blew and the storms began,
    when the rain fell and the floods rose –
    men, women, children everywhere –
    yelling,

screaming,
   sobbing,
   dying.
It was awful,
   a sight I pray never to see again,
   and despite what some may say,
   I swear it broke God's heart as much as mine.
It could have been me, that's the sobering thing –
   had I given in to the pressure,
   swallowed my principles and followed the crowd,
   I'd have shared the same fate –
   me and my loved ones.
They thought I was mad,
   a religious nutcase,
   and I'd begun to believe they might be right;
   but I realise now,
   painful though the lesson was,
   that to this world, all too often,
   the wisdom of God looks like foolishness.

Prayer

Loving God,
   you call us to distinctive discipleship,
   a way of life that sets us apart from others;
   not a self-righteous superiority
   based on judgemental intolerance,
   but a quality of love and willingness to serve
   which shows itself in everything we say and do.
Forgive us that we fall so far short of that calling,
   compromising what we believe for fear of mockery.
Forgive us that we go along with the way of the crowd
   rather than follow the demanding way of Christ.
Speak to us now,
   challenge our complacency,
   and give us the courage to be different.
Amen.

5
HANG ON A MINUTE, I SAID

Abram

Reading – Genesis 12:1-5a

Now the Lord said to Abram, 'Go from your country and your kindred and your father's house to the land that I will show you. I will make of you a great nation, and I will bless you, and make your name great, so that you will be a blessing. I will bless those who bless you, and the one who curses you I will curse; and in you all the families of the earth shall be blessed.'

So Abram went, as the Lord had told him; and Lot went with him. Abram was seventy-five years old when he departed from Haran. Abram took his wife Sarai and his brother's son Lot, and all the possessions that they had gathered, and the persons whom they had acquired in Haran; and they set forth to go to the land of Canaan.

Meditation

Hang on a minute, I said,
    let's get this straight:
    you're not serious, surely?
A trifle familiar, you might say,
    and you'd be right, I realise that now,
    but at the time I'd no idea who I was talking to,
    just this inner conviction
    that I should pick up sticks,
    head off to goodness knows where,
    and start again.
It was a lot to ask, wasn't it? –
    enough to make anyone in their right mind think twice.
Yet that's how it was for me,
    just this voice in my head
    telling me to pack my bags
    and head off into the wilderness,
    away to a land he would show me.

Was I simply restless, I wondered –
   the years bringing with them the urge to move on?
No, it wasn't that –
   deep down I knew, despite the doubts,
   that God was speaking to me –
   God as I'd never known him,
   never imagined him,
   never encountered him before.
And I was hooked, pure and simple,
   for here was a God unlike any other –
   mighty,
   majestic,
   mysterious –
   not *shaped* by our hands but *shaping* our lives,
   not *ours* to control but controlling *all*;
   a God beyond expression,
   sovereign over history,
   ruler over heaven and earth.
It was exhilarating and terrifying,
   a moment of promise, yet also of dread,
   for here was a call to leave home and livelihood,
   to tear up roots and forsake everything familiar –
   then venture out into the unknown.
Do you realise what that meant?
It wasn't just *me* involved, but my loved ones,
   them too asked to make the sacrifice
   and take the step of faith.
A lot to expect of anyone,
   even had we known the way ahead.
Yet they agreed,
   willingly,
   gladly,
   without a moment's hesitation,
   for they saw, so they told me,
   a light in my eyes
   and a flame in my heart,
   impossible to resist.
It was a hard journey,
   longer than we ever expected,
   with many a trial and tribulation along the way,
   but there were blessings too,
   surprises I could never have dreamt of,

and the greatest of all
is the lesson I've learned never to fear the future,
for however uncertain it may be,
and whatever it may bring,
I realise now we must keep on travelling,
journeying in faith,
until our dying day.

Prayer

Lord,
    you do not call us to a destination
    but a journey;
    a journey of continual new discoveries
    and new experiences of your love.
Save us from ever thinking we have arrived,
    from imagining we know all there is to know
    or that we have exhausted the riches
    of everything you would reveal to us.
Open our eyes to the great adventure of life
    and to the unfathomable mysteries of your purpose,
    and so help us to be a pilgrim people,
    travelling in faith as Abraham travelled before us,
    until we reach at last the kingdom
    you hold in store for all your people.
Amen.

6

COULD I HAVE GONE THROUGH WITH IT?

Abraham

Reading – Genesis 22:1-13

After these things God tested Abraham. He said to him, 'Abraham!' And he said, 'Here I am.' He said, 'Take your son, your only son Isaac, whom you love, and go to the land of Moriah, and offer him there as a burnt offering on one of the mountains that I shall show you.' So Abraham rose early in the morning, saddled his donkey, and took two of his young men with him, and his son Isaac; he cut the wood for the burnt offering, and set out and went to the place in the distance that God had shown him. On the third day Abraham looked up and saw the place far away. Then Abraham said to his young men, 'Stay here with the donkey; the boy and I will go over there; we will worship, and then we will come back to you. Abraham took the wood of the burnt offering and laid it on his son Isaac, and he himself carried the fire and the knife. So the two of them walked on together. Isaac said to his father Abraham, 'Father!' And he said, 'Here I am, my son.' He said, 'The fire and the wood are here, but where is the lamb for a burnt offering?' Abraham said, 'God himself will provide the lamb for a burnt offering, my son.' So the two of them walked on together.

When they came to the place that God had shown him, Abraham built an altar there and laid the wood in order. He bound his son Isaac, and laid him on the altar, on top of the wood. Then Abraham reached out his hand and took the knife to kill his son. The angel of the Lord called to him from heaven, and said, 'Abraham, Abraham!' And he said, 'Here I am.' He said, 'Do not lay your hand on the boy or do anything to him; for now I know that you fear God, since you have not withheld your son, your only son, from me.' And Abraham looked up and saw a ram, caught in a thicket by its horns. Abraham went and took the ram and offered it up as a burnt offering instead of his son.

Meditation

Could I have gone through with it –
    slaughtered my son as a sacrifice to God?
If I'm honest, no,
    the very idea horrific,
    unimaginable!
I loved that boy more than my own self,
    the most precious thing in the world to me,
    and to think of plunging in the knife,
    watching the flames consume him –
    it was too much,
    more than I could ever bear.
So I shut the thought out,
    hoping and praying
    that when the moment of truth came
    God would call a halt,
    come up with something else I could sacrifice instead.
What if he hadn't, I hear you ask?
And the answer? –
    I think I'd have killed *myself*,
    for there was no way I could have lived with my conscience
    had I harmed the lad.
But it didn't come to that, God be praised –
    at the last moment a ram caught my eye,
    its horns caught in a thicket –
    and I knew that God had simply been testing me all along,
    measuring the depth of my devotion
    and the extent of my faith.
But I'll never forget that expression on my son's face –
    that heart-breaking mixture
    of fear, confusion and disbelief
    as I stood over him,
    knife poised,
    sweat pouring from my brow,
    looking down with such dreadful anguish.
I think I was shaking more than him!
We laughed about it afterwards,
    made out it was all a joke,
    and thankfully he believed me –
    or wanted to anyway –
    but it took a long time

before I could look him in the eye again.
And as for Sarah, I never breathed a word of it,
    nor Isaac either, thank God.
I passed the test though, so it seems,
    God having blessed me since more than I deserve.
Yet I know in my heart,
    as I'm sure he knows too,
    that though I love him dearly,
    with heart and soul and mind,
    I love my boy more.
I'm just grateful that, in his mercy, God understood,
    pushing me hard, but not beyond my limit,
    for let's face it, offering your love is one thing,
    but giving your own son to show it –
    surely nobody could love enough for that!

Prayer

Gracious God,
    you call us to a life of self-sacrifice,
    service and dedication to you.
Yet you know our weakness,
    and understand how hard we find it
    to offer even a little, let alone much.
We thank you that in your mercy
    you came to us through your only Son,
    the Word made flesh,
    and through him
    made the sacrifice we are incapable of making;
    an offering which alone can atone for our sin.
Gracious God,
    we praise you for your love which knows no bounds,
    which gave all
    so that we may receive life in all its fullness.
Receive our grateful worship,
    and consecrate our lives to your service.
Amen.

7

LET'S FACE IT, I WAS A COMPLETE FOOL

Esau

Reading – Genesis 25:29-30; 27:30-38

Once when Jacob was cooking a stew, Esau came in from the field, and he was famished. Esau said to Jacob, 'Let me eat some of that red stuff, for I am famished!' . . . Jacob said, 'First sell me your birthright.' Esau said, 'I am about to die; of what use is a birthright to me?' Jacob said, 'Swear to me first.' So he swore to him, and sold his birthright to Jacob. Then Jacob gave Esau bread and lentil stew, and he ate and drank, and rose and went his way. Thus Esau despised his birthright . . .

(Some time later, Jacob, with the connivance of his mother, has successfully appropriated his father's blessing.)

As soon as Isaac had finished blessing Jacob, when Jacob had scarcely gone out from the presence of his father Isaac, his brother Esau came in from his hunting. He also prepared savoury food, and brought it to his father. And he said to his father, 'Let my father sit up and eat of his son's game, so that you may bless me.' His father Isaac said to him, 'Who are you?' He answered, 'I am your firstborn son, Esau.' Then Isaac trembled violently, and said, 'Who was it then that hunted game and brought it to me, and I ate it all before you came, and I have blessed him? – yes, and blessed he shall be!' When Esau heard his father's words, he cried out with an exceedingly great and bitter cry, and said to his father, 'Bless me, me also, father!' But he said, 'Your brother came deceitfully, and he has taken away your blessing.' Esau said, 'Is he not rightly named Jacob? For he has supplanted me these two times. He took away my birthright; and look, now he has taken away my blessing.' Then he said, 'Have you not reserved a blessing for me?' Isaac answered Esau, 'I have already made him your lord, and I have given him all his brothers as servants, and with grain and wine I have sustained him. What then can I do for you, my son?' Esau said to his father, 'Have you only one blessing, father? Bless me, me also, father!' And Esau lifted up his voice and wept.

Meditation

Let's face it, I was a complete fool.
It doesn't help much to admit it,
    for I still feel angry sometimes,
    even bitter –
    cheated so shamelessly out of my rightful inheritance –
    but I had it coming to me, it has to be said,
    victim finally of my own folly.
Yes, there was a certain naiveté, fair enough,
    a simple, almost childish, trust
    ruthlessly taken advantage of;
    but it ran deeper than that,
    exposing a lazy careless streak I could never conquer,
    hard though I tried.
You see, I had everything I could ever want –
    heir to my father's inheritance,
    security and prosperity guaranteed,
    and what did I do with it? –
    I threw it all away for a bowl of soup!
Talk about casting pearls before swine!
It was crass stupidity,
    unforgivable,
    but I was ravenous that morning,
    fit to drop,
    at the time filling my belly all that seemed to matter,
    so I traded away my birthright
    for a moment's fleeting satisfaction.
Exploited? Certainly!
And you may well call that brother of mine
    a devious twisted opportunist.
But he understood the things in life which really matter
    more than I ever could;
    while I dwelt on my stomach
    he looked to the future,
    an eye for tomorrow as well as today.
I thought I'd undone the damage even then,
    that morning when Dad called me in
    and promised his blessing.
It was the chance I'd been looking for,
    and I raced off excitedly to prepare the meal he'd asked for,
    heart skipping,

hope bubbling anew.
I should have noticed that look in Mother's eye,
    the thoughtful, scheming gleam,
    but I didn't;
    and while my back was turned, my brother nipped in,
    pulling the wool over my father's eyes
    with no sign of remorse.
It was a dastardly trick,
    just about finishing the poor fellow off,
    and when I learned the truth I was seething,
    intent only on revenge.
God knows, I'd have killed him given half the chance,
    torn him limb from limb without a shred of conscience,
    but he made himself scarce until my temper cooled,
    knowing full well I'd come round in time.
And I did, sure enough.
Call me a fool if you like,
    but when he slunk back to meet me all those years later,
    tail between his legs,
    I hadn't the heart to have a go at him;
    welcoming him instead like a long-lost brother.
Yes, it still rankles occasionally, even now –
    when I think what might have been,
    what I could have had,
    but, you see, it was mine for the taking,
    and I let it go,
    a priceless treasure allowed to slip through my fingers.
He wanted it most,
    and made it his,
    fixing his eyes not on a passing pleasure
    but an eternal promise,
    and much though it pains me to say it,
    that difference between us says it all.

Prayer

Lord,
   you have given us so much to enjoy –
   a world full of infinite variety and fascination.
We thank you for everything within it
   that gives us pleasure,
   that interests and excites us,
   that fills our minds with wonder
   and our hearts with joy.
Teach us to appreciate all you have given
   and to celebrate accordingly.
But teach us also to recognise
   those things in life which matter most of all,
   which alone can satisfy not just the body
   but also the soul.
Help us to crave your blessing
   and hunger for your kingdom;
   then give us the resolve we need
   to reach out and make these ours.
Amen.

8

HAVE YOU EVER BEEN BROUGHT DOWN TO EARTH WITH A BUMP?

Jacob

Reading – Genesis 28:10-17

Jacob left Beer-sheba and went toward Haran. He came to a certain place and stayed there for the night, because the sun had set. Taking one of the stones of the place, he put it under his head and lay down in that place. And he dreamed that there was a ladder set up on earth, the top of it reaching to heaven; and the angels of God were ascending and descending on it. And the Lord stood beside him and said, 'I am the Lord, the God of Abraham your father and the God of Isaac; the land on which you lie I will give to you and to your offspring; and your offspring shall be like the dust of the earth, and you shall spread abroad to the west and to the east and to the north and to the south; and all the families of the earth shall be blessed in you and in your offspring. Know that I am with you and will keep you wherever you go, and will bring you back to this land; for I will not leave you until I have done what I have promised you.' Then Jacob woke from his sleep and said, 'Surely the Lord is in this place – and I did not know it!' And he was afraid, and said, 'How awesome is this place! This is none other than the house of God, and this is the gate of heaven.'

Meditation

Have you ever been brought down to earth with a bump?
I was last night,
    and strangely enough
    by – of all things – a vision of heaven!
I was feeling so pleased with myself,
    so smug and self-satisfied,
    for I'd secured the future I'd always wanted,
    the inheritance of my dreams –
    or so I thought.
Only suddenly, as I lay on that makeshift pillow of mine,

tossing and turning in fitful sleep,
I realised it wasn't that simple,
the awful truth hitting me
that my trickery and treachery had all been in vain,
for the blessing I'd so wantonly filched
was as nothing beside the riches I glimpsed then,
the blessing of God himself,
the Lord of heaven and earth.
I'd given him little thought until then –
faith pretty much academic,
failing to touch the daily business of life –
but in that astonishing vision I felt him close,
challenging,
confronting,
calling me to account –
an unexpected day of reckoning.
I'd believed I could control the future,
shape my destiny,
but now I saw I couldn't.
I'd imagined wealth and success spelt happiness,
yet I understood suddenly that it wasn't true.
I'd thought I could act with impunity,
never mind the consequences,
only then the voice of conscience reared its head.
It was an eerie moment,
exhilarating yet terrifying,
bringing supreme joy and agonising humiliation,
for I was suddenly naked before God,
the folly of my actions,
the smallness of my vision,
laid bare,
and life was changed for ever.
I was brought down to earth with a vengeance,
everything I thought I'd achieved
exposed for the illusion it was.
But I tell you this,
I left that place rejoicing,
spirit dancing within me,
for I was touched by the sheer wonder of grace,
and I met there the God who not only brings us low
but who is able to lift us up
to heights beyond our imagining.

Prayer

Living God,
   so often we spend our lives
   chasing after empty dreams with no power to satisfy.
We allow ourselves to be swallowed up
   by the material and trivial,
   and all the time our souls ache within us,
   crying out for life-giving water.
Help us to catch sight of your kingdom,
   to glimpse your glory,
   to hunger and thirst after righteousness.
Bring us low,
   that through your grace we might rise high.
Amen.

9

HE WAS LIVID WHEN HE FOUND OUT

Rachel

Reading – Genesis 29:16-23, 25-28, 30

Now Laban had two daughters; the name of the elder was Leah, and the name of the younger was Rachel. Leah's eyes were lovely, and Rachel was graceful and beautiful. Jacob loved Rachel; so he said, 'I will serve you seven years for your younger daughter Rachel.' Laban said, 'It is better that I should give her to you than that I should give her to any other man; stay with me.' So Jacob served seven years for Rachel, and they seemed to him but a few days because of the love he had for her. Then Jacob said to Laban, 'Give me my wife that I may go in to her, for my time is completed.' So Laban gathered together all the people of the place, and made a feast. But in the evening he took his daughter Leah and brought her to Jacob; and he went in to her.

When morning came, it was Leah! And Jacob said to Laban, 'What is this you have done to me? Did I not serve with you for Rachel? Why then have you deceived me? Laban said, 'This is not done in our country – giving the younger before the firstborn. Complete the week of this one, and we will give you the other also in return for serving me another seven years.' Jacob did so, and completed her week; then Laban gave him his daughter Rachel as a wife.

So Jacob went in to Rachel also, and he loved Rachel more than Leah. He served Laban for another seven years.

Meditation

He was livid when he found out,
    more angry than I have ever known him,
    and with good cause.
It was a shabby trick they played –
    one that could have destroyed all our futures,
    not just mine –
    and when I realised what they were up to
    I was beside myself,

begging them to think again, though to no avail.
Poor Jacob, what a shock it must have been,
    to wake up that morning –
    head still throbbing from the night before –
    to find my sister there instead of me.
And poor Leah,
    to see that look of fury,
    disgust,
    disappointment on his face,
    more eloquent and damning than words could ever be.
She loved him, you see,
    as much as I did,
    worshipping the very ground he walked on,
    so when the plot was hatched
    she couldn't believe her luck –
    it was like a dream come true.
I felt sorry for her later, I really did,
    for she'd have done anything for just one of his smiles,
    a word of affection,
    a peck on the cheek;
    but it was me he wanted, all too clearly,
    and at the time it was Jacob my heart bled for,
    so cruelly and wickedly deceived.
Seven years he'd worked for me,
    seven long years of unmitigated slog –
    my father a hard taskmaster, kinsman or no kinsman –
    but he did it willingly,
    an act of devotion,
    longing for that moment when we could be together,
    husband and wife at last.
It was snatched from his grasp,
    and I dreaded the consequences,
    petrified he might walk away,
    our dream destroyed for ever.
But he didn't;
    he promised to stay,
    just as my father had bargained on,
    seven more years' hard graft to make me his –
    could any girl ask for more?
He was bitter afterwards, understandably,
    determined to exact revenge,
    and I couldn't blame him,

for I felt hurt myself.
But do you know what? A funny thing happened yesterday.
We were together, just the two of us,
    talking about old times,
    and I happened to mention that fateful night,
    his being taken in like that –
    duped into mistaking Leah for me –
    and then swallowing that feeble excuse
    about the firstborn deserving their rights.
I was only teasing him,
    just a bit of harmless fun really,
    but suddenly Jacob looked at me,
    a look of wonder and comprehension in his eyes,
    as though a light had dawned,
    a mystery been unravelled,
    and the next moment he threw back his head,
    and laughed till the tears rolled down his face.
He saw a joke somewhere that I'd never intended,
    a sense in which God was having the last laugh.
Can you see it?
I wish I could.

Prayer

Lord,
    there are times when life doesn't seem fair,
    when those who openly flout your will
    seem to prosper,
    while those who follow you
    gain scant reward.
We know this shouldn't matter to us –
    that our treasure should be in heaven
    rather than on earth,
    our hearts set on things eternal
    rather than the riches of this world –
    yet it's hard sometimes not to feel frustrated,
    even resentful,
    at the apparent injustice of life.
Forgive us the times we have made that mistake,
    setting ourselves up as judge and jury.

Forgive us the times we have doubted you in consequence,
    questioning your justice and resenting your grace.
Teach us to understand that, whoever we are,
    our actions will finally catch up with us,
    and so help us to live faithfully as your people,
    rejoicing in the blessings you have given,
    and anticipating the joy yet to come.
Amen.

10

There was no way I deserved it

Jacob

Reading – Genesis 32:9-12, 22-31

Jacob said, 'O God of my father Abraham and God of my father Isaac, O Lord who said to me, "Return to your country and to your kindred, and I will do you good", I am not worthy of the least of all the steadfast love and all the faithfulness that you have shown to your servant, for with only my staff I crossed this Jordan; and now I have become two companies. Deliver me, please, from the hand of my brother, from the hand of Esau, for I am afraid of him; he may come and kill us all, the mothers with the children. Yet you have said, "I will surely do you good, and make your offspring as the sand of the sea, which cannot be counted because of their number".'

The same night he got up and took his two wives, his two maids, and his eleven children, and crossed the ford of Jabbok. He took them and sent them across the stream, and likewise everything that he had. Jacob was left alone; and a man wrestled with him until daybreak. When the man saw that he did not prevail against Jacob, he struck him on the hip socket, and Jacob's hip was put out of joint as he wrestled with him. Then he said, 'Let me go, for the day is breaking.' But Jacob said, 'I will not let you go, unless you bless me.' So he said to him, 'What is your name?' And he said, 'Jacob.' Then the man said, 'You shall no longer be called Jacob, but Israel, for you have striven with God and with humans, and have prevailed.' Then Jacob asked him, 'Please tell me your name.' But he said, 'Why is it that you ask my name?' And there he blessed him. So Jacob called the place Penuel, saying, 'For I have seen God face to face, and yet my life is preserved.' The sun rose upon him as he passed Penuel, limping because of his hip.

Meditation

There was no way I deserved it,
   no reason God should have blessed me.
I was under no illusions about that,
   no false sense of my own worthiness.

I was a two-faced, scheming swindler,
    and I knew it as well as any,
    but if that was down to me it was also down to God,
    for he made me that way,
    the responsibility at least his in part.
So I reckoned he owed me something –
    a place in his purpose,
    a share in his promise.
Only it cut both ways,
    for he reckoned *I* owed *him* something too –
    obedience,
    worship,
    faith.
And the result was inevitable –
    somewhere,
    some time,
    we had to clash,
    thrash the whole business out,
    sort out once and for all exactly where we stood.
And that's what happened,
    one dark night by the ford of Jabbok,
    a night I shall never forget as long as I live.
Did it really happen as I remember it?
I can't be sure.
Perhaps it was just a dream,
    perhaps a vision,
    perhaps simply a crisis of conscience,
    but suddenly this stranger blocked my path,
    daring me to pass –
    and we were locked in mortal combat,
    wrestling for grim death as the hours ticked away.
Did I defeat him?
I thought so at the time,
    refusing to let him go until he blessed me,
    but I realised later he could have destroyed me
    had he wished,
    tossed me aside with a flick of the wrist.
He was testing my resolve,
    assessing my commitment,
    measuring my determination to grasp the future
    come what may;
    and if I was willing to play my part, he'd play his.

I knew for sure then what I'd suspected all along –
    I'd been grappling with God,
    and myself,
    wrestling with my inner doubts and hidden fears,
    struggling with my stubborn greed,
    my troubled mind, my aching soul.
I could have backed away, of course,
    turned aside and ignored the challenge,
    but the time for running was over –
    I was on the spot,
    face to face with God,
    face to face with self –
    a time to decide.
It changed my life, that moment,
    a new beginning from which I never looked back.
Yes, the encounter was bruising,
    but it brought me a wholeness I have never known before,
    impossible to describe –
    an inner health of body, mind and spirit –
    whole, at last!

Prayer

Gracious God,
    you created us in your image
    to enjoy a living relationship with you.
And though we fail you time and again,
    you continually reach out to us,
    longing to break down the barriers which keep us apart
    so that you can call us your children.
We have no claim on your love,
    no reason to feel we deserve it,
    for we are false and faithless in so much.
Forgive us for sometimes forgetting that truth,
    imagining that we are better than we really are.
Teach us to face ourselves openly and honestly,
    to wrestle with the harsh realities of life
    and the vast mysteries of faith;
    and, above all, teach us to recognise
    our dependence on your divine grace.
Amen.

11

WAS IT A PUNISHMENT FOR THOSE MISTAKES LONG AGO?

Jacob

Reading – Genesis 37:3-4, 12-13a, 14, 17b-20, 22-24a, 26-28, 31-35

Now Israel loved Joseph more than any other of his children, because he was the son of his old age; and he had made him a long robe with sleeves. But when his brothers saw that their father loved him more than all his brothers, they hated him, and could not speak peaceably to him.

Now his brothers went to pasture their father's flock near Shechem. And Israel said to Joseph, 'Go now, see if it is well with your brothers and with the flock; and bring word back to me.'

So Joseph went after his brothers, and found them at Dothan. They saw him from a distance, and before he came near to them, they conspired to kill him. They said to one another, 'Here comes this dreamer. Come now, let us kill him and throw him into one of the pits; then we shall say that a wild animal has devoured him, and we shall see what will become of his dreams.'

Reuben said to them, 'Shed no blood; throw him into this pit here in the wilderness, but lay no hand on him' – that he might rescue him out of their hand and restore him to their father. So when Joseph came to his brothers, they stripped him of his robe, the long robe with sleeves that he wore; and they took him and threw him into a pit.

Then Judah said to his brothers, 'What profit is it if we kill our brother and conceal his blood? Come, let us sell him to the Ishmaelites, and not lay our hands on him, for he is our brother, our own flesh.' And his brothers agreed. When some Midianite traders passed by, they drew Joseph up, lifting him up out of the pit, and sold him to the Ishmaelites for twenty pieces of silver. And they took Joseph to Egypt.

Then they took Joseph's robe, slaughtered a goat, and dipped the robe in the blood. They had the long robe with sleeves taken to their father, and they said, 'This we have found; see now whether it is your son's robe or not.' He recognised it, and said, 'It is my son's robe! A wild animal has devoured him; Joseph is without doubt torn to pieces.' Then Jacob tore his garments, and put sackcloth on his loins, and mourned for his son many days. All his sons and all his daughters sought to comfort him; but he refused to be comforted, and said, 'No, I shall go down to Sheol to my son, mourning.'

Meditation

Was it a punishment for those mistakes long ago –
    God paying me back
    for having cheated and connived
    to make his blessing mine?
I thought so at the time,
    when my boys came back, all bar Joseph,
    heads bowed low,
    tears streaming down their faces,
    wringing their hands in sorrow.
I believed the worst at once,
    heart lurching within me.
Call me gullible, if you like,
    but what reason did I have to doubt their word?
They produced his robe, remember,
    dripping in blood,
    ripped to shreds,
    and I assumed immediately he'd been torn to pieces,
    my precious boy set upon by a wild beast.
All right, so they'd had their disagreements,
    even come to blows occasionally,
    but which boys don't? –
    it's a part of growing up.
They must have known he was harmless,
    despite those crazy dreams of his;
    conceited, perhaps,
    but innocent enough beneath it all.
I never dreamt for a moment they hated him,
    still less that they might do him in,
    so when they broke the news
    I accepted it without question –
    shattered,
    inconsolable,
    yet convinced it was true.
Divine judgement, it seemed, had come at last.
Only it wasn't God I should have blamed,
    nor his brothers, come to that –
    it was me,
    for I was the cause of it all.
I spoiled him, you see, that lad of mine,
    from the day he was born,

thrusting him forward,
pandering to his whims,
not just accepting his airs and graces,
but in many ways positively encouraging them.
Can you believe that? –
me of all people to make such a mistake,
after Father had doted on Esau
and Mother had time only for me!
It had torn us apart, their favouritism,
the seeds they sowed bearing terrible fruit,
and they'd died of a broken heart, the pair of them,
grieving for what might have been.
I should have learned from that,
remembered the bitterness and anger it caused,
and the dreadful steps it drove me to.
But I was blind,
and the wheel turned full circle.
It was fitting, I realised afterwards,
that I should be deceived in turn,
hoist, you might say, by my own petard,
but I couldn't have argued had the lad been dead,
for I deserved punishment after everything I'd done,
no sentence too severe.
Yet God was gracious.
his hand upon Joseph,
upon us all,
and I realise now that though in a sense
the past *did* catch up with me that day –
so much heartache of my own making –
it wasn't the past God was thinking of,
not for a moment,
but the future!

Prayer

Lord,
we find it hard to escape from the past.
It has shaped our lives in so many ways,
helping to make us what we are today.
And though there have been successes,

there have been mistakes also,
   too many of which continue to haunt us.
We find it hard to let go of regrets,
   hard to forgive,
   hardest of all to put past failures behind us
   and start again.
Yet you are the God who holds the future,
   always ready to forget what has been
   and lead us on to what shall be.
You are a God of new beginnings,
   new hope, new life.
Help us to grasp the full implications of what that means,
   and so help us to accept each day you give us
   and live it to the full,
   secure in the knowledge of your unfailing love.
Amen.

12

WAS I TEMPTED? YOU BET I WAS!

Joseph

Reading – Genesis 39:6b-20

Now Joseph was handsome and good-looking. And after a time his master's wife cast her eyes on Joseph and said, 'Lie with me.' But he refused and said to his master's wife, 'Look, with me here, my master has no concern about anything in the house, and he has put everything that he has in my hand. He is not greater in this house than I am, nor has he kept back anything from me except yourself, because you are his wife. How then could I do this great wickedness, and sin against God?' And although she spoke to Joseph day after day, he would not consent to lie beside her or to be with her. One day, however, when he went into the house to do his work, and while no one else was in the house, she caught hold of his garment, saying, 'Lie with me!' But he left his garment in her hand, and fled and ran outside. When she saw that he had left his garment in her hand and had fled outside, she called out to the members of her household and said to them, 'See, my husband has brought among us a Hebrew to insult us! He came in to me to lie with me, and I cried out with a loud voice; and when he heard me raise my voice and cry out, he left his garment beside me and fled outside.' Then she kept his garment by her until his master came home, and she told him the same story, saying, 'The Hebrew servant, whom you have brought among us, came in to me to insult me; but as soon as I raised my voice and cried out, he left his garment beside me, and fled outside.'

When his master heard the words that his wife spoke to him, saying, 'This is the way your servant treated me,' he became enraged. And Joseph's master took him and put him into the prison, the place where the king's prisoners were confined; he remained there in prison.

Meditation

Was I tempted? You bet I was!
She was an attractive woman, let's face it,
    suave,

sophisticated,
    sexy,
    and I was a young man in my prime,
    flattered and excited by her attentions.
I felt my pulse racing when she looked at me,
    my palms sweating with anticipation,
    and I could have yielded so easily,
    my body crying out to surrender.
But I couldn't, despite myself,
    for both our sakes, not just mine.
Oh, I'd have enjoyed it, no doubt,
    for a moment, in the heat of passion,
    nothing else seeming to matter;
    but then the guilt would have started,
    the regrets,
    the sordid subterfuge,
    and finally, punishment!
She was married, you see,
    my master's wife,
    and the vows she'd taken were sacred,
    whichever god she'd made them by.
So I refused her, time and again,
    keeping my distance whenever I could.
Only she wouldn't take no for an answer,
    waiting patiently to seize her chance.
I should have it seen it coming, I suppose,
    for I knew she was put out –
    you could see that a mile off –
    unused, apparently, to being turned down,
    but I never thought she'd come on that strong,
    not after all I'd said.
It was a close call eventually,
    too close for comfort,
    costing me my clothes, if not my virtue.
And it wasn't just my clothes I lost that day;
    it was my freedom,
    my position,
    my reputation,
    for she turned the tables as I knew she would,
    making *me* out to be the guilty party –
    'hell hath no fury . . .' as they say.
But whatever I lost, I kept far more,

my integrity,
my self-respect,
and, above all, my faith.
A price worth paying, wouldn't you say?

Prayer

Loving God,
    you know what it is to be tempted,
    for you took on human flesh,
    making yourself frail and vulnerable,
    just as we are.
You know what it is to lose everything,
    for you gave your only Son
    for the life of the world.
For our sakes you became poor,
    enduring humiliation,
    yet you stood firm,
    refusing to be swayed
    or to contemplate compromise.
Teach us, in our turn,
    to hold fast, come what may.
When temptation comes,
    help us to look to you rather than self,
    to *your* kingdom rather than *our* gratification.
Show us the way you would have us take,
    and help us to walk it faithfully,
    now and always.
Amen.

13

IT COULDN'T BE, I TOLD MYSELF

Joseph

Reading – Genesis 42:6-9, 15-16a, 21, 23-24a; 45:1-3, 14-15

Now Joseph was governor over the land; it was he who sold to all the people of the land. And Joseph's brothers came and bowed themselves before him with their faces to the ground. When Joseph saw his brothers, he recognised them, but he treated them like strangers and spoke harshly to them. 'Where do you come from?' he said. They said, 'From the land of Canaan, to buy food.' Although Joseph had recognised his brothers, they did not recognise him. Joseph also remembered the dreams that he had dreamed about them. He said to them, 'You are spies; you have come to see the nakedness of the land. . . . Here is how you shall be tested: as Pharaoh lives, you shall not leave this place unless your youngest brother comes here! Let one of you go and bring your brother, while the rest of you remain in prison, in order that your words may be tested . . .'

They said to one another, 'Alas, we are paying the penalty for what we did to our brother; we saw his anguish when he pleaded with us, but we would not listen. That is why this anguish has come upon us.' They did not know that Joseph understood them, since he spoke with them through an interpreter. He turned away from them and wept . . .

(Later, on their way home to Israel a second time, having returned once again to Egypt as the famine in Israel intensified, the twelve brothers were placed under arrest as a cup which Joseph had secretly ordered to be planted there was found in Benjamin's sack. Grovelling before Joseph in terror, they pleaded for mercy, begging him to spare Benjamin, their father's favourite son, and offering to stand in his place if necessary.)

Then Joseph could no longer control himself before all those who stood by him, and he cried out, 'Send everyone away from me.' So no one stayed with him when Joseph made himself known to his brothers. And he wept so loudly that the Egyptians heard it, and the household of Pharaoh heard it. Joseph said to his brothers, 'I am Joseph. Is my father still alive?' But his brothers could not answer him, so dismayed were they at his presence.

Then he fell upon his brother Benjamin's neck and wept. And he

kissed all his brothers and wept upon them; and after that his brothers
talked with him.

Meditation

It couldn't be, I told myself –
   not here in Egypt,
   not my long-lost brothers,
   surely!
But it was!
Believe it or not, there they were,
   kneeling before me,
   prostrating themselves in homage.
It was astonishing,
   heart-rending,
   and it was all I could do not to break down in tears,
   such was the poignancy of the moment.
Only I couldn't, not yet,
   not after all they'd put me through.
Can you imagine what it was like,
   your own brothers plotting to kill you?
And then, sensing a reprieve, only to be sold into slavery,
   condemned to years of servitude
   in a strange and distant land.
I wasn't blameless, I knew that.
God knows, I'd given cause enough for resentment
   with those dreams of mine –
   even if they *were* coming true
   then and there before my eyes.
But though I could understand what they did, and why,
   I could never excuse it,
   not a betrayal as vile as that.
So, you see, I had to test them,
   see if they'd learned their lesson
   or were still the same.
I made them sweat, to put it mildly,
   their hunted expression as I quizzed them saying it all;
   and when that cup turned up in Benjamin's sack,
   you should have seen their faces –

it was as though their world had collapsed in pieces.
There seemed little doubt after that,
 their sincerity plain to all.
But I had to be sure,
 so I strung them along further,
 tormenting,
 teasing,
 until the perspiration poured off them
 and they begged for mercy.
It was my father's name which did it –
 when they spoke of him and all he'd suffered.
I broke down then,
 all the pain of those long and lonely years apart flooding out;
 and as the truth slowly dawned on them,
 breaking through their guilt,
 we held each other close,
 laughter mingling with tears,
 old feuds forgotten.
Was that the way it had to be,
 the way God planned it?
It's hard to believe –
 too many questions left unanswered –
 yet I tell you this,
 it wasn't just my brothers I found changed that day,
 it was me as much as any of them,
 each of us stronger and wiser for all we'd faced.
Suddenly life was sweeter and richer
 than we had ever imagined,
 as though somehow, despite everything we'd faced,
 it all made sense!

Prayer

Lord,
    so often we don't understand what is happening to us.
We are swept along by a tide of circumstances,
    and we look in vain to find any pattern
    which might give meaning to it all.
This fleeting span of ours is a confusing riddle
    from which you can seem painfully absent.
Yet you are there even though we cannot see you,
    patiently weaving the broken strands of life
    into an intricate tapestry.
Teach us, then, to trust in you and live by faith
    until that day when the picture is complete
    and we understand at last
    all the ways you have been working
    to bring order out of chaos.
Amen.

14

THEY HATED US

A Hebrew slave

Reading – Exodus 1:8-16

Now a new king arose over Egypt, who did not know Joseph. He said to his people, 'Look, the Israelite people are more numerous and more powerful than we. Come, let us deal shrewdly with them, or they will increase and, in the event of war, join our enemies and fight against us and escape from the land.' Therefore they set taskmasters over them to oppress them with forced labour. They built supply cities, Pithom and Rameses, for Pharaoh. But the more they were oppressed, the more they multiplied and spread, so that the Egyptians came to dread the Israelites. The Egyptians became ruthless in imposing tasks on the Israelites, and made their lives bitter with hard service in mortar and brick and in every kind of field labour. They were ruthless in all the tasks that they imposed on them.

The king of Egypt said to the Hebrew midwives, one of them named Shiphrah and the other Puah, 'When you act as midwives to the Hebrew women, and see them on the birthstool, if it is a boy, kill him; but if it is a girl, she shall live.'

Meditation

They hated us –
    not because we'd done wrong,
    nor through any fault on our part,
    but because we were different –
    another culture,
    another faith,
    another race.
It was as simple as that.
Immigrants, they called us – and worse;
    good-for-nothing layabouts, sponging off their state,
    stealing their women,
    taking their jobs,

sapping their wealth,
spoiling their country.
It was nonsense, of course, everybody knew it –
we'd become part of their land,
our lives and destiny interwoven;
pursuing our own faith, admittedly,
worshipping our own God,
but loyal, law-abiding citizens.
Oh yes, they knew,
but they preferred to forget it,
for they wanted someone to blame for their troubles –
someone to hound,
someone to hate,
someone to hurt –
and we were the ones chosen,
the luckless scapegoats herded off for sacrifice.
What did they do to us? You wouldn't believe it.
Things too unspeakable, too terrible to mention!
Yet they were people, that's what I can't understand,
ordinary people like you or me;
folk we'd walked with, talked with,
worked with, laughed with,
suddenly cruel, cold, callous monsters.
One day we were human,
the next, objects;
one day, friend,
the next, foe.
Who'd have believed things could change so quickly,
the world turn upside down?
We were different, that's all,
another tongue,
another creed,
but, for all that, we were still people, just as they were,
flesh and blood feeling joy and sorrow, pleasure and pain.
I thought that mattered,
that whatever divided us, more must unite,
but I was wrong,
so hideously, hopelessly wrong.
Was God to blame?
I believed so at the time,
asking myself, day after day,
how he could stand by and let it happen,

remote in heaven from such dreadful crimes on earth.
And it troubled me deeply,
   as much as the suffering itself,
   my faith shaken,
   dangling on a thread.
But it wasn't God, I realise that now –
   it was man,
   man as I never dreamt he could be;
   one human being destroying another,
   life counting for nothing –
   and that disturbs me yet more.

Prayer

Lord,
   you have made us all different,
   with different characters, different gifts,
   different opinions, different insights.
Yet you have made us also, every one of us,
   in your own image,
   uniquely precious to you.
Forgive us that we allow our differences to come between us
   rather than draw us together;
   that we see them as a threat rather than a gift.
Forgive us that we find it so hard to change.
We do our best to overcome the prejudice within us,
   but it runs deep,
   emerging in ways we fail to recognise,
   poisoning our very souls.
Teach us to look at ourselves and others with your eyes,
   seeing the good and the bad,
   the lovely and the unlovely,
   the strengths and the weaknesses,
   the truths and the falsehoods,
   yet seeing always our common humanity.
Open our hearts and minds to one another,
   and so also to you.
Amen.

15

I CAN'T DO IT, LORD

Moses

Reading – Exodus 3:1-15

Moses was keeping the flock of his father-in-law Jethro, the priest of Midian; he led his flock beyond the wilderness, and came to Horeb, the mountain of God. There the angel of the Lord appeared to him in a flame of fire out of a bush; he looked and the bush was blazing, yet it was not consumed. Then Moses said, 'I must turn aside and look at this great sight, and see why the bush is not burned up.' When the Lord saw that he had turned aside to see, God called to him out of the bush, 'Moses, Moses!' And he said, 'Here I am.' Then he said, 'Come no closer! Remove the sandals from your feet, for the place on which you are standing is holy ground.' He said further, 'I am the God of your father, the God of Abraham, the God of Isaac, and the God of Jacob.' And Moses hid his face, for he was afraid to look at God.

Then the Lord said, 'I have observed the misery of my people who are in Egypt; I have heard their cry on account of their taskmasters. Indeed, I know their sufferings, and I have come down to deliver them from the Egyptians, and to bring them up out of that land to a good and broad land, a land flowing with milk and honey, to the country of the Canaanites, the Hittites, the Amorites, the Perizzites, the Hivites, and the Jebusites. The cry of the Israelites has now come to me; I have also seen how the Egyptians oppress them. So come, I will send you to Pharaoh to bring my people, the Israelites, out of Egypt.' But Moses said to God, 'Who am I that I should go to Pharaoh, and bring the Israelites out of Egypt?' He said, 'I will be with you; and this shall be the sign for you that it is I who sent you: when you have brought the people out of Egypt, you shall worship God on this mountain.'

But Moses said to God, 'If I come to the Israelites and say to them, "The God of your ancestors has sent me to you", and they ask me, "What is his name?" what shall I say to them?' God said to Moses, 'I AM WHO I AM.' He said further, 'Thus you shall say to the Israelites, "I AM has sent me to you".' God also said to Moses, 'Thus you shall say to the Israelites, "The Lord the God of your ancestors, the God of Abraham, the God of Isaac, and the God of Jacob, has sent me to you": This is my name for ever, and this my title for all generations.'

Meditation

I can't do it, Lord,
　out of the question!
That's what I thought,
　and that's what I told him,
　eventually.
All right, so it took me a while to get to the point, I admit it,
　but would you have been any different?
It's not easy to say no when God asks you to do something,
　not easy at all.
So I hummed and ha'd a bit at first,
　hoping he'd see reason,
　realise he was asking too much of me.
I had good grounds, let's face it –
　I wasn't even a gifted speaker for a start,
　not even at the best of times,
　and before Pharaoh? –
　well, I knew I'd be a bag of nerves,
　scarcely able to put two words together to save my life.
Anyway, why should he listen to me,
　or anyone else for that matter?
He was the one in charge,
　the one calling the shots,
　so why listen to some jumped-up nobody
　poking his nose in where it wasn't wanted?
But more to the point was my past record –
　I'd killed a man, remember, back there in Egypt,
　battered his head in and buried him in the sand.
A crime of passion, perhaps, if that can justify such a thing,
　yet for all that it was murder,
　and if anyone there was to recognise me
　and put two and two together,
　who's to say what the outcome might have been?
It could have spelt the end for me.
So when the excuses ran out
　and he still wouldn't take no for an answer,
　I told him straight:
　'Not me, Lord, get someone else to do it.'
But would you believe it, he was ready for that one,
　ready it seemed to counter any objection I could come up with.
So I finally gave in,

no option left but to do it his way.
No, I didn't relish facing Pharaoh, too right,
    not with the message I had to deliver,
    but the prospect of facing God,
    having gone against his will,
    appealed still less.
And, do you know what? –
I need never have worried,
    for he gave me the words I needed when I needed them,
    courage such as I'd never have dreamt of,
    and faith to move mountains.
I went to Pharaoh eventually, not once,
    not twice,
    but ten times,
    cool as you like,
    with the same message: 'Let my people go!'
And finally, despite himself, the tyrant gave in,
    unable to battle any longer against the living God.
It took some doing, I can tell you,
    standing there that first time,
    but when God calls again,
    however daunting the challenge,
    however stacked against me the odds might seem,
    I won't think twice,
    for I realise now that whatever he may ask of you,
    he will more than help you do it.

Prayer

Lord,
    all too often we feel daunted
    by the challenges facing us.
Whether it be the everyday pressures of life
    or the unique responsibilities of Christian discipleship,
    we feel inadequate to cope
    with the demands put upon us,
    lacking either the qualities, the courage
    or the commitment needed to meet them successfully.
Yet you have promised that whatever you call us to do,

you will enable us to fulfil it,
your Spirit always within us
and your hand always beside us.
Inspire us, then, to respond in faith,
confident that with you to support us
no task is too hard to take on.
Amen.

16

I WAS READY TO CALL IT A DAY

Moses

Reading – Exodus 11:1, 4-10

The Lord said to Moses, 'I will bring one more plague upon Pharaoh and upon Egypt; afterwards he will let you go from here; indeed, when he lets you go, he will drive you away . . .'

Moses said, 'Thus says the Lord: About midnight I will go out through Egypt. Every firstborn in the land of Egypt shall die, from the firstborn of Pharaoh who sits on his throne to the firstborn of the female slave who is behind the handmill, and all the firstborn of the livestock. Then there will be a loud cry throughout the whole land of Egypt, such as has never been or will ever be again. But not a dog shall growl at any of the Israelites – not at people, not at animals – so that you may know that the Lord makes a distinction between Egypt and Israel. Then all these officials of yours shall come down to me, and bow low to me, saying, "Leave us, you and all the people who follow you." After that I will leave.' And in hot anger he left Pharaoh.

The Lord said to Moses, 'Pharaoh will not listen to you, in order that my wonders may be multiplied in the land of Egypt.' Moses and Aaron performed all these wonders before Pharaoh: but the Lord hardened Pharaoh's heart, and he did not let the people of Israel go out of his land.

Meditation

I was ready to call it a day,
    to throw in the towel and give the whole thing up.
What more could I do?
I'd tried, hadn't I? –
    given my all as God had commanded –
    but despite everything,
    the words I'd spoken,
    the signs he'd given,
    it still apparently wasn't enough.
I'd been reluctant to get involved from the start,

don't forget that,
every audience filling me with dread,
but I'd gone,
and I'd kept on going,
determined to play my part.
Only by then I wasn't so sure,
   for time and again my hopes had been raised
   only to be dashed before I knew it.
Could I take any more?
I really wasn't sure.
Perhaps I'd been mistaken all along,
   God not wanting to use me at all.
Perhaps I'd said the wrong things,
   given the wrong message,
   tried the wrong tack –
   who could say?
Whatever the reasons, I'd had enough,
   after all, how many times can a man be knocked down
   and keep on coming back for more?
Yet still I couldn't escape his call, try though I might.
He was urging me on,
   back to the same place
   with the same message
   on the same mission.
And suddenly, I had my answer,
   for our prayer was answered –
   an end to the long years of slavery,
   freedom at last!
I was a celebrity after that,
   for a time anyway, until the next crisis came along.
And yes, if I'm honest, I was proud of what I'd achieved,
   for it hadn't come easy to me,
   not easy at all.
Yet you won't find me getting carried away,
   for I know had it been left to me alone
   it would have been a very different story,
   and a much less happy ending.
I'd have given up long before, sooner rather than later,
   our deliverance still but a dream.
No, it's not me who deserves the glory –
   it's God,
   for while *I* cared a little *he* cared completely,

passionate enough about his people's freedom
to keep on fighting for it
despite the setbacks and disappointments;
nothing finally able to withstand his purpose
or frustrate his love.

Prayer

Lord,
    it's hard to keep striving sometimes
    when all our efforts meet with failure;
    hard to keep praying
    when all our prayers seem to be unanswered;
    hard to keep believing
    when so much in life seems to undermine our faith.
Yet it is at such times as those
    that we need to hold firmly to you,
    discovering the strength that you alone can give
    and trusting in your sovereign purpose.
Teach us to persevere
    even when the odds seem hopelessly stacked against us,
    confident that your will shall finally prevail
    despite all which conspires against it.
Help us to know
    that though we may be tempted to give up on you,
    you will never give up on us!
Amen.

17

IT WAS THE WORST MOMENT OF MY LIFE

Moses

Reading: Exodus 14:8-14, 21-28

The Lord hardened the heart of Pharaoh king of Egypt and he pursued the Israelites, who were going out boldly. The Egyptians pursued them, all Pharaoh's horses and chariots, his chariot drivers and his army; they overtook them camped by the sea, by Pi-hahiroth, in front of Baal-zephon.

As Pharaoh drew near, the Israelites looked back, and there were the Egyptians advancing on them. In great fear the Israelites cried out to the Lord. They said to Moses, 'Was it because there were no graves for us in Egypt that you have taken us away to die in the wilderness? What have you done to us, bringing us out of Egypt? Is this not the very thing we told you in Egypt, "Let us alone and let us serve the Egyptians"? For it would have been better for us to serve the Egyptians than to die in the wilderness.' But Moses said to the people, 'Do not be afraid, stand firm, and see the deliverance that the Lord will accomplish for you today; for the Egyptians whom you see today you shall never see again. The Lord will fight for you, and you have only to keep still.'

Then Moses stretched out his hand over the sea. The Lord drove the sea back by a strong east wind all night, and turned the sea into dry land; and the waters were divided. The Israelites went into the sea on dry ground, the waters forming a wall for them on their right and their left. The Egyptians pursued them, and went into the sea after them, all of Pharaoh's horses, chariots, and chariot drivers. At the morning watch the Lord in the pillar of fire and cloud looked down upon the Egyptian army, and threw the Egyptian army into panic. He clogged the chariot wheels so that they turned with difficulty. The Egyptians said, 'Let us flee from the Israelites, for the Lord is fighting for them against Egypt.'

Then the Lord said to Moses, 'Stretch out your hand over the sea, so that the water may come back upon the Egyptians, upon their chariots and chariot drivers. So Moses stretched out his hand over the sea, and at dawn the sea returned to its normal depth. As the Egyptians fled before it, the Lord tossed the Egyptians into the sea. The waters returned and covered the chariots and chariot drivers, the entire army of Pharaoh that had followed them into the sea; not one of them remained.

Meditation

It was the *worst* moment of my life –
   that sudden desperate shout,
   and then the dust rising in the distance,
   the dull but unmistakable thud of hooves,
   and the sight of that mighty army appearing over the horizon.
We knew what it meant immediately,
   and our blood ran cold –
   the Egyptians were coming!
And then the shouting started,
   sounds I will never forget –
   the screams of terror,
   the howls of disbelief,
   the explosions of anger –
   our mood changing from one of celebration to panic,
   from unbridled joy to utter, abject despair.
I wanted to cry out too,
   my fear as acute as any,
   but I couldn't, could I? –
   not as the one who'd brought them out there,
   the one who'd got them into such a hopeless mess.
I had to seem strong,
   cool, calm, collected,
   even if I didn't feel it.
But inside my stomach was churning,
   for our situation looked hopeless,
   destined to be cut down there in the wilderness,
   our brief taste of freedom ruthlessly terminated.
No wonder some of them chose to curse me,
   for I'd promised them a new beginning,
   a fresh start,
   only to lead them out there to their deaths.
How could God let it happen?
What did he think he was doing?
I shouldn't have asked, I know, but I couldn't help it.
How could he have brought us this far,
   only to abandon us now?
It couldn't be.
Somehow,
   some way,
   he would surely help us.

And then the idea came to me,
   ridiculous,
   impossible,
   unthinkable,
   yet there was no doubt in my mind
   that it was the voice of God urging us forward.
We were to cross the sea,
   to walk through the water
   and on to liberty!
Yes, I told you it sounded ridiculous,
   but I knew better than to argue,
   for time and again God had confounded our expectations,
   making the impossible look easy.
So I stretched out my hand as the Lord commanded,
   and the waters parted,
   as if rolled back by some hidden hand –
   a sight more stunning than any you could ever hope to see –
   and there before us a valley between the waves,
   a pathway to liberty.
We walked spellbound,
   eyes wide,
   mouths agape,
   hearts pounding,
   scarcely daring to breathe.
But then we were over,
   the last of us safely across,
   and as I turned and stretched out my hands again
   the waters broke on our pursuers,
   a mighty torrent,
   a thundering, awesome cascade,
   crashing over their heads and sweeping them away.
We stood for a moment gazing in wonder,
   unable to take in what had happened.
But then the truth sank home,
   the reality of our deliverance,
   and we were leaping like new-born lambs,
   skipping for joy,
   running,
   laughing,
   dancing,
   unable to contain our jubilation.
The Lord had heard our cry

and delivered us from the Egyptians;
    we were set free,
    our slavery over,
    safe at last.
And yes, I have to say it –
    it was the *best* day of my life!

Prayer

Lord,
    it is easy to follow you when life is going well;
    much harder when we come up against problems.
Our faith then evaporates so quickly,
    and we find ourselves overwhelmed by confusion,
    consumed by doubt,
    uncertain where to turn next.
Forgive us for the weakness of our faith,
    for being fair-weather disciples,
    swift to turn when the going gets rough.
Help us to recognise
    that there are times when we must face challenges
    and overcome apparently insurmountable obstacles,
    and teach us that you are as much there
    in moments such as those
    as at any other time.
Give us courage to trust in you always
    and walk wherever you might lead,
    confident that you will never fail us or forsake us.
Amen.

18
WHAT ON EARTH WAS I THINKING OF?

Aaron

Reading – Exodus 24:12-13, 18; 32:1-8, 19-20, 35

The Lord said to Moses, 'Come up to me on the mountain, and wait there; and I will give you the tablets of stone, with the law and the commandment, which I have written for their instruction. So Moses went up . . . into the mountain of God. Moses was on the mountain for forty days and forty nights.

When the people saw that Moses delayed to come down from the mountain, the people gathered around Aaron, and said to him, 'Come, make gods for us, who shall go before us; as for this Moses, the man who brought us up out of the land of Egypt, we do not know what has become of him.' Aaron said to them, 'Take off the gold rings that are on the ears of your wives, your sons, and your daughters, and bring them to me.' So all the people took off the gold rings from their ears, and brought them to Aaron. He took the gold from them, formed it in a mould, and cast an image of a calf; and they said, 'These are your gods, O Israel, who brought you up out of the land of Egypt!' When Aaron saw this, he built an altar before it; and Aaron made proclamation and said, 'Tomorrow shall be a festival to the Lord.' They rose early the next day, and offered burnt offerings and brought sacrifices of well-being; and the people sat down to eat and drink, and rose up to revel.

The Lord said to Moses, 'Go down at once! Your people, whom you brought up out of the land of Egypt, have acted perversely; they have been quick to turn aside from the way that I commanded them; they have cast for themselves an image of a calf, and have worshipped it and sacrificed to it, and said, "These are your gods, O Israel, who brought you up out of the land of Egypt!"'

As soon as he came near the camp and saw the calf and the dancing, Moses' anger burned hot, and he threw the tablets from his hands and broke them at the foot of the mountain. He took the calf that they had made, burned it with fire, ground it to powder, scattered it on the water, and made the Israelites drink it.

Then the Lord sent a plague on the people, because they made the calf – the one that Aaron made.

Meditation

What on earth was I thinking of?
How could I have been so foolish?
It's all a blur now, looking back,
    a grim and ghastly memory.
But it was real at the time,
    and I curl up in shame at the merest mention of it.
I must have been out of my mind,
    driven to distraction by the constant carping,
    the incessant complaints,
    but though that may explain, it can never excuse –
    not a folly as deep as mine.
It's just that they were growing desperate,
    restlessness giving way to panic
    as the hours ticked by and still no sign of Moses.
What was he up to, I wondered?
How much longer could he need up that blessed mountain?
And that's when the doubts got to me too,
    a sneaking suspicion taking hold
    that he wouldn't come back,
    some ghastly fate having surely befallen him.
I should have waited, I know that,
    but it's easy to say that with hindsight;
    for me there, on the spot, it was a different story.
I had to rebuild confidence,
    calm things down somehow,
    and what better way than a visible symbol,
    tangible proof that all was well.
That's all I wanted to do, believe me,
    to make the unseen, seen,
    the unknown, known –
    the idea of building an idol was the last thing on my mind.
Yet that's what it amounted to, there's no denying it.
And you can guess what happened next, can't you?
Exactly! Trust Moses to return then of all times,
    as we knelt in worship offering our sacrifices!
You should have seen the look he gave us,
    from the face of an angel when he arrived
    to a face like thunder;
    not just anger in his eyes,
    but horror, disgust, disappointment.

Not that I could blame him,
    for he'd met God there on that mountain,
    the God of Abraham, Isaac and Jacob,
    Lord of heaven and earth.
He'd glimpsed his glory,
    heard his voice, and received his word –
    the sacred covenant engraved in stone –
    and here we were, grovelling before a lump of metal,
    flouting the most important commandment of all:
    to love the Lord our God with heart and mind and soul,
    and have no other gods before him.
It was a day to forget,
    the most humiliating moment of my life,
    and I was lucky to escape unscathed –
    many didn't.
But it wasn't wasted, not entirely,
    for as I watched that image I'd made being ground to dust,
    I remembered that, from the dust of the ground,
    God had made me,
    each one of us fashioned by his hand,
    created in his likeness, formed by his power.
To think I presumed to shape him with human hands –
    what on earth was I thinking of!

Prayer

Sovereign God,
    you are the Creator of all,
    the Lord of history,
    ruler over space and time.
You are greater than our minds can fathom,
    your ways not our ways
    nor your thoughts our thoughts.
You alone deserve praise and worship.
Yet all too often, without realising it,
    we pay homage to other gods,
    idols of material wealth and worldly satisfaction
    which have no power to satisfy.
Forgive us for our folly,

for inadvertently bringing you down to our level
and losing sight of who you are.
Help us to open our lives
to your living and searching presence,
and so may we honour you
in all we are and all we do.
Amen.

19

I'VE SEEN IT!

Moses

Reading – Deuteronomy 34:1-5

Then Moses went up from the plains of Moab to Mount Nebo, to the top of Pisgah, which is opposite Jericho, and the Lord showed him the whole land: Gilead as far as Dan, all Naphtali, the land of Ephraim and Manasseh, all the land of Judah as far as the Western Sea, the Negeb, and the Plain – that is, the valley of Jericho, the city of palm trees – as far as Zoar. The Lord said to him, 'This is the land of which I swore to Abraham, to Isaac, and to Jacob, saying, "I will give it to your descendants"; I have let you see it with your eyes, but you shall not cross over there.' Then Moses, the servant of the Lord, died there in the land of Moab, at the Lord's command.

Meditation

I've seen it!
After all this time I've seen the promised land!
At a distance, true,
    just the briefest of glimpses,
    yet to me the most beautiful sight in the world.
You see, I'd longed for that moment as long as I can remember,
    the thought of it keeping me going across the years.
When my spirit sagged and my body ached,
    when my patience was tested and my nerve began to fail,
    that hope was always there to spur us on –
    the land which God had promised.
Would it have mattered if I hadn't made it,
    if I hadn't caught a snatch before I died?
I don't think so,
    for though the details were sketchy
    and the picture sometimes blurred,
    the goal was always clear enough,
    imprinted on my mind not as some futuristic kingdom
    but an ever-present reality.

God had been with me, each moment, each step,
    his love and guidance ever sure,
    so I'd lived every day as it came,
    content to leave the next in his hands,
    confident that whatever it might bring
    it was more special,
    more wonderful,
    than I could even begin to contemplate.
Not that it was always easy, I'm not saying that,
    for inevitably there were questions,
    times when it was hard to keep believing
    as the years went by and the journey unfolded.
So yes, I had my moments, as anyone would,
    and I'd have liked to see more, of course I would –
    to have set foot in those fertile fields
    and tasted the milk and honey,
    all questions answered,
    all details clear.
But I'm not complaining,
    for I *have* seen it,
    a glimpse perhaps, but enough and more than enough.
God has led me to the gates of his kingdom,
    led me the whole way through,
    and I know now, if I ever doubted it before,
    his promise will not fail.
What more could I ask!

Prayer

Lord,
    you call us to live by faith, not by sight.
You tell us to trust in things unseen,
    realities we cannot grasp.
We do our best, Lord, but it's not easy,
    for we like to have everything cut and dried,
    spelt out for us down to the finest detail.
It's true of everyday matters,
    the routine business of life,
    let alone our eternal destiny.
Yet we know deep down there is no other way,

for the joys you hold in store for us
are beyond our imagining,
too awesome for the human mind to comprehend.
Teach us, then, to leave all things in your hands,
trusting for tomorrow
through what we know of you today.
Teach us to work for your kingdom
until that day we enter ourselves
into the wonder of your presence.
Amen.

20

BE STRONG, HE SAID

Joshua

Reading – Joshua 1:1-9

After the death of Moses the servant of the Lord, the Lord spoke to Joshua son of Nun, Moses' assistant, saying, 'My servant Moses is dead. Now proceed to cross the Jordan, you and all this people, into the land that I am giving them, to the Israelites. Every place that the sole of your foot will tread upon I have given to you, as I promised to Moses. From the wilderness and the Lebanon as far as the great river, the river Euphrates, all the land of the Hittites, to the Great Sea in the west shall be your territory. No one shall be able to stand against you all the days of your life. As I was with Moses, so I will be with you; I will not fail you or forsake you. Be strong and courageous; for you shall put this people in possession of the land that I swore to their ancestors to give them. Only be strong and very courageous, being careful to act in accordance with all the law that my servant Moses commanded you; do not turn from it to the right hand or to the left, so that you may be successful wherever you go. This book of the law should not depart out of your mouth; you shall meditate on it day and night, so that you may be careful to act in accordance with all that is written in it. For then you shall make your way prosperous, and then you shall be successful. I hereby command you: Be strong and courageous; do not be frightened or dismayed, for the Lord your God is with you wherever you go.'

Meditation

Be strong, he said,
    be very courageous,
    and I will be with you wherever you go.
It was a wonderful promise,
    an unchanging hope in an uncertain world,
    and I needed that then, more than I can tell you.

For suddenly I was on my own, or that's how it seemed;
    our leader, Moses, taken from us,
    man of God,
    man of the people,
    man we would see no more.
He'd be a hard act to follow,
    we'd realised that from the beginning,
    each of us dreading the day
    when the end must finally come,
    but when it did I never dreamt for a moment
    I'd be the one they'd turn to,
    the one chosen by the great man himself.
I felt lost,
    bewildered –
    we all did –
    a ship without a rudder,
    an ox without a yoke.
For he'd always been there, as long as we could remember,
    leading us safely on through thick and thin.
And we'd made it, so we thought,
    our destination reaching out to greet us,
    a land flowing with milk and honey,
    peace, prosperity, at last.
Only it wasn't,
    for though the journey was over
    the conquest had just begun,
    and I was petrified,
    overwhelmed by the scale of the challenge,
    awed by the responsibility.
Who was I to take it on? –
    nothing special,
    no one gifted,
    a plain ordinary man
    with a quite extraordinary mission.
I couldn't have done it,
    not alone,
    no way.
But I didn't have to, of course,
    for God was with us as he promised,
    every step of the way;
    there to challenge,
    there to guide,

there to bless.
When my spirit failed, he was with me,
    when my foot slipped, he picked me up,
    always helping,
    always leading,
    a never-failing stream of love.
He asked one thing, that's all,
    and it wasn't much,
    hard though we found it,
    often though we failed.
It was to stay true to the commandments he had given
    in the book of the Law,
    holding them fast in our minds,
    meditating on them day and night –
    never swerving,
    never turning,
    but walking in faith, come what may.
We had our moments, like I say,
    still do, sadly –
    even now some people looking back with regret
    and ahead with consternation.
Well, it's up to them, I've done my bit –
    it's their choice, no one else's –
    but as for me and my family,
    there's no question,
    no doubt in our minds:
    we will serve the Lord.

Reading – Joshua 24:15-17a, 18b

'Now if you are unwilling to serve the Lord, choose this day whom you will serve, whether the gods your ancestors served in the region beyond the River or the gods of the Amorites in whose land you are living; but as for me and my household, we will serve the Lord.' Then the people answered, 'Far be it from us that we should forsake the Lord to serve other gods; for it is the Lord our God who brought us and our ancestors up from the land of Egypt, out of the house of slavery . . . Therefore we also will serve the Lord, for he is our God.'

Prayer

Lord,
    it's hard to bounce back from disappointment,
    to find new reserves and fresh inspiration
    to try and try again.
When we've given our all
    and believe we've achieved something,
    when we've kept on battling
    despite the obstacles in our way,
    it hurts to accept that there are still more hurdles to face,
    yet more setbacks to overcome.
Yet though we may sometimes feel weary at the demands,
    we know in our hearts that life is made of such challenges;
    no achievement, however special,
    sufficient to answer all our dreams.
Renew us, then, through your Holy Spirit,
    and give us the faith and commitment we need
    to live each day as your pilgrim people,
    pressing on towards the prize.
Amen.

CONQUEST AND KINGDOM

21

YOU KNOW WHAT THEY'D HAVE CALLED ME

Rahab

Reading – Joshua 2:1-14

Then Joshua son of Nun sent two men secretly from Shittim as spies, saying, 'Go, view the land, especially Jericho.' So they went, and entered the house of a prostitute whose name was Rahab, and spent the night there. The king of Jericho was told, 'Some Israelites have come here tonight to search out the land.' Then the king of Jericho sent orders to Rahab, 'Bring out the men who have come to you, who entered your house, for they have come only to search out the whole land.' But the woman took the two men and hid them. Then she said, 'True, the men came to me, but I did not know where they came from. And when it was time to close the gate at dark, the men went out. Where the men went I do not know. Pursue them quickly, for you can overtake them.' She had, however, brought them up to the roof and hidden them with the stalks of flax that she had laid out on the roof. So the men pursued them on the way to the Jordan as far as the fords. As soon as the pursuers had gone out, the gate was shut.

Before they went to sleep, she came up to them on the roof and said to the men: 'I know that the Lord has given you the land, and that dread of you has fallen on us, and that all the inhabitants of the land melt in fear before you. For we have heard how the Lord dried up the water of the Red Sea before you when you came out of Egypt, and what you did to the two kings of the Amorites that were beyond the Jordan, to Sihon and Og, whom you utterly destroyed. As soon as we heard it, our hearts melted, and there was no courage left in any of us because of you. The Lord your God is indeed God in heaven above and on earth below. Now then, since I have dealt kindly with you, swear to me by the Lord that you in turn will deal kindly with my family. Give me a sign of good faith that you will spare my father and mother, my brothers and sisters, and all who belong to them, and deliver our lives from death.' The men said to her, 'Our life for yours! If you do not tell this business of ours, then we will deal kindly and faithfully with you when the Lord gives us the land.'

Meditation

You know what they'd have called me
    had they found out, don't you?
That's right, a traitor!
And with good cause,
    for I was precisely that,
    sheltering sworn enemies of my country,
    selling my own people down the river.
I know what you're going to say,
    that I did it to save my own skin,
    but you'd be wrong, for it was more than that,
    much more.
Yes, of course I wanted to live –
    wouldn't you have?
And when I saw the chance
    of protecting my loved ones into the bargain,
    that in itself was persuasion enough.
But what finally decided me
    was listening to those men as they sat in my home.
I could tell they were different the moment they walked in –
    not a bit like those I usually meet in my line of business –
    and if I had any doubts why they'd come,
    they soon dispelled them:
    it wasn't my body they were after,
    it was information.
They had a sense of purpose like I'd never seen before,
    a confidence, an inner conviction,
    which I could only envy,
    and I realised then it was true
    what people said of these Israelites:
    their God was with them –
    a God like none other, ruler of heaven and earth –
    and no one could stand in their way.
Hold on, you might argue,
    I could still have handed them over,
    done my best to frustrate their plans –
    but what difference would it have made?
None at all,
    for had they been stopped, there would have been others,
    always someone else to step into their place,
    until finally they achieved their goal and the end came.

No, I had to choose, that day,
 and believe me, it wasn't easy;
 not one moment has passed since
 when I haven't questioned the decision I made.
But though the memory still troubles me,
 I still believe I did what I had to.
Had it been men I was up against
 I'd have taken my chance,
 for I was used to them, wasn't I,
 able to look after myself?
But a God like that?
Well, you resist him if you want to –
 for me there was no other way!

Prayer

Living God,
 we have prayed countless times,
 'Your will be done',
 but exactly what your will is can be hard to fathom.
We read, even in the Scriptures,
 of actions which seem to run counter
 to everything we believe about you,
 yet which are attributed to your purpose.
We see warring factions, competing traditions,
 even divided churches,
 each claiming they have understood your will correctly
 yet exposing through their actions
 the hollowness of any such claim.
In our own lives there have equally been times
 when we have been convinced of your guidance,
 only to find we have followed our own inclinations.
But we know, despite all this,
 that your will shall finally triumph,
 no obstacle able to stand against it.
Help us, then,
 though we see imperfectly at present,
 and understand only in part,
 to offer our service as best we can,
 until your kingdom comes and your will is done,
 on earth as it is in heaven.
Amen.

22

POOR OLD BALAK,
YOU SHOULD HAVE SEEN HIS FACE

Balaam

Reading – Numbers 22:1-8, 12; 23:7a, 8-12

The Israelites set out, and camped in the plains of Moab across the Jordan from Jericho. Now Balak son of Zippor saw all that Israel had done to the Amorites. Moab was in great dread of the people, because they were so numerous; Moab was overcome with fear of the people of Israel. And Moab said to the elders of Midian, 'This horde will now lick up all that is around us, as an ox licks up the grass of the field.' Now Balak son of Zippor was king of Moab at that time. He sent messengers to Balaam son of Beor at Pethor, which is on the Euphrates, in the land of Amaw, to summon him, saying, 'A people has come out of Egypt; they have spread over the face of the earth, and they have settled next to me. Come now, curse this people for me, since they are stronger than I; perhaps I shall be able to defeat them and drive them from the land; for I know that whomever you bless is blessed, and whomever you curse is cursed.'

So the elders of Moab and the elders of Midian departed with the fees for divination in their hand; and they came to Balaam, and gave him Balak's message. He said to them, 'Stay here tonight, and I will bring back word to you, just as the Lord speaks to me'; so the officials of Moab stayed with Balaam.

God said to Balaam, 'You shall not go with them; you shall not curse the people, for they are blessed.'

Then Balaam uttered his oracle, saying: 'How can I curse whom God has not cursed? How can I denounce those whom the Lord has not denounced? For from the top of the crags I see him, from the hills I behold him; here is a people living alone, and not reckoning itself among the nations! Who can count the dust of Jacob, or number the dust-cloud of Israel? Let me die the death of the upright, and let my end be like his!'

Then Balak said to Balaam, 'What have you done to me? I brought you to curse my enemies, but now you have done nothing but bless them.' He answered, 'Must I not take care to say what the Lord puts into my mouth?'

Meditation

Poor old Balak, you should have seen his face –
   a look of sheer disbelief coupled with abject misery –
   and why not, for his plans were in tatters,
   not just thwarted, but blown up in his face.
Yet I couldn't feel sorry for him,
   for it was no more than he deserved,
   caught like that in a web of his own making.
I understood why he did it, mind you,
   why he turned to me in desperation for my services,
   for they were special, those Israelites,
   something about them
   which set them apart from any nation, any people I'd seen before.
He realised that as well as any,
   more than most, I'd say,
   but what he hadn't begun to grasp was the cause,
   the secret of their success.
'One curse,' he said, 'that's all I ask.
   One simple pronouncement to bring them down.
   You can do it!'
But I couldn't, not when it came to it –
   there was no way, even had I wanted to,
   that I could speak one word against them.
It was as though a voice were whispering in my ear,
   giving me the words to say,
   closing my mind to all others,
   and I could do nothing but obey.
It took Balak by surprise, I can tell you.
He was there on the mountain, ready and waiting,
   almost rubbing his hands with glee,
   and I could see he could scarcely contain his excitement.
Not long, he thought,
   and victory would be his for the taking,
   an end to all his worries,
   the future assured.
But then I spoke –
   not to curse but to bless –
   and I've never seen a face fall so quickly.
I shouldn't laugh, I really shouldn't,
   yet it's hard not to,
   for if he'd only stopped to think

he'd have seen it coming.
Like I made clear at the beginning,
    I would speak God's word,
    just as it was given,
    and that's what I did,
    no more, no less.
It cost me my wages,
    and could have cost more –
    if looks could kill I'd be dead now!
But I didn't care.
Danger or no danger, it would have made no difference –
    God had given me his word;
    what else could I do but speak it?

Prayer

Living God,
    it is uncomfortable sometimes having to choose.
We prefer to sit on the fence,
    to hedge our bets,
    to take the path of compromise
    in the hope of pleasing all.
Even when we know the right way
    we turn aside from it,
    fearful of the cost which may be involved.
Yet there are times when that response simply won't do;
    times when failing to decide *for* you
    means deciding *against* you.
Help us to recognise when choices must be made,
    and give us the courage then to stand firm in faith,
    whatever it may cost.
Amen.

23

I WASN'T SURE EVEN THEN!

Gideon

Reading – Judges 6:36-40

Then Gideon said to God, 'In order to see whether you will deliver Israel by my hand, as you have said, I am going to lay a fleece of wool on the threshing floor; if there is dew on the fleece alone, and it is dry on all the ground, then I shall know that you will deliver Israel by my hand, as you have said.' And it was so. When he rose early next morning and squeezed the fleece, he wrung enough dew from the fleece to fill a bowl with water. Then Gideon said to God, 'Do not let your anger burn against me, let me speak one more time; let me, please, make trial with the fleece just once more; let it be dry only on the fleece, and on all the ground let there be dew.' And God did so that night. It was dry on the fleece only, and on all the ground there was dew.

Meditation

I wasn't sure even then!
After all God had done,
   the signs he'd given,
   I still couldn't get the questions out of my head.
I tried, heaven knows,
   but the truth was,
   whatever signs he may have given,
   they could never silence the doubts inside.
Yet I needed assurance –
   a protective arm around my shoulder,
   a quiet word of encouragement –
   for I was as human as the next man,
   unsure of myself despite the bravado,
   and the task before me was onerous by any standards,
   a challenge I could do without.
So I dared to bargain.
It sounds presumptuous, I know,

even arrogant, some might say,
   for who was I, a mere mortal,
   to make demands of God?
Surely he was the one to set conditions, not me?
But, incredibly, he not only listened to my terms,
   he accepted them,
     happy to offer the proof I needed!
You'd have thought I'd be happy then, wouldn't you,
   sure of my destiny?
And I was –
   for a time –
   ready and raring to go.
But only for a moment, that's what grieves me –
   a brief burst of faith
   and then the fears returned,
   nibbling away at my hard-won confidence,
   so that before I knew it I was back on my knees,
   hands clasped in prayer:
   'Lord, give me a sign.'
He could have brushed me aside without compunction,
   struck me down had he wished,
   for there were plenty of others just as able,
   just as gifted,
   and probably far more faithful than I could ever be.
But he didn't.
With touching patience and awesome grace
   he responded again,
   once more the sign I asked for
   just as I'd asked for it.
I went then, out into battle –
   I could hardly do otherwise, could I?
But I still wasn't sure,
   for though a sign may say much
   it finally proves nothing.
There was no other way, I realised it then,
   no choice but to throw caution to the wind
   and step out in faith –
   though I still hedged my bets,
   reluctant to let go to the end.
But the funny thing is, once I did, everything changed –
   no more need for signs,
   no asking for reassurance –

I *knew* God was with me
not because of any sign he had given,
but through the touch of his hand,
the closeness of his presence,
and the knowledge of his love with me day by day.
What more proof could I ever need!

Prayer

Gracious God,
like your servant Gideon
we often feel uncertain about the way ahead.
We see problems rather than the opportunities.
We remember failure instead of success.
We are filled with doubt rather than faith.
And, like Gideon once again,
we crave for a sign,
some assurance that you will see us safely through.
Forgive us for finding it so hard to trust you,
for so easily forgetting all you have done for us.
We do not deserve any proof,
yet so often in your mercy
you provide the sign we are looking for.
Teach us at such times to follow without reserve,
and grant that we may draw closer to you
until we need no further confirmation of your purpose
than the daily, living reality of your presence.
Amen.

24

DO YOU KNOW WHAT THEY TOLD ME? LOVE IS BLIND!

Samson

Reading – Judges 16:4-22

After this he fell in love with a woman in the valley of Sorek, whose name was Delilah. The lords of the Philistines came to her and said to her, 'Coax him, and find out what makes his strength so great, and how we may overpower him, so that we may bind him in order to subdue him; and we will each give you eleven hundred pieces of silver.' So Delilah said to Samson, 'Please tell me what makes your strength so great, and how you could be bound, so that one could subdue you.' Samson said to her, 'If they bind me with seven fresh bowstrings that are not dried out, then I shall become weak, and be like anyone else.' Then the lords of the Philistines brought her seven fresh bowstrings that had not dried out, and she bound him with them. While men were lying in wait in an inner chamber, she said to him, 'The Philistines are upon you, Samson!' But he snapped the bowstrings, as a strand of fibre snaps when it touches the fire. So the secret of his strength was not known.

Then Delilah said to Samson, 'You have mocked me and told me lies; please tell me how you could be bound.' He said to her, 'If they bind me with new ropes that have not been used, then I shall become weak, and be like anyone else.' So Delilah took new ropes and bound him with them, and said to him, 'The Philistines are upon you, Samson!' (The men lying in wait were in an inner chamber.) But he snapped the ropes off his arms like a thread.

Then Delilah said to Samson, 'Until now you have mocked me and told me lies; tell me how you could be bound.' He said to her, 'If you weave the seven locks of my head with the web and make it tight with the pin, then I shall become weak, and be like anyone else.' So while he slept, Delilah took the seven locks of his head and wove them into the web, and made them tight with the pin. Then she said to him, 'The Philistines are upon you Samson!' But he awoke from his sleep, and pulled away the pin, the loom, and the web.

Then she said to him, 'How can you say, "I love you", when your heart is not with me? You have mocked me three times now and have not told me what makes your strength so great.' Finally, after she had nagged him with her words day after day, and pestered him, he was tired to death. So he told her his whole secret, and said to her, 'A razor has never come upon my head; for I have been a nazirite to God from my mother's womb. If my head were shaved, then my strength would leave me; I would become weak, and be like anyone else.'

When Delilah realised that he had told her his whole secret, she sent and called the lords of the Philistines, saying, 'This time come up, for he has told his whole secret to me.' Then the lords of the Philistines came up to her, and brought the money in their hands. She let him fall asleep on her lap; and she called a man, and had him shave off the seven locks of his head. He began to weaken, and his strength left him. Then she said, 'The Philistines are upon you, Samson!' When he awoke from his sleep, he thought, 'I will go out as at other times, and shake myself free.' But he did not know that the Lord had left him. So the Philistines seized him and gouged out his eyes. They brought him down to Gaza and bound him with bronze shackles; and he ground at the mill in the prison. But the hair of his head began to grow again after it had been shaved.

Meditation

Do you know what they told me?
Love is blind!
Well, I've learned that now, haven't I, all too literally.
If only I'd listened!
They told me not to marry her,
    warned time and again what it might lead to;
    but I just didn't care.
What did they know of life, I told myself?
What right had they to interfere?
That was me all over, I'm afraid,
    always certain I knew best,
    and woe betide anyone who dared suggest otherwise.
There was nothing too hard for me, so I thought –
    my arrogance knowing no bounds –
    so I went ahead and tied the knot,
    a life-changing decision on a moment's impulse,
    and I've regretted the consequences ever since,
    just as they said I would.
It's still hard to believe,
    me, Samson, slayer of lions,
    scourge of the Philistines,

humbled by a woman's persuasive tongue!
But that's what happened,
   and all finally down to my own stupidity.
I thought I could handle her, you see –
   whatever she might throw at me
   a piece of cake beside wrestling with lions –
   only I'd no idea how hard it could be,
   the incessant nagging, day in day out,
   never a moment's peace,
   and always the same old refrain: 'Tell me your secret.'
I knew she was up to something, and I tried to resist,
   but she wouldn't be fobbed off,
   and at last, for the sake of peace, I told her all.
Was that so wrong? – I hear you ask;
   what harm in a simple haircut?
And, of course, you're right, for it wasn't the hair which mattered;
   if anyone thinks that then they're more of a fool than I was!
No, it wasn't the hair itself but what it stood for –
   my promise to God,
   my oath of allegiance,
   which, believe it or not, despite my many lapses, I still took seriously.
It was there my true strength lay,
   for it was my faith in his purpose which gave strength to my arm,
   and in that pathetic moment's madness I betrayed it all;
   not just myself, my friends and family,
   but God himself.
I recognise it now, all too clearly,
   how one false step led to another,
   one stupid failing to an indescribable folly.
I've learned my lesson,
   and made my peace – vows once broken now restored –
   and though they're smirking now, those enemies of mine,
   gloating over my downfall,
   they won't much longer, for I'll wipe that smile from their faces,
   one last effort to absolve the past.
It's a funny old world, isn't it,
   for when I had eyes to see, I saw so little,
   yet now, with my eyes made blind, I see all.

Prayer

Gracious God,
   in different ways we have promised to serve you,
   yet so often, when the moment of testing comes,
   we let you down.
The spirit is willing but the flesh is weak,
   and before we realise it
   we find we have failed you again,
   betraying the vows of obedience we have made.
Forgive us our inability
   to live up to the goals we set ourselves,
   let alone the goals you set before us.
Through your love strengthen our resolve
   and deepen our faith
   so that we serve you better
   to the glory of your name.
Amen.

25

WAS I MAKING A MISTAKE STAYING WITH HER LIKE THAT?

Ruth

Reading – Ruth 1:8-17

But Naomi said to her two daughters-in-law, 'Go back each of you to your mother's house. May the Lord deal kindly with you, as you have dealt with the dead and with me. The Lord grant that you may find security, each of you in the house of your husband.' Then she kissed them, and they wept aloud. They said to her, 'No, we will return with you to your people.' But Naomi said, 'Turn back, my daughters, why will you go with me? Do I still have sons in my womb that they may become your husbands? Turn back, my daughters, go your way, for I am too old to have a husband. Even if I thought there was hope for me, even if I should have a husband tonight and bear sons, would you then wait until they were grown? Would you then refrain from marrying? No, my daughters, it has been far more bitter for me than for you, because the hand of the Lord has turned against me.' Then they wept aloud again. Orpah kissed her mother-in-law, but Ruth clung to her.

So she said, 'See, your sister-in-law has gone back to her people and to her gods; return after your sister-in-law.' But Ruth said, 'Do not press me to leave you or to turn back from following you! Where you go, I will go; where you lodge, I will lodge; your people shall be my people, and your God my God. Where you die, I will die – there will I be buried. May the Lord do thus and so to me, and more as well, if even death parts me from you!'

Meditation

Was I making a mistake staying with her like that?
My sister thought so, plain enough,
    Naomi too, mother-in-law or not.
And I could see why,
    for I was a Moabite, not a Jew,
    belonging, so they thought, with my own people,

my own family,
  instead of a distant town in a foreign land.
What were my prospects there, you have to say?
What hope of finding a new husband,
  starting a new home,
  building a new life?
Precious little, there was no point denying it –
  I would be a stranger with no place in their history,
  their faith or their customs.
So when she told us to turn back,
  I knew why she said it,
  her only concern for our welfare,
  thoughts all for us and none for her.
Quite simply, she was exhausted,
  mentally and spiritually –
  life having dished out one heartbreak too many –
  and though she tried to mask the sorrow with a smile,
  I knew she'd given up,
  ready now to suffer whatever fate might throw at her.
But for us it could be different –
  that's what she hoped anyway –
  just because her future seemed grim
  why should ours be too?
So yes, like my sister Orpah I could have left in good conscience,
  gone back to the place of my birth.
There'd be a welcome there of sorts,
  and no reason to feel guilty –
  simply doing what was best for all.
Yet when I looked at her standing there,
  so alone,
  so helpless,
  I couldn't walk away,
  not after all we'd shared together.
There were too many memories,
  moments which bound us inseparably together –
  triumphs and tragedies, pleasure and pain –
  each uniting us in a way formal ties could never begin to.
So I stayed, hard though she tried to dissuade me;
  I pledged my love,
  my loyalty,
  come what may.
It looked foolish, you're quite right,

the wild impulse of a headstrong youngster,
but, you see, she wasn't simply a mother-in-law to me,
she was a friend,
the one I'd turned to so often in time of need –
and this time she needed me.
I had a choice, in theory anyway,
but when it came to it there was no question,
none at all.
There was just one answer I could make,
one response which would do.
Could you have acted differently in my place?
I hope not.

Prayer

Lord,
we thank you today for family and friends,
those who have been part of our lives,
sharing significant moments with us.
We thank you for those we feel especially close to,
who we know will stand by us
even when life is difficult and our fortunes low.
We thank you for the fellowship we share in Christ,
the love we share together through him.
And, above all, we thank you for the friendship *you* bring,
watching over us every moment of every day
and working for good
through all the changing circumstances of our lives.
Teach us to put our trust in you always,
knowing that whatever we may face,
you will be by our side, to the end of time.
Amen.

26
DID I EVER REGRET THAT VOW?

Hannah

Reading – 1 Samuel 1:1-11

There was a certain man of Ramathaim, a Zuphite from the hill country of Ephraim, whose name was Elkanah son of Jeroham son of Elihu son of Tohu son of Zuph, an Ephraimite. He had two wives; the name of the one was Hannah, and the name of the other Peninnah. Peninnah had children, but Hannah had no children.

Now this man used to go up year by year from his town to worship and to sacrifice to the Lord of hosts at Shiloh, where the two sons of Eli, Hophni and Phinehas, were priests of the Lord. On the day when Elkanah sacrificed, he would give portions to his wife Peninnah and to all her sons and daughters; but to Hannah he gave a double portion, because he loved her, though the Lord had closed her womb. Her rival used to provoke her severely, to irritate her, because the Lord had closed her womb. So it went on year by year; as often as she went up to the house of the Lord, she used to provoke her. Therefore Hannah wept and would not eat. Her husband Elkanah said to her, 'Hannah, why do you weep? Why do you not eat? Why is your heart sad? Am I not more to you than ten sons?'

After they had eaten and drunk at Shiloh, Hannah rose and presented herself before the Lord. Now Eli the priest was sitting on the seat beside the doorpost of the temple of the Lord. She was deeply distressed and prayed to the Lord, and wept bitterly. She made this vow: 'O Lord of hosts, if only you will look on the misery of your servant, and remember me, and not forget your servant, but will give to your servant a male child, then I will set him before you as a nazirite until the day of his death. He shall drink neither wine nor intoxicants, and no razor shall touch his head.'

Meditation

Did I ever regret that vow?
After the initial euphoria,
    the spontaneous outburst of praise and thanksgiving,

did I ever stop to wonder just what I'd done –
how I could ever have made so wild a promise,
so huge a commitment?
Well yes, there's been the odd moment, of course there has,
I'd hardly be human if there hadn't, would I?
Yet it wasn't as simple as you might think,
not as simple at all.
You see, it may sound shocking
but I didn't want the child for its own sake anyway –
it was more to get back at my rival,
to wipe that smug grin off her face
and silence that wicked tongue of hers once and for all.
Can you blame me?
I'd borne it with good grace, at the beginning –
the jibes,
the jeers,
the jests –
believing that love could conquer all.
But as the years passed, so that pain grew sharper,
the hurt harder to bear,
until I could stand it no longer.
I broke down, there at the temple,
sobbing my heart out,
begging God to do something whatever it might cost –
and, you've guessed it, he heard my prayer,
then, of all times.
It's so ironic for, could I only have seen it,
she was as unhappy as I was,
perhaps more, if anything.
She felt unloved,
unwanted,
resentful of the love Elkanah showed me,
little knowing it was her malice
which drove him ever further from her side.
And there was me feeling much the same,
convinced I was imperfect,
less than a woman,
all because I had no child.
He told me it made no difference,
that he loved me just as much despite it,
but I wouldn't listen,
reason blinded by resentment.

And even though he proved his care, time and again,
 I refused to see it,
 pleasure dulled by pain,
 blinded to the person I *was*
 by the person I thought I *should* be.
So I made my vow,
 believing a child would bring me happiness,
 and I paid the highest price.
I can see that now, but I didn't then, not for a moment.
There were no regrets,
 just a wonderful feeling of exultation,
 and an overwhelming desire to praise him,
 for God had heard my prayer and taken away my sorrow.
Now? – I'm not so sure,
 for I can't help wondering occasionally what might have been,
 the love I might have shared,
 the joys I could have known.
Remember that next time you pray,
 and if you want to bargain with God,
 consider the consequences.
It's easy to make a promise,
 but it may cost you more than you think to honour it.

Prayer

Lord,
 there are some things we want so much
 we would give almost anything to get them.
They can fill our minds night and day,
 until we think of nothing else
 except making them our own.
And the temptation is to sacrifice all else
 in pursuit of that goal,
 however great the cost may be to ourselves and others.
Lord, you understand such feelings,
 and you know how great the pain can be
 when hopes are dashed and dreams brought to nothing.
Yet you know also that life has more to offer
 than any one ambition,

however special it may be.
Forgive us when we dwell so much on what we haven't got
     that we lose sight of the blessings we have.
Teach us to rejoice in each moment you give us,
     and to trust you for what is yet to be.
Amen.

27

THREE TIMES HE CALLED ME

Samuel

Reading – 1 Samuel 3:4-18

The Lord called, 'Samuel! Samuel!' and he said, 'Here I am!' and ran to Eli, and said, 'Here I am, for you called me.' But he said, 'I did not call; lie down again.' So he went and lay down. The Lord called again, 'Samuel!' Samuel got up again and went to Eli, and said, 'Here I am, for you called me.' But he said, 'I did not call, my son; lie down again.' Now Samuel did not yet know the Lord, and the word of the Lord had not yet been revealed to him. The Lord called Samuel again, a third time. And he got up and went to Eli, and said, 'Here I am, for you called me.' Then Eli perceived that the Lord was calling the boy. Therefore Eli said to Samuel, 'Go, lie down; and if he calls you, you shall say, "Speak, Lord, for your servant is listening".' So Samuel went and lay down in his place.

Now the Lord came and stood there, calling as before, 'Samuel! Samuel!' And Samuel said, 'Speak, for your servant is listening.' Then the Lord said to Samuel, 'See, I am about to do something in Israel that will make both ears of anyone who hears of it tingle. On that day I will fulfill against Eli all that I have spoken concerning his house, from beginning to end. For I have told him that I am about to punish his house forever, for the iniquity that he knew, because his sons were blaspheming God, and he did not restrain them. Therefore I swear to the house of Eli that the iniquity of Eli's house shall not be expiated by sacrifice or offering forever.

Samuel lay there until morning; then he opened the doors of the house of the Lord. Samuel was afraid to tell the vision to Eli. But Eli called Samuel and said, 'Samuel, my son.' He said, 'Here I am.' Eli said, 'What was it that he told you? Do not hide it from me. May God do so to you and more also, if you hide anything from me of all that he told you.' So Samuel told him everything and hid nothing from him. Then he said, 'It is the Lord; let him do what seems good to him.'

Meditation

Three times he called me,
    three times that same compelling voice calling my name –
    and I was baffled,

unable to make sense of what was happening.
Was I slow on the uptake?
Perhaps; but the voice of God!
The possibility never crossed my mind –
    why should it have?
It had to be *Eli*, that's what I assumed –
    no reason to think different.
But when I went to him that third time,
    and still he stared at me blankly,
    we both realised something strange was going on –
    this voice unlike any I'd heard before.
I was still puzzled,
    still struggling to take it all in,
    but I could see Eli had grasped something I hadn't,
    a curious mixture of joy and apprehension in his eyes.
It's the Lord, he told me,
    go back and be ready to answer.
So I went, and I waited, and I listened;
    tense, but eager; nervous, yet excited,
    wondering what God could possibly want
    from a youngster like me.
I soon knew, for he spoke again,
    as unmistakably as before,
    and this time I was all ears,
    receptive to whatever he might say.
But I wish I hadn't been.
I wish now I'd buried my head in my pillow
    and thrust that voice aside,
    for the message it brought was one of warning –
    stern, solemn, forbidding –
    about justice, pain and punishment . . . about Eli.
I wanted to keep it quiet, pretend I'd never heard,
    but Eli would have none of it,
    insisting I tell him every word.
So I spat it out,
    and from the way he took it I realised it came as no surprise,
    almost as though he knew what I'd say
    even before I told him.
It was dreadful nonetheless,
    perhaps the worst moment of my life,
    having to break news like that,
    and it would have been so much easier to hide the truth,

or dress it up more kindly.
But I didn't –
    I came straight out with it in all the clumsiness of youth –
    and strangely Eli was grateful,
    as if, painful though it was,
    he needed to hear that message,
    almost glad, in a way, to get it done with.
And I realised why, later,
    for though the words were grim and the message harsh,
    it gave him the courage he'd been looking for,
    which he'd tried to find for so long,
    to be honest with himself and honest with God –
    and so finally find peace.

Prayer

Living God,
    we ask you time and again to speak to us,
    to reveal your will and give us your guidance,
    but all too often when your call comes
    we fail to recognise it.
You take us by surprise,
    for though we talk of prayer being a two-way encounter,
    the reality is usually different,
    few of us seriously expecting to hear your voice.
Even when we do hear we do not always listen,
    for your word can be disturbing,
    bringing a message very different
    from the one we want to hear.
Give us a true sense of anticipation
    when we come to you in prayer.
Give us sensitivity to discern your voice
    in the daily business of life.
Give us courage to hear what you would say to us.
And give us faith to respond willingly
    to whatever challenge you bring,
    however demanding it may seem.
Amen.

28
WAS IT A FOOL'S ERRAND?

Samuel

Reading – 1 Samuel 16:1, 4a, 5b-13

The Lord said to Samuel, 'How long will you grieve over Saul? I have rejected him from being king over Israel. Fill your horn with oil and set out; I will send you to Jesse the Bethlehemite, for I have provided for myself a king among his sons.'

Samuel did what the Lord commanded, and came to Bethlehem. . . . And he sanctified Jesse and his sons and invited them to the sacrifice.

When they came, he looked on Eliab and thought, 'Surely the Lord's anointed is now before the Lord.' But the Lord said to Samuel, 'Do not look on his appearance or on the height of his stature, because I have rejected him; for the Lord does not see as mortals see; they look on the outward appearance, but the Lord looks on the heart.' Then Jesse called Abinadab, and made him pass before Samuel. He said, 'Neither has the Lord chosen this one.' Then Jesse made Shammah pass by. And he said, 'Neither has the Lord chosen this one.' Jesse made seven of his sons pass before Samuel, and Samuel said to Jesse, 'The Lord has not chosen any of these.' Samuel said to Jesse, 'Are all your sons here?' And he said, 'There remains yet the youngest, but he is keeping the sheep.' And Samuel said to Jesse, 'Send and bring him; for we will not sit down until he comes here.' He sent and brought him in. Now he was ruddy, and had beautiful eyes, and was handsome. The Lord said, 'Rise and anoint him; for this is the one.' Then Samuel took the horn of oil, and anointed him in the presence of his brothers; and the spirit of the Lord came mightily upon David from that day forward. Samuel then set out and went to Ramah.

Meditation

Was it a fool's errand?
I began to wonder after a time,
    as one by one they trooped before me,
    and one by one God turned them down.
It was disconcerting, to say the least,

for they all looked acceptable to me, every one of them,
    especially the eldest – that young fellow Eliab.
He had all it took, to my mind –
    tall, strapping, handsome,
    a budding king if ever there was one –
    and I was all set to anoint him,
    oil poised over his head,
    until God stepped in to correct me:
    a gentle but firm ticking-off.
'Who's choosing here?' – that's what he said, near enough;
    and with good reason,
    for I'd overstepped the mark good and proper.
It wasn't just my presuming to choose,
    though that was foolish;
    it was the way my choice had been made –
    judging by the outside,
    the external veneer,
    instead of looking beneath at the inner man.
I was swayed by show –
    a pleasing face,
    an imposing presence –
    never thinking to ask what it all might hide,
    and the result was general embarrassment all round.
I can picture them still,
    those seven lads licking their wounds in a corner,
    furious their hopes had been raised one moment
    to be dashed the next –
    and as for their father, I had this distinct feeling
    I might soon outstay my welcome.
But I turned to him one last time,
    more in hope than expectation,
    and asked if there were any more I'd not yet seen –
    and that's when they sent for David.
You could tell at once why they'd overlooked him,
    for he was only a boy,
    bright-eyed admittedly, but a mere strip of a lad.
Yet though *we'd* passed him by,
    God had set him apart,
    seeing in that youthful frame the seeds of greatness.
I learned then a truth which I've never forgotten –
    that God sees deeper than most of us ever begin to,
    beneath the mask to the person behind –

but what disturbs me to this day
is the fact that I never thought to question,
never imagined the accepted order might be open to debate,
and it's made me realise that even when I think I see,
I may be more blind than I could possibly imagine.

Prayer

Gracious God,
    we know how foolish it is to judge by the outside,
    yet time and again we catch ourselves doing it.
Our minds say one thing,
    but our hearts tell us another.
Even when we think we are looking deeper,
    we are still conditioned to look at the world
    in a way which we find almost impossible to escape from.
All too often we are deceived by superficial impressions,
    failing to see the good in some and the evil in others.
Help us to see with your eyes.
Grant us the ability to look beyond the obvious
    to the deeper realities of life,
    and to recognise the true worth of all those around us.
Amen.

29

YOU SHOULD HAVE SEEN THEIR FACES AS I WALKED OUT THERE

David

Reading – 1 Samuel 17:4, 8, 32, 38-40, 42-45, 48-49

And there came out from the camp of the Philistines a champion named Goliath, of Gath, whose height was six cubits and a span. . . . He stood and shouted to the ranks of Israel, 'Why have you come out to draw up for battle? Am I not a Philistine, and are you not servants of Saul? Choose a man for yourselves, and let him come down to me.'

David said to Saul, 'Let no one's heart fail because of him; your servant will go and fight with this Philistine.'

Saul clothed David with his armour; he put a bronze helmet on his head and clothed him with a coat of mail. David strapped Saul's sword over the armour, and he tried in vain to walk, for he was not used to them. Then David said to Saul, 'I cannot walk with these; for I am not used to them.' So David removed them. Then he took his staff in his hand, and chose five smooth stones from the wadi, and put them in his shepherd's bag, in the pouch; his sling was in his hand, and he drew near to the Philistine.

When the Philistine looked and saw David, he disdained him, for he was only a youth, ruddy and handsome in appearance. The Philistine said to David, 'Am I a dog, that you come to me with sticks?' And the Philistine cursed David by his gods. The Philistine said to David, 'Come to me, and I will give your flesh to the birds of the air and to the wild animals of the field.' But David said to the Philistine, 'You come to me with sword and spear and javelin; but I come to you in the name of the Lord of hosts, the God of the armies of Israel, whom you have defied.'

When the Philistine drew nearer to meet David, David ran quickly towards the battle line to meet the Philistine. David put his hand in his bag, took out a stone, slung it, and struck the Philistine on his forehead; the stone sank into his forehead, and he fell face down on the ground.

Meditation

You should have seen their faces as I walked out there –
    a look of sheer disbelief on every one of them –
    amused,
    appalled,
    astonished!
Honestly, they didn't know whether to laugh or cry,
    a mere boy like me
    going out to meet a monster like him.
And as for Goliath, he was furious,
    convinced it was all some dirty trick,
    some devious scheme to humiliate him before his own men.
If looks could kill I'd be dead now, no doubt about that!
They all thought it would be over in a moment,
    not one of them giving a fig for my chances
    once battle commenced.
Was I scared?
Well, that's one way of putting it!
Petrified, more like,
    shaking like a leaf beneath that cool facade of mine,
    for I was no soldier,
    just an ordinary boy, fresh from the fields.
Yet I couldn't just stand by, could I,
    and see our people humiliated?
It reflected on us all –
    our nation,
    our faith,
    our God.
I'd watched them jeering day after day,
    sniggering behind our backs, hurling their insults,
    and it was too much to bear,
    so I went to Saul and begged him, 'Let me fight!'
He laughed at first, along with the rest of them,
    even tried to talk me out of it –
    men against boys, you know the sort of thing.
And humanly speaking he was right, of course,
    I didn't stand a chance,
    the odds hopelessly stacked against me.
But he was reckoning without God,
    seeing the scale of the problem,
    instead of the immensity of our resources.

They'd lost sight of that, every one of them,
    trusting in human brawn rather than divine power,
    and had I taken their advice,
    I'd have staggered out to fight with armour I couldn't walk in,
    a shield I couldn't carry,
    and a sword I couldn't lift!
Better that, you may say, than a sling and five stones,
    but you'd be wrong,
    for it proved to be four stones too many,
    just the one all I needed.
They saluted me afterwards,
    welcomed me back like a conquering hero.
But they shouldn't have, not if they'd stopped to think,
    for it wasn't me they owed their lives to,
    it was God,
    he alone who gave me strength.
It took some doing, don't think otherwise,
    to swallow my doubts and take up the fight,
    but when the call came I had to respond,
    for, let's face it, if God was with me,
    who could be against?

Prayer

Gracious God,
    there are times in our lives when we feel up against it,
    when everything seems to conspire against us.
We look at the problems confronting us,
    and we feel small and helpless,
    powerless to do anything about them.
Yet you are a God who time and again has used
    what seems insignificant in this world
    to achieve great things;
    a God who has overcome the strong through the weak;
    and a God who is able to accomplish within us
    far more than we can ask or even imagine.
Help us, then,
    when we are faced by obstacles which seem insurmountable,
    to put our trust in you,
    knowing that you will give us the strength we need,
    when we need it.
Amen.

30
DO YOU KNOW HOW IT FELT?

Jonathan

Reading – 1 Samuel 20:1-3, 12-17

David fled from Naioth in Ramah. He came before Jonathan and said, 'What have I done? What is my guilt? And what is my sin against your father that he is trying to take my life?' He said to him, 'Far from it! You shall not die. My father does nothing either great or small without disclosing it to me, and why should my father hide this from me? Never!' But David also swore, 'Your father knows well that you like me; and he thinks, "Do not let Jonathan know this, or he will be grieved." But truly, as the Lord lives and as you yourself live, there is but a step between me and death.'

Jonathan said to David, 'By the Lord, the God of Israel! When I have sounded out my father, about this time tomorrow, or on the third day, if he is well disposed towards David, shall I not then send and disclose it to you? But if my father intends to do you harm, the Lord do so to Jonathan, and more also, if I do not disclose it to you, and send you away, so that you may go in safety. May the Lord be with you, as he has been with my father. If I am still alive, show me the faithful love of the Lord; but if I die, never cut off your faithful love from my house, even if the Lord were to cut off every one of the enemies of David from the face of the earth.' Thus Jonathan made a covenant with the house of David, saying, 'May the Lord seek out the enemies of David.' Jonathan made David swear again by his love for him; for he loved him as he loved his own life.

Meditation

Do you know how it felt?
Have you any idea of the agonies I went through,
    the torment of indecision?
It was terrible,
    like a spear thrust into my side,
    and there was no way of escaping it.

A choice had to be made –
   David, or my father –
   and I was torn in two,
   my mind saying one thing,
   my heart another.
What could I do?
I loved my father, despite his faults,
   too many happy memories, too much shared together,
   for those to come between us.
Yet I loved David too,
   not through ties of blood,
   but as a friend,
   a brother in arms,
   almost, you might say, another self.
It's hard to describe it adequately,
   but there was a bond between us,
   a special affinity,
   each trusting the other implicitly.
I'd have put my life in his hands, if necessary,
   just as he, finally, had to do with me.
We never expected that, for all my father's raving.
I suppose we thought it would pass;
   that it was a temporary aberration,
   a moment's madness born of jealousy;
   only, of course, it wasn't.
It went much deeper than that –
   a malaise not just of mind, but of heart and soul,
   eating away inside until it finally consumed him.
I can't defend what he did, but I do ask this:
   don't be too hard on him,
   for it *wasn't* my father at the end,
   not the man I knew and loved –
   it was a pale shadow,
   a cruel imitation,
   robbed of reason and self-respect.
I've told myself that so many times,
   and it helps a little,
   for I know my helping David is what he'd have wanted,
   what he'd have asked me to do in happier days.
But I still can't help feeling I betrayed him,
   for I protected the man who would take away his crown,
   the man he admired yet feared more than any other –

and that knowledge is hard to live with.
Yet, despite the pain, it was the right decision,
    for though it cost me much, it gave me more –
    the chance to serve a friend in need,
    and a glimpse of what friendship really means.

Prayer

Living God,
    there are many we call our friends,
    few with whom we share real friendship.
We keep most of our relationships on a superficial level,
    rarely opening the secret places of our heart
    and showing ourselves as we truly are.
Thank you for that small circle of people,
    whether family or friends,
    among whom we can show such openness;
    deepen the bond between us
    and strengthen our commitment to each other.
Thank you, too,
    for wanting us to enjoy such a relationship with you,
    for accepting us as we really are;
    draw us closer to you,
    so that, inspired by your love which gave everything,
    we may offer our faithful service in return.
Teach us the meaning of friendship,
    and help us, through accepting its challenge,
    to discover also its joy.
Amen.

31

HE COULD HAVE KILLED ME, HAD HE WANTED TO

Saul

Reading – 1 Samuel 24:1-10, 16-20

When Saul returned from following the Philistines, he was told, 'David is in the wilderness of En-gedi.' Then Saul took three thousand chosen men out of all Israel, and went to look for David and his men in the direction of the Rocks of the Wild Goats. He came to the sheepfolds beside the road, where there was a cave; and Saul went in to relieve himself. Now David and his men were sitting in the innermost parts of the cave. The men of David said to him, 'Here is the day of which the Lord said to you, "I will give your enemy into your hand, and you shall do to him as it seems good to you".' Then David went and stealthily cut off a corner of Saul's cloak. Afterwards David was stricken to the heart because he had cut off a corner of Saul's cloak. He said to his men, 'The Lord forbid that I should do this thing to my lord, the Lord's anointed, to raise my hand against him, for he is the Lord's anointed.' So David scolded his men severely and did not permit them to attack Saul. Then Saul got up and left the cave, and went on his way.

Afterwards David also rose up and went out of the cave and called after Saul, 'My lord the king!' When Saul looked behind him, David bowed with his face to the ground, and did obeisance. David said to Saul, 'Why do you listen to the words of those who say, "David seeks to do you harm"? This very day your eyes have seen how the Lord gave you into my hand in the cave; and some urged me to kill you, but I spared you. I said, "I will not raise my hand against my lord; for he is the Lord's anointed".'

When David had finished speaking these words to Saul, Saul said, 'Is this your voice, my son David?' Saul lifted up his voice and wept. He said to David, 'You are more righteous than I; for you have repaid me good, whereas I have repaid you evil. Today you have explained how you have dealt well with me, in that you did not kill me when the Lord put me into your hands. For who has ever found an enemy, and sent the enemy safely away? So may the Lord reward you with good for what you have done to me this day. Now I know that you shall surely be king, and that the kingdom of Israel shall be established in your hand.'

Meditation

He could have killed me, had he wanted to –
    one thrust of his sword,
    one twist of his dagger,
    and it would have all been over,
    my reign history,
    his troubles at an end.
God knows, he'd good reason to wish me dead,
    for I'd wronged him shamefully,
    hunting him day and night like a petty thief,
    a common criminal,
    with never a moment's respite.
And with no cause, that's the irony,
    for he'd done me no wrong,
    his loyalty unquestionable
    and his conduct toward me beyond reproach.
But when the crowds shouted his name instead of mine,
    and when I recalled how God had chosen him
    and rejected me,
    it was as though a demon took control,
    a madness coursing through my every vein.
I felt let down,
    cheated,
    for it had been *me* once the crowd had idolised,
    me whom God had anointed,
    and I'd revelled in the privilege,
    the prestige,
    the responsibility of it all.
Who was this youngster,
    this nobody from Bethlehem,
    to march in and take my place?
What right had he,
    what reason, to presume he could step into my shoes
    and make my kingdom his?
The very thought made my blood boil.
All right, so he'd killed Goliath,
    seen off the threat of the Philistines.
And yes, maybe I had made mistakes,
    listened to the wrong counsel,
    but why should that cost me my throne?
I was as ready to listen as any man,

ready to learn,
    ready to make amends, if only God would let me.
Only it wasn't to be,
    and as the realisation sunk home
    so a plan took shape in my mind –
    get rid of David and it might all be different,
    the threat extinguished,
    my future secure.
I should have known better, of course,
    for it wasn't David I had to fear,
    it was God.
He would decide the future, not me,
    the fate of everyone, not simply David, in his hands.
I'd had my chance, and I'd thrown it away,
    sacrificing divine blessing for material reward,
    and though I could fool *myself* it would be different next time,
    I couldn't fool him.
The time had come for a change,
    and as I stood there with David it was all too clear why.
He'd had the chance to kill me,
    and he knew full well I'd have killed *him* in his shoes,
    but he preferred to let God have the final say.
There was the difference.

Prayer

Gracious God,
    we talk of giving *you* the glory,
    but all too often it is *ours* which really concerns us.
We speak of doing *your* will,
    yet it is *ours* we invariably follow.
Forgive us that we pay lip service to high ideals
    which are repeatedly denied by the way we live.
Teach us the secret of true humility and genuine trust,
    so that you may be able to take and use us
    for the work of your kingdom
    in your own way and your own time.
Amen.

32

I'M ASHAMED NOW, LOOKING BACK

David

Reading – 2 Samuel 11:2-6, 14-17, 26-27

It happened, late one afternoon, when David rose from his couch and was walking about on the roof of the king's house, that he saw from the roof a woman bathing; the woman was very beautiful. David sent someone to enquire about the woman. It was reported, 'This is Bathsheba daughter of Eliam, the wife of Uriah the Hittite.' So David sent messengers to get her, and she came to him, and he lay with her. (Now she was purifying herself after her period.) Then she returned to her house. The woman conceived; and she sent and told David, 'I am pregnant.'

So David sent word to Joab, 'Send me Uriah the Hittite.' And Joab sent Uriah to David.

In the morning David wrote a letter to Joab, and sent it by the hand of Uriah. In the letter he wrote, 'Set Uriah in the forefront of the hardest fighting, and then draw back from him, so that he may be struck down and die.' As Joab was besieging the city, he assigned Uriah to the place where he knew there were valiant warriors. The men of the city came out and fought with Joab; and some of the servants of David among the people fell. Uriah the Hittite was killed as well.

When the wife of Uriah heard that her husband was dead, she made lamentation for him. When the mourning was over, David sent and brought her to his house, and she became his wife, and bore him a son.

Meditation

I'm ashamed now, looking back,
   sickened that I could have been so cold,
   so callous,
   so calculating in making the prize I coveted mine.
Yet I felt no compunction at the time,
   that's what frightens me –
   no sense of remorse,
   still less regret.

I saw that woman,
 and I wanted her,
 all reason, all common sense,
 thrown to the wind in that fateful moment.
It was wrong, I knew it,
 a contradiction of everything I believed,
 but that didn't matter,
 nothing of any consequence save sating my desire.
So I connived and cheated,
 sending an innocent man to his death.
I stole and murdered,
 blind to all else in my passion, save making her mine.
Oh, you can split hairs if you want to –
 argue that she was to blame as much as I was,
 that I never struck the blow which killed her husband –
 but it's no use,
 I know in my heart I was responsible, no one else,
 the whole sordid business down to me.
It haunted us, afterwards, did you know that? –
 a shadow over our relationship,
 an ugly blot on our happiness.
But I can't complain, for I deserved what I got,
 and I'm only grateful that God, in his mercy, spared me more.
I'd like to think I'm different now,
 older and wiser,
 less ready to go off the rails on a moment's impulse.
But I'm not convinced,
 not convinced at all,
 for I can remember like it was only yesterday
 how I tossed everything aside,
 even my faith,
 when temptation raised its head.
I'm ashamed of it, believe me,
 disgusted by my own folly,
 but I know though the spirit is willing, the flesh is weak.
God be merciful to me, a sinner!

Prayer

Lord,
    it's easy to condemn.
We do it all the time,
    always ready to see the worst,
    to point the accusing finger,
    to throw the first stone.
But we know in our hearts we have nothing to boast about,
    no reason to set ourselves up in judgement over others.
We are all fallible, all make mistakes,
    each one of us vulnerable to temptation when it strikes;
    and we are all finally dependent on your grace
    to offer us forgiveness beyond our deserving.
Teach us, then, to show mercy to others
    as you have shown it to us,
    and to see our own faults
    as clearly as we see theirs.
Amen.

33

SHOULD I HAVE KEPT QUIET?

Nathan

Reading – 2 Samuel 12:1-7

The Lord sent Nathan to David. He came to him, and said to him, 'There were two men in a certain city, the one rich and the other poor. The rich man had very many flocks and herds; but the poor man had nothing but one little ewe lamb, which he had bought. He brought it up, and it grew up with him and with his children; it used to eat of his meagre fare, and drink from his cup, and lie in his bosom, and it was like a daughter to him. Now there came a traveller to the rich man, and he was loath to take one of his own flock or herd to prepare for the wayfarer who had come to him, but he took the poor man's lamb, and prepared that for the guest who had come to him.' Then David's anger was greatly kindled against the man. He said to Nathan, 'As the Lord lives, the man who has done this deserves to die; he shall restore the lamb fourfold, because he did this thing, and because he had no pity.'

Nathan said to David, 'You are the man!'

Meditation

Should I have kept quiet?
I was tempted, I have to admit it,
 for there was no knowing the sort of reception I'd get,
 whether I'd pay for my temerity with my life.
We don't like being criticised, any of us,
 and when you're a king, well, it's just not the done thing.
An affront to his dignity, that's how he could have seen it,
 or worse still, an act of treason –
 dress my words up how I like,
 they were bound to cause offence.
So why bother, I hear you say?
Why stick my neck out like that
 when it wasn't even my problem?

After all, the damage had been done,
    an innocent man sent to his death,
    and no amount of recrimination or remorse
    could bring him back,
    so why get involved?
I knew that,
    and, believe me, there's nothing I'd have liked more
    than to wash my hands of the whole sorry saga,
    look the other way and pretend it had never happened.
But I couldn't, could I? –
    for, like it or not, it *was* my problem,
    mine, and everyone else's,
    whether they recognised it or not.
It wasn't just that I was a prophet,
    entrusted with special responsibility
    and expected to give a lead to others.
It was the fact that I cared about my country,
    the society I lived in,
    and, equally important, I cared about David.
What he had done was wrong, there was no escaping it –
    a blot on our nation,
    a stain on his character –
    and though I tried my best to understand,
    put myself in his shoes,
    I couldn't just let it go,
    for what signal would that have given,
    and where would it finally have led?
Carry on, it would have said,
    and never mind the consequences.
Do what you like,
    and if someone gets hurt, that's their bad luck.
Is that the sort of world you want?
I don't.
But if it wasn't to be like that it was down to me,
    for why should others speak out if I kept silent?
I didn't relish the prospect one bit,
    and as I stood before David
    my knees were knocking and my mouth was dry.
But I tell you what,
    even if the outcome had been different,
    if my worst fears had been realised,
    I'd still have gone, and gone gladly,

for there are some things too important to let go,
some things you must be ready to die for
if life is to be worth living.

Prayer

Sovereign God,
  there is much in our world which is corrupt
  and much in our own society which is unjust,
  but we are afraid to speak out against it
  for fear of the consequences.
Even when wrongdoing affects us personally
  we are reluctant to protest in case the result proves costly.
We do not want to risk hostility or damage our credibility.
We are afraid that once we nail our colours to the mast
  there may be no going back.
And we are cautious also about throwing the first stone
  in case it turns out we have misunderstood the situation.
Sovereign God,
  you do not want us to judge,
  but you do want us to stand up for what is right
  and oppose what is evil.
Help us to recognise when those times are,
  and give us the courage then
  to be true to our convictions,
  and true to you.
Amen.

34

DID SHE IMAGINE I'D GO THROUGH WITH IT?

Solomon

Reading – 1 Kings 3:16-22, 24-28

Two women who were prostitutes came to the king and stood before him. The one woman said, 'Please, my Lord, this woman and I live in the same house; and I gave birth while she was in the house. Then on the third day after I gave birth, this woman also gave birth. We were together; there was no one else with us in the house. Then this woman's son died in the night, because she lay on him. She got up in the middle of the night and took my son from beside me while your servant slept. She laid him at her breast, and laid her dead son at my breast. When I rose in the morning to nurse my son, I saw that he was dead; but when I looked at him closely in the morning, clearly it was not the son I had borne.' But the other woman said, 'No, the living son is mine, and the dead son is yours.' The first said, 'No, the dead son is yours, and the living son is mine.' So they argued before the king.

So the king said, 'Bring me a sword,' and they brought a sword before the king. The king said, 'Divide the living boy in two; then give half to the one, and half to the other.' But the woman whose son was alive said to the king – because compassion for her son burned within her – 'Please, my Lord, give her the living boy; certainly do not kill him!' The other said, 'It shall be neither mine nor yours; divide it.' Then the king responded: 'Give the first woman the living boy; do not kill him. She is his mother.' All Israel heard of the judgement that the king had rendered, and they stood in awe of the king, because they perceived that the wisdom of God was in him, to execute justice.

Meditation

Did she imagine I'd go through with it?
From the look on her face it was clear that she did –
    a mixture of horror and sheer disbelief
    contorting her features.
I've never seen a woman so changed,
    her passion and devotion clear to all.

She loved that child with every ounce of her being,
    enough if necessary to condemn herself to a living death
    if it meant life for him.
There could be no question after that,
    not a shred of doubt left as to which was the true mother,
    and though her rival screamed in protest,
    she knew well enough she was beaten,
    her duplicity exposed for what it was.
I suppose, by rights, I should have punished her
    as many urged me to,
    for it was a shabby trick she'd tried to play,
    the cruellest deception imaginable,
    but as I looked deep into her eyes,
    I realised she'd suffered enough,
    whatever anyone might do to her was nothing
    compared with the torture she already endured.
You see, she'd loved just as much as the other,
    with the same ferocity, the same dedication,
    and, had the roles been reversed,
    I'm sure she'd have shown the same willingness
    to give her all to save her little one.
But for her that wasn't an option, was it?
Her child was dead,
    plucked from her,
    and her life was suddenly bereft,
    a bleak and barren wilderness, devoid of meaning.
Could I blame her after that for one moment's madness?
I'm not saying it excused her actions,
    but what she needed was comfort instead of rebuke,
    an arm around her shoulders
    rather than a whip across her back –
    I only hope someone, somewhere,
    had the heart to give it to her.
It caught the public imagination, that incident,
    helped more than any other to build my reputation
    as a man of God and fount of wisdom,
    and I can see why,
    for it brought a sticky situation to a just conclusion.
But don't imagine, as some seem to have done,
    that it all ended happily,
    for, whatever else, it didn't do that.
It did for the one, of course, and rightly so,

but the other? –
for her the pain and sorrow continued,
day after day,
year after year,
until her dying day.
So if you must remember what I did that day, that's fine,
only please,
please,
remember her too,
and pray for anyone who suffers as she has.

Prayer

Lord,
when we look beneath the veneer of our world
there is so much hurt, so much tragedy.
We cocoon ourselves from it, most of the time,
happy that such pain does not touch us,
and hoping we can get through life before it ever does.
But, of course, finally, as well as joy
we must all taste sorrow,
and when that comes we need the love, support
and understanding of others to see us through.
Forgive us, then, those times
when we have turned our backs on others
and added to their pain.
Forgive us for failing to respond
because we cannot find the words to say,
so making their sense of isolation all the more acute.
Forgive us for being so wrapped up in ourselves
that we are blind to needs even on our own doorstep.
Open our hearts to all who suffer,
and make real to them the extent of your love
through our willingness both to share and to care.
Amen.

35

WAS IT WORTH CARRYING ON?

Elijah

Reading – 1 Kings 19:9-13

At that place he came to a cave, and spent the night there. Then the word of the Lord came to him, saying, 'What are you doing here, Elijah?' He answered, 'I have been very zealous for the Lord, the God of hosts; for the Israelites have forsaken your covenant, thrown down your altars, and killed your prophets with the sword. I alone am left, and they are seeking my life, to take it away.'

He said, 'Go out and stand on the mountain before the Lord, for the Lord is about to pass by.' Now there was a great wind, so strong that it was splitting mountains and breaking rocks in pieces before the Lord, but the Lord was not in the wind; and after the wind an earthquake, but the Lord was not in the earthquake; and after the earthquake a fire, but the Lord was not in the fire; and after the fire a sound of sheer silence. When Elijah heard it, he wrapped his face in his mantle and went out and stood at the entrance of the cave. Then there came a voice to him that said, 'What are you doing here, Elijah?'

Meditation

Was it worth carrying on?
I couldn't help but wonder,
   for, despite everything God had done,
   the countless signs he'd given,
   it seemed I was the last one left,
   the only one in all Israel ready to honour his name.
I'd bounced back before from such moments –
   just when all had seemed hopeless
   his power bringing fresh hope –
   but this time there seemed no grounds for such confidence,
   for though he'd humiliated their prophets,
   poured scorn on their gods,
   still my enemies pursued me,

more determined than ever to do me in.
So I took myself off and went into hiding,
    waiting for the inevitable end.
And that's where he found me,
    the God who never lets go,
    calling me back on to my feet,
    back into active service.
What could I do?
After all the setbacks, the innumerable false dawns,
    it seemed pointless,
    yet he was my one firm hold in an ever-shifting world.
So I went, as he told me, up on to the mountain,
    and there I met him as never before,
    not in the wind,
    nor in the earthquake,
    nor in the fire,
    but in a soft and gentle whisper –
    almost, you might call it, the sound of silence.
It was a moment I never expected,
    but one I shall always treasure,
    for I realised God was telling me something special,
    something I so badly needed to hear.
No need for signs and wonders, this time,
    no call for displays of power to get the message home –
    he was speaking in the stillness,
    teaching me that though I might not see him,
    and though his voice may seem strangely silent,
    he'd be with me always,
    close by my side to my journey's end.
I returned eagerly after that,
    heart singing,
    spirit soaring.
And do you know what? –
    I *wasn't* the last one left, the only one serving the Lord;
    there were *others*,
    more than I had dared dream,
    still loyal to his cause.
I should have known, shouldn't I? –
    should have trusted he would not fail.
Well, I know now, and I tell you this,
    even though I cry and hear no answer,
    even though I look and see no sign,

I won't lose heart, still less give up;
I'll take time to be still,
to savour the quietness,
and to rejoice that God is God.

Prayer

Gracious God,
    you do not always answer our prayers as we ask
    or work in the way we hope.
Your purpose can be hard to fathom
    and your will difficult to understand,
    so that we wonder at times
    if you have heard our prayer
    or care about our plight.
At our lowest moments
    we even question the point of praying at all.
Yet you do answer,
    not simply through your word of old,
    nor solely through the channels we lay down for you,
    but through your still small voice –
    your word even in the silence.
Amen.

36

THE TIME HAD COME

Elisha

Reading – 2 Kings 2:1, 9-13

Now when the Lord was about to take Elijah up to heaven by a whirlwind, Elijah and Elisha were on their way from Gilgal.

Elijah said to Elisha, 'Tell me what I may do for you before I am taken from you.' Elisha said, 'Please let me inherit a double share of your spirit.' He responded, 'You have asked a hard thing; yet, if you see me as I am being taken from you, it will be granted you; if not, it will be not.' As they continued walking and talking, a chariot of fire and horses of fire separated the two of them, and Elijah ascended in a whirlwind into heaven. Elisha kept watching and crying, 'Father, father! The chariots of Israel and its horsemen!' But when he could no longer see him, he grasped his own clothes and tore them in two pieces.

Meditation

The time had come,
    the moment I'd dreaded for so long,
    which I'd steadfastly thrust to the back of my mind,
    hoping it need never happen –
    suddenly there before me –
    and there was no escape!
No longer could I follow in the master's footsteps,
    watching him at work from the safety of the shadows.
I was on my own now,
    carrying on from where he had left off –
    and the prospect was terrifying,
    more daunting than I can tell you.
All right, so I'd watched and listened, like I say,
    drinking in his every word and action day after day;
    and, yes, we'd talked together long and often,
    sometimes into the small hours of the night,
    discussing first this point, then that.
But he'd always been the boss,

the one I looked up to,
    my childhood hero for as long as I could remember.
Me? I was just his servant,
    nothing more,
    and scarcely qualified for that,
    let alone to step into the great man's shoes.
Yet I'd known for a long time he had other ideas,
    so when he turned to me that morning to break the news,
    I went cold with dread,
    overcome by the responsibility he was giving to me.
I didn't feel ready,
    nowhere near;
    just a rank beginner, still cutting my teeth.
Some day, if I had to –
    that's what I felt like saying –
    but not yet, please!
Only I couldn't, could I? –
    not given that look in his eyes,
    the confidence he so clearly placed in me.
So I did the next best thing –
    took a deep breath and nodded acceptance . . .
    on one condition:
    that he give me a double share,
    an extra portion of his spirit.
Does that sound greedy?
It wasn't meant to be.
It's simply that I was desperate –
    painfully aware of my own weakness beside his strength –
    and without help I knew I'd be sunk,
    lost without trace in my own mediocrity.
Was he surprised at my audacity?
I think he was rather.
But I think, more than that, he was disappointed,
    as though after all I'd seen and heard
    I should know better than to ask such a thing.
So did I get what I asked for?
Well, let me put it this way,
    I watched just as I'd been told to,
    eyes on him like a hawk,
    and as he disappeared from sight
    it suddenly dawned on me what he wanted me to see.
It wasn't *his* spirit which had sustained his ministry

and brought such power,
it was God's –
and that same spirit which had filled him all those years
now flowed through me.
Does that answer your question?
It did mine,
for I wasn't on my own now as I'd feared I might be;
I was still following in the Master's footsteps,
as the great man had done before me!

Prayer

Loving God,
it is not easy to carry responsibilities.
We prefer to share the burden with others,
to have someone else we can lean on,
knowing that they will always be there to support us.
But there are times
when we have to stand on our own two feet
and accept the challenges life brings.
Help us, when those moments come,
to recognise that, however helpless we may feel,
we are never alone,
for you are always with us, giving us the help we need
to meet those challenges head on.
Teach us to trust in your strength,
and through the power of the Holy Spirit
faithfully to discharge the responsibilities you give us.
Amen.

37

WHO DID HE TAKE ME FOR?

Naaman

Reading – 2 Kings 5:1-5, 9-15

Naaman, commander of the army of the king of Aram, was a great man and in high favour with his master, because by him the Lord had given victory to Aram. The man, though a mighty warrior, suffered from leprosy. Now the Arameans on one of their raids had taken a young girl captive from the land of Israel, and she served Naaman's wife. She said to her mistress, 'If only my lord were with the prophet who is in Samaria! He would cure him of his leprosy.' So Naaman went in and told his lord just what the girl from the land of Israel had said. And the king of Aram said, 'Go then, and I will send along a letter to the king of Israel.'

So Naaman came with his horses and chariots, and halted at the entrance of Elisha's house. Elisha sent a messenger to him, saying, 'Go, wash in the Jordan seven times, and your flesh shall be restored and you shall be clean.' But Naaman became angry and went away, saying, 'I thought that for me he would surely come out, and stand and call on the name of the Lord his God, and would wave his hand over the spot, and cure the leprosy! Are not Abana and Pharpar, the rivers of Damascus, better than all the waters of Israel? Could I not wash in them, and be clean?' He turned and went away in a rage. But his servants approached him and said to him, 'Father, if the prophet had commanded you to do something difficult, would you not have done it? How much more, when all he said to you was, "Wash, and be clean"?' So he went down and immersed himself seven times in the Jordan, according to the word of the man of God; his flesh was restored like the flesh of a young boy, and he was clean.

Then he returned to the man of God, he and all his company; he came and stood before him and said, 'Now I know that there is no God in all the earth except in Israel.'

Meditation

Who did he take me for? – that's what I wanted to know!
Honestly, I wasn't just any old visitor,
   one of his average clientele;

I was a national celebrity,
    commander of the Aramean army,
    accepted in the highest circles of the land.
And why not? –
    for, against all the odds, I'd led them to victory,
    distinguished myself both in leadership and valour.
So when this so-called prophet from Israel
    ordered me to take a dip in the Jordan,
    quite frankly, I was livid.
It was an insult,
    a deliberate attempt to humiliate me,
    at least that's how it seemed –
    and had I been back in my own country
    I'd have clapped the fellow in irons,
    either that or had him flogged there on the spot.
Not that I was surprised, mind you,
    for I'd had my doubts from the beginning,
    the moment that servant girl of mine
    dreamt up the hair-brained scheme.
Oh, she meant well, no doubt,
    and I was touched by her devotion;
    but, I ask you,
    Israel – hardly the centre of the universe, is it?
So there I was, stomping back home in a rage,
    telling myself I'd been a fool to listen to her,
    when one of my men took me quietly aside.
It took some doing, tackling me in a mood like that,
    and I could see he half-expected me
    to bite his head off at any moment,
    but even as the oaths were forming on my lips
    so his words sunk home.
In all honesty, what had I to lose –
    surely anything was better
    than the fate which lay in store for me?
And let's face it, whether it be Aram or Judea,
    a river is just a river.
It was my pride holding me back, nothing more,
    a misplaced sense of my own importance preventing me
    from taking perhaps the most important step of my life.
So I went back,
    and went down into the water,
    just as he'd told me to;

and when I came up that seventh time,
it wasn't just my skin made new,
it was my mind,
my soul,
my everything –
life more precious than it had ever been before!
Who did he think he was? –
that's what I asked at the beginning,
but as I made my way home,
I realised it was the wrong question,
to the wrong person,
for I'd been touched by that God of his,
a God unlike any I'd met before,
and a God who was asking me, quite simply,
who did *I* think *he* was?

Prayer

Gracious God,
you call us to walk humbly with you,
open to your voice and the voice of others,
yet the reality is that all too often
we are full of our own importance.
We believe we know best,
and resent ideas different from our own.
We think we can cope, and resist offers of support.
We talk of your glory,
but it is our own which concerns us,
so much of our time spent nursing or bolstering our egos.
Forgive us for looking inwards instead of outwards;
for letting our preoccupation with self
blind us to who you would have us be.
Teach us to humble ourselves under your mighty hand,
knowing that when we do that
you will lift us up to live life in all its fullness.
Amen.

38

WHAT GROUNDS DID I HAVE FOR CONFIDENCE?

Hezekiah

Reading – 2 Kings 18:1, 3, 5-7, 13, 17a, 28-32a; 19:15-19

In the third year of King Hoshea son of Elah of Israel, Hezekiah son of King Ahaz of Judah began to reign. . . . He did what was right in the sight of the Lord just as his ancestor David had done. . . . He trusted in the Lord the God of Israel; so that there was no one like him among all the kings of Judah after him, or among those who were before him. For he held fast to the Lord; he did not depart from following him but kept the commandments that the Lord commanded Moses. The Lord was with him; wherever he went, he prospered. He rebelled against the king of Assyria and would not serve him.

In the fourteenth year of King Hezekiah, King Sennacherib of Assyria came up against all the fortified cities of Judah and captured them. . . . The king of Assyria sent the Tartan, the Rabsaris, and the Rabshakeh with a great army from Lachish to King Hezekiah at Jerusalem.

Then the Rabshakeh stood and called out in a loud voice in the language of Judah, 'Hear the word of the great king, the king of Assyria! Thus says the king: "Do not let Hezekiah deceive you, for he will not be able to deliver you out of my hand. Do not let Hezekiah make you rely on the Lord by saying, The Lord will surely deliver us, and this city will not be given into the hand of the king of Assyria." Do not listen to Hezekiah; for thus says the king of Assyria: "Make your peace with me and come out to me; that every one of you will eat from your own vine and your own fig tree, and drink water from your own cistern, until I come and take you away to a land like your own land, a land of grain and wine, a land of bread and vineyards, a land of olive oil and honey, that you may live and not die."'

And Hezekiah prayed before the Lord, and said: 'O Lord the God of Israel, who are enthroned above the cherubim, you are God, you alone, of all the kingdoms of the earth; you have made heaven and earth. Incline your ear, O Lord, and hear; open your eyes, O Lord, and see; hear the words of Sennacherib, which he has sent to mock the living God. Truly, O Lord, the kings of Assyria have laid waste the nations and their lands, and have hurled their gods into the fire, though they were no gods but the work of human hands – wood and stone – and so they were destroyed. So now, O Lord our God, save us, I pray you, from his hand, so that all the kingdoms of the earth may know that you, O Lord, are God alone.'

Meditation

What grounds did I have for confidence?
You may well ask, for there were precious few;
    none at all, according to many!
We were a tiny fish in a vast ocean;
    the prospect of being swallowed up
    seeming more likely every minute.
So why struggle on, some wanted to know;
    surely the time had come to face facts.
Better to bend a little than be broken completely,
    that's what they thought;
    nothing too shocking –
    just a willingness to move with the times,
    go with the wind –
    God would understand.
And, yes, he probably would,
    despite what some may tell you,
    for he's always been more patient,
    more loving,
    more understanding than most of us ever dare imagine.
Yet it was no good,
    for, you see, we'd given way too much already,
    and if we went any further down the road of compromise
    it was obvious where it would end.
We'd survive, after a fashion,
    but any life left to us would be a pale shadow,
    a pathetic reflection of what once had been,
    for no matter what they might tell us
    I knew peace would be at a price.
Could we have stomached that –
    our faith desecrated,
    our convictions neutered,
    our identity lost for ever?
I couldn't.
And deep down, despite their misgivings,

I didn't think my people could either.
So I made my stand,
 threw down the gauntlet,
 dug in my heels.
There were few grounds for confidence, it's true,
 little reason, humanly speaking,
 to hold any kind of hope for the future.
Our enemies were closing in, sensing the kill,
 and I knew they had the power to strip us bare,
 plunder our homes, our wealth and our freedom.
Yet, whatever else, we would still have God,
 nobody but ourselves could take *him* from us,
 and it seemed to me, so long as that were true,
 though the cost would be hard to bear
 we'd still have the best of the bargain,
 the one prize that really counted.

Prayer

Living God,
 faced by the complexities of life,
 we are uncertain sometimes as to the right way forward.
We wish issues were black and white,
 but so often they are shades of grey,
 making it impossible to offer categorical answers.
Give us guidance
 so that we will know when we ought to bend
 and when we should make a stand.
Grant us humility
 to recognise that others have insights as valid as our own,
 but grant us also courage
 to hold on to our principles when it is necessary.
Above all, help us to stay faithful to you,
 despite the pressures to compromise,
 knowing that you will always stay faithful to us.
Amen.

39

DO YOU KNOW WHAT WE FOUND TODAY?

Josiah

Reading – 2 Chronicles 34:14-21

While they were bringing out the money that had been brought into the house of the Lord, the priest Hilkiah found the book of the Law of the Lord given through Moses. Hilkiah said to the secretary Shaphan, 'I have found the book of the Law in the house of the Lord'; and Hilkiah gave the book to Shaphan. Shaphan brought the book to the king, and further reported to the king, 'All that was committed to your servants they are doing. They have emptied out the money that was found in the house of the Lord and have delivered it into the hand of the overseers and the workers.' The secretary Shaphan informed the king, 'The priest Hilkiah has given me a book.' Shaphan then read it aloud to the king.

When the king heard the words of the Law he tore his clothes. Then the king commanded Hilkiah, Ahikam son of Shaphan, Abdon son of Micah, the secretary Shaphan, and the king's servant Asaiah: 'Go, enquire of the Lord for me and for those who are left in Israel and in Judah, concerning the words of the book that has been found; for the wrath of the Lord that is poured out on us is great, because our ancestors did not keep the word of the Lord, to act in accordance with all that is written in this book.'

Meditation

Do you know what we found today,
    hidden away in the temple?
Go on, have a guess?
A priestly robe?
A sacred relic?
A heavenly messenger?
No, none of those.
Something much more simple,
    yet much more shocking.
A scroll, that's what it was,
    neatly rolled,

carefully bound,
　　locked away.
'So what?' I hear you say,
　　'What's so exciting about that?'
And you'd have a point, had it been any old scroll.
But it wasn't –
　　it was the book of the Law,
　　God's word to Moses,
　　the founding document of our nation –
　　and we'd forgotten it even existed!
Can you imagine what it felt like,
　　hearing those words read to me –
　　God suddenly speaking again,
　　setting out his will and purpose for his people?
I could scarcely take it in,
　　overwhelmed by sheer emotion,
　　an uncanny mixture of wonder and dread.
To think that such a priceless heritage
　　could have been locked away for so many years,
　　untouched,
　　unread,
　　unheeded.
How had it happened, I wanted to know?
How could something so vital for our people,
　　so central to our faith,
　　be forgotten like that,
　　out of sight and out of mind?
It seemed beyond belief,
　　yet it was true,
　　the evidence there before my very eyes,
　　crying out in eloquent accusation.
What did I do about it?
Well, I acted, didn't I?
Took steps, immediately,
　　to ensure it should never happen again,
　　that from then on the book of the covenant
　　should receive its rightful place.
Yet, I wonder, will those steps be enough?
We've learned our lesson, believe me,
　　but will those who come after us learn from our mistakes?
We had God's word there in our possession,
　　his gracious word of life,

but for so long we failed to read it,
  leaving it instead to gather dust in a cupboard.
Surely no one else could be so foolish as to do the same . . .
  could they?

Prayer

Gracious God,
  you have spoken to us not just through the Law,
  but through the prophets,
  through words of wisdom, history and psalms,
  and through the testimony of Evangelists and Apostles
  to Jesus Christ, the Word made flesh.
We can turn to the Bible whenever we wish to
  and read it freely in our own tongue.
We can read new translations
  which help bring the age-old message to life,
  and we have access to all kinds of resources
  designed to deepen our understanding of all we read.
Forgive us that all too often
  we leave your word sitting on a shelf,
  unopened, unexplored.
Help us to recognise the priceless treasure
  you have given us in the Scriptures,
  and teach us in the clamour of each day
  to make time to read them reverently and thoughtfully,
  so that your voice may speak again,
  offering light to our path
  and the way to life in all its fullness.
Amen.

40

COULD I HONESTLY MAKE A DIFFERENCE?

Esther

Reading – Esther 3:8-10; 4:1, 5, 9-16

Then Haman said to King Ahasuerus, 'There is a certain people scattered and separated among the peoples in all the provinces of your kingdom; their laws are different from those of every other people, and they do not keep the king's laws, so that it is not appropriate for the king to tolerate them. If it pleases the king, let a decree be issued for their destruction, and I will pay ten thousand talents of silver into the hands of those who have charge of the king's business, so that they may put it into the king's treasures.' So the king took his signet ring from his hand and gave it to Haman son of Hammedatha the Agagite, the enemy of the Jews.

When Mordecai learned all that had been done, Mordecai tore his clothes and put on sackcloth and ashes, and went through the city, wailing with a loud and bitter cry.

Then Esther called for Hathach, one of the king's eunuchs, who had been appointed to attend her, and ordered him to go to Mordecai to learn what was happening and why . . . Hathach went and told Esther what Mordecai had said. Then Esther spoke to Hathach and gave him a message for Mordecai, saying, 'All the king's servants and the people of the king's provinces know that if any man or woman goes to the king inside the inner court without being called, there is but one law – all alike are to be put to death. Only if the king holds out the golden sceptre to someone, may that person live. I myself have not been called to come in to the king for thirty days.' When they told Mordecai what Esther had said, Mordecai told them to reply to Esther, 'Do not think that in the king's palace you will escape any more than all the other Jews. For if you keep silence at such a time as this, relief and deliverance will rise for the Jews from another quarter, but you and your father's family will perish. Who knows? Perhaps you have come to royal dignity for just such a time as this.' Then Esther said in reply to Mordecai, 'Go, gather all the Jews to be found in Susa, and hold a fast on my behalf, and neither eat nor drink for three days, night or day. I and my maids will also fast as you do. After that I will go to the king, though it is against the law; and if I perish, I perish.'

Meditation

Could I honestly make a difference?
It seemed hard to believe,
    the very idea preposterous,
    but I had to do something,
    for surely anything in the circumstances was worth a go?
My people were under threat,
    not just the odd one or two, but every one of them,
    facing the prospect of wholesale slaughter.
I couldn't just stand by and let them face their doom,
    however ineffectual my efforts might be,
    for we were inseparably bound,
    the same culture,
    the same faith,
    the same God.
If anyone could help them, I could.
Not that there were any guarantees, I knew that –
    the fact that I was his wife counted for nothing.
He was the king,
    ruler of a mighty empire,
    the difference between life and death
    dependent on his whim;
    and I was but one of many,
    each vying for his favour,
    each waiting for his call.
I'd pleased him once –
    could I do so again?
It wasn't just *my* future which rested on the answer,
    it was my nation's,
    the fate of us all hanging by a thread.
Yet I had no qualms,
    no second thoughts;
    incredible though it seemed,
    I realised God had put me there for such a time as that.
It was my chance to serve him,
    to do my bit for his kingdom,
    and I couldn't afford to waste it.
So I went –
    ignoring tradition,
    flouting every rule in the book,
    I entered his chamber and stood before him.

Was he surprised?
I was too terrified to notice,
    but to my amazement he listened –
    attention personified –
    and when I'd finished he gave the order,
    sentencing not *us* to death,
    but those who would have seen us killed!
We were safe,
    free to walk the streets with heads held high.
    and together we gave thanks to God.
But do you know what happened next?
I'm afraid so – they made me a celebrity,
    much to my embarrassment.
No, I'm not being modest, despite what some may think.
I took a risk, it's true,
    and yes, it could have cost me my life,
    but no more than if I'd closed my eyes and done nothing,
    my fate irrevocably tied to theirs.
I did what I could, that's all,
    what God would have asked of anyone –
    the rest was down to him.

Prayer

Living God,
    for us all there come opportunities to serve you;
    to use our gifts, position or circumstances
    to further your purpose.
You do not force us to respond,
    but invite us to share
    in making your love real on earth.
We can offer ourselves freely,
    or hold back,
    afraid of the cost, reluctant to let go.
Forgive us that all too often we choose the latter;
    that through our failure to give *to* you
    we deny our claim to live *for* you.
Inspire us through the example
    of those who have risked everything

in the cause of your kingdom,
and help us,
remembering the One who sacrificed all,
to give the little you ask from us.
Amen.

WISDOM, SONGS AND STORIES

41

WHAT DID I DO WRONG, CAN YOU TELL ME?

Job

Reading – Job 23:2-17

Today also my complaint is bitter;
his hand is heavy despite my groaning.
Oh, that I knew where I might find him,
that I might come even to his dwelling!
I would lay my case before him,
and fill my mouth with arguments.
I would learn what he would answer me,
and understand what he would say to me.
Would he contend with me in the greatness of his power?
No; but he would give heed to me.
There an upright person could reason with him,
and I should be acquitted for ever by my judge.

If I go forward, he is not there;
or backward, I cannot perceive him;
on the left he hides, and I cannot behold him;
I turn to the right, but I cannot see him.
But he knows the way that I take;
when he has tested me, I shall come out like gold.
My foot has held fast to his steps;
I have kept his way and have not turned aside.
I have not departed from the commandment of his lips;
I have treasured in my bosom the words of his mouth.
But he stands alone and who can dissuade him?
What he desires, that he does.
For he will complete what he appoints for me;
and many such things are in his mind.
Therefore I am terrified at his presence;
when I consider, I am in dread of him.
God has made my heart faint;
the Almighty has terrified me.
If only I could vanish in darkness,
and thick darkness would cover my face!

Meditation

What did I do wrong, can you tell me?
What terrible crime did I commit to deserve such pain,
    such sorrow,
    such suffering?
I've asked myself that day after day,
    year after year –
    the question always there,
    adding yet more torment to my private hell –
    and it's with me still,
    refusing to be silenced
    despite my every attempt to lance its poison.
Yet for all my searching I find no answer,
    not one moment of madness
    to explain these endless months of misery.
Oh, I've made my mistakes like anyone else –
    foolish words,
    foolish thoughts,
    foolish deeds –
    but nothing especially shocking,
    no worse than anything others do all around me,
    so why is it that I suffer and they don't,
    I endure such agony and they enjoy such blessing?
It makes no sense, for I've tried to be faithful,
    day after day seeking the Lord's will,
    studying his word,
    following his commandments,
    so why does he hide his face from me
    in my hour of despair?
Repent, that's what they tell me,
    acknowledge my weakness,
    confess my mistakes,
    and all shall be well.
They mean well, I know that,
    each one, in their own way,
    trying to make sense of the inexplicable,
    but if they only knew the added pain they cause me,
    the extra burden they impose,
    perhaps then, like me, they'd learn to be silent,
    accepting that the ways of God are beyond us all.
I don't blame them, for they want answers,

easy solutions to uncomfortable questions,
but you can take it from me –
from someone who's experienced
depths of suffering I pray you'll never know –
it's not that simple,
not that simple at all.

Prayer

Living God,
  there is so much suffering in this world of ours;
  so much pain, so much sorrow, so much evil.
It is hard sometimes to reconcile all this
  with it being your world too,
  created by you and precious in your sight.
We search desperately for answers,
  clinging first to this and then to that,
  and underneath there are times
  when our faith begins to crumble.
Teach us, though we cannot always see it,
  that you are there,
  sharing in our anguish,
  carrying in yourself the agony of creation
  as it groans under the weight of imperfection.
Teach us that you will not rest
  until that day when all suffering is ended,
  when evil is no more
  and your kingdom is established;
  and in that assurance give us strength to face each day,
  whatever it might bring.
Amen.

42

I USED TO LAUGH ONCE, LONG AGO

Job

Reading – Job 29:1-6; 30:16-23

Job again took up his discourse and said:
'O that I were as in the months of old,
as in the days when God watched over me;
when his lamp shone over my head,
and by his light I walked through darkness;
when I was in my prime,
when the friendship of God was upon my tent;
when the Almighty was still with me,
when my children were around me;
when my steps were washed with milk,
and the rock poured out for me streams of oil!

Now my soul is poured out within me;
days of affliction have taken hold of me.
The night racks my bones,
and the pain that gnaws me takes no rest.
With violence he seizes my garment;
he grasps me by the collar of my tunic.
He has cast me down into the mire,
and I have become like dust and ashes.
I cry to you and you do not answer me;
I stand, and you merely look at me.
You have turned cruel to me;
with the might of your hand you persecute me.
You lift me up on the wind, make me ride on it,
and you toss me about in the roar of the storm.
I know that you will bring me to death,
and to the house appointed for all the living.

Meditation

I used to laugh once, long ago,
    life overflowing with happiness,
    brimful with joy.
You find that hard to believe?
I'm not surprised,
    for to see me now –
    the lines of misery on my forehead,
    the despair deep in my eyes –
    you'd think I must have known only sorrow,
    a lifetime of perpetual shadow and endless pain.
Yet it wasn't always like that, not by a long way.
There was a time when my spirit soared and my heart skipped,
    when the sun rose rich with promise, new every morning,
    each day a priceless treasure,
    each moment a gift to be savoured.
I rejoiced then in the beauty of it all,
    overwhelmed by the wonder of creation
    and the sweetness of life,
    and I lifted my voice to God in exultation,
    his praise always on my lips.
Only that was then, and this is now,
    such carefree moments a distant memory,
    troubling my thoughts like some half-remembered dream,
    so that I question if they ever truly were.
Yet it's no good looking back;
    no answers to be found there.
It's the future that matters,
    and despite all I've faced I await it with confidence,
    convinced that God will be with me to lead me forward;
    for, believe it or not, through all the pain and heartache
    somehow I've grown,
    my faith stronger,
    refined through fire,
    able to withstand whatever may be thrown against it.
I may not celebrate quite as I used to,
    for I will bear the scars within me until my dying day,
    but I will laugh with a greater understanding,
    I will love with a deeper passion,
    and I will live with a richer sense of purpose,
    for I have stared into the darkness,

a blackness beyond words,
and I've found God coming to meet me,
his light reaching out, even there!

Reading – Job 38:1-2; 40:7-9; 42:1-6

Then the Lord answered Job out of the whirlwind: 'Who is this that darkens counsel by words without knowledge? . . . Gird up your loins like a man: I will question you, and you declare to me. Will you even put me in the wrong? Will you condemn me that you may be justified? Have you an arm like God, and can you thunder with a voice like his?'

Then Job answered the Lord: 'I know that you can do all things, and that no purpose of yours can be thwarted. "Who is this that hides counsel without knowledge?" Therefore I have uttered what I did not understand, things too wonderful for me, which I did not know. "Hear, and I will speak; I will question you, and you declare to me." I had heard of you by the hearing of the ear, but now my eye sees you; therefore I despise myself, and repent in dust and ashes.'

Prayer

Gracious God,
   you came to our world through Jesus Christ,
   and despite everything that conspires against you,
   your love continues to shine through him.
You conquered the forces of evil,
   you overcame the sting of death,
   and you brought joy out of sorrow,
   hope out of despair.
Teach us, whatever we may face,
   to hold on to that truth,
   confident that you will always lead us out of darkness
   into your marvellous light.
Hold on to us when life is hard,
   and assure us that you are present
   even in the bleakest moments,
   able to use every moment of each day
   in ways beyond our imagining.
Amen.

43
Is it possible?

David

Reading – Psalm 8

O Lord, our Sovereign,
how majestic is your name in all the earth!

You have set your glory above the heavens.
Out of the mouths of babes and infants
you have founded a bulwark because of your foes,
to silence the enemy and the avenger.

When I look at your heavens, the work of your fingers,
the moon and the stars that you have established;
what are human beings that you are mindful of them,
mortals that you care for them?

Yet you have made them a little lower than God,
and crowned them with glory and honour.
You have given them dominion over the works of your hands;
you have put all things under their feet,
all sheep and oxen,
and also the beasts of the field,
the birds of the air, and the fish of the sea,
whatever passes along the paths of the seas.

O Lord, our Sovereign,
how majestic is your name in all the earth!

Meditation

Is it possible?
Can it really be true that God has time for you and me?
It seems preposterous,
    stretching credulity to the limit,

for what place can we have in the grand scheme of things;
   what reason for God to concern himself about our fate?
I look at the vastness of the heavens
   and the awesome tapestry of creation,
   and we're nothing,
   just the tiniest speck against the great backdrop of history.
And yet amazingly,
   astonishingly,
   we matter!
Not just *noticed* by God,
   but *precious* to him,
   special,
   unique,
   holding an unrivalled place in his affections and purpose.
Can it be true? –
   a little lower than God himself,
   made in his image?
It sounds fantastic,
   almost blasphemous,
   for who are we –
   weak, sinful, fatally flawed humanity –
   to be likened to the sovereign God,
   creator of the ends of the earth,
   enthroned in splendour,
   perfect in his holiness?
Yet there it is,
   incredible yet true,
   not just part of creation but stewards over it –
   the beasts of the field,
   the birds of the air,
   the fish of the sea –
   their future in our hands;
   this wonderful world,
   so beautiful,
   so fragile,
   placed into our keeping,
   held on trust.
That's how much he loves us,
   the ultimate proof of his care.
What a wonderful privilege!
What an awesome responsibility!

Prayer

Lord of all,
    your love for us involves responsibility
    as well as privilege.
Our place in creation carries a duty to nurture
    rather than simply exploit it.
Forgive us for our part in a society
    that has too often lived for today
    with no thought of tomorrow,
    plundering this world's resources
    with little care as to the consequences.
Challenge the hearts and minds of people everywhere,
    that they and we may understand more fully
    both the wonder and the fragility
    of this planet you have given us,
    and so honour our calling to be faithful stewards of it all.
In the name of Christ we pray.
Amen.

44

I'M A LUCKY MAN

David

Reading – Psalm 16

Protect me, O God, for in you I take refuge.
I say to the Lord, 'You are my Lord;
I have no good apart from you.'
As for the holy ones in the land, they are the noble,
in whom is all my delight.

Those who choose another god multiply their sorrows;
their drink offerings of blood I will not pour out
or take their names upon my lips.

The Lord is my chosen portion and my cup;
you hold my lot.
The boundary lines have fallen for me in pleasant places;
I have a goodly heritage.

I bless the Lord who gives me counsel;
in the night also my heart instructs me.
I keep the Lord always before me;
because he is at my right hand, I shall not be moved.

Therefore my heart is glad, and my soul rejoices;
my body also rests secure.
For you do not give me up to Sheol,
or let your faithful one see the Pit.

You show me the path of life.
In your presence there is fullness of joy;
in your right hand are pleasures for evermore.

Meditation

I'm a lucky man –
    so much to be thankful for,
    so much to celebrate,
    my life running over with good things!
All right, I've not got everything, admittedly,
    and yes, perhaps I would change the odd detail
    given the chance,
    but nothing major,
    certainly nothing to fret over,
    for when I stop to count my blessings,
    weigh things up in the balance,
    I realise how truly fortunate I am.
I should never have forgotten, of course,
    but I did,
    and I do,
    time after time,
    to my shame not only failing to be thankful
    but actually complaining,
    bemoaning my lot,
    dwelling on the bad rather than the good.
It's crazy, I know,
    but we all do it, don't we? –
    so much taken for granted,
    unrecognised,
    unappreciated;
    so feeble a response to so vast a treasure.
Probably it will always be the same,
    despite my best intentions,
    the gratitude I feel now
    evaporating yet again before I know it.
Probably I'll still end up feeling sorry for myself,
    looking enviously at my neighbour,
    muttering that life's not fair.
But today at least I want to give thanks,
    I want to celebrate everything in life that is good and special,
    and, above all, I want to praise God,
    to whom I owe it all.

Prayer

Lord,
    we have so much to thank you for,
    yet all too often we take it for granted.
Instead of counting our blessings,
    we dwell on our problems.
Instead of celebrating all you have given,
    we brood about what we might yet have.
In our pursuit of illusory dreams of happiness
    we lose sight of the gifts each day brings,
    the countless reasons we have to rejoice.
Forgive us for forgetting how fortunate we are,
    and help us to appreciate the wonder
    of all we have received from your loving hands.
In the name of Christ.
Amen.

45

I FELT ALONE

David

Reading – Psalm 22:1-2, 7-11, 16b-19, 23-24

My God, my God, why have you forsaken me?
Why are you so far from helping me,
from the words of my groaning?
O my God, I cry by day, but you do not answer;
and by night, but find no rest.

All who see me mock at me;
they make mouths at me, they shake their heads;
'Commit your cause to the Lord; let him deliver –
let him rescue the one in whom he delights!'

Yet it was you who took me from the womb,
you who kept me safe on my mother's breast.
On you I was cast from my birth,
and since my mother bore me you have been my God.
Do not be far from me,
for trouble is near
and there is no one to help.

A company of evildoers encircles me.
My hands and feet have shrivelled;
I can count all my bones.
They stare and gloat over me;
they divide my clothes among themselves,
and for my clothing they cast lots.

But you, O Lord, do not be far away!
O my help, come quickly to my aid!

You who fear the Lord, praise him!
All you offspring of Jacob, glorify him;
stand in awe of him, all you offspring of Israel!
For he did not despise or abhor

the affliction of the afflicted;
he did not hide his face from me,
but heard when I cried to him.

Meditation

I felt alone,
   utterly abandoned,
   not just by man but by God,
   and I was bereft,
   desolate,
   broken in body, mind and spirit.
How could it be happening, I asked myself?
Why had God brought me thus far,
   always by my side,
   always there to guide me,
   only to desert me when I needed him most?
It made no sense,
   faith itself thrown into turmoil,
   for it denied everything:
   the love, the purpose, the mercy I'd trusted in so long.
Yet when I cried out in agony of spirit,
   there was nothing –
   not a word,
   not a sign –
   nothing;
   and it was crushing,
   the bleakest, blackest moment of my life.
I wanted to let go,
   give up,
   for surely anything, even the oblivion of death,
   was preferable to this.
Yet somehow I held on.
Despite the emptiness,
   the awful silence,
   I kept praying,
   remembering all that God had done.
And somewhere, deep within, hope flickered again,
   spluttering,
   tremulous,
   like a smouldering candle,

a flame caught in the breeze,
yet alight once more,
refusing to be extinguished.
It took time, mind you, before the cloud lifted;
not just days, but weeks, months –
a long and lonely struggle in the wilderness –
and I often wondered if I would ever taste joy again,
my heart dance once more to the familiar tunes of old.
I was wrong, of course,
for I came through finally,
stronger and tougher through the experience.
God hadn't forsaken me;
he'd been there all along,
right there in the darkness
sharing my sorrow,
bearing my pain.
But for a time I'd believed him lost to me,
I'd glimpsed the agony of separation,
and it was more terrible than you can imagine.
God save anyone from facing that again.

Prayer

Gracious God,
there are times when life seems dark
and your purpose hard to fathom;
when try as we might to make sense of it,
so much is impossible to understand.
We call to you but you do not seem to answer,
we seek your presence but feel utterly alone.
Help us, when such moments strike,
to remember all the ways you have been with us
and the guidance you have given.
Help us to recall the coming of your light into the world,
and the promise that nothing shall ever overcome it.
Gracious God, when we lose hold of you,
keep hold of us and see us safely through,
in the name of Jesus Christ,
the crucified yet risen Lord.
Amen.

46
I MET HIM OUT ON THE HILLS

David

Reading – Psalm 23

The Lord is my shepherd, I shall not want.
He makes me lie down in green pastures;
he leads me beside still waters;
he restores my soul.
He leads me in right paths for his name's sake.

Even though I walk through the darkest valley,
I fear no evil;
for you are with me;
your rod and your staff –
they comfort me.

You prepare a table before me
in the presence of my enemies;
you anoint my head with oil;
my cup overflows.
Surely goodness and mercy shall follow me
all the days of my life,
and I shall dwell in the house of the Lord
my whole life long.

Meditation

I met him out on the hills,
   night drawing in,
   the wind, chill –
   a solitary shepherd,
   brow furrowed,
   searching for a sheep gone astray.
And suddenly it all came flooding back,
   those long hours I had spent as a boy

out in the fields tending my father's flock.
Good days, on the whole –
    time to think,
    to pray,
    or simply to enjoy the beauty of this world God has given.
But demanding also,
    even dangerous sometimes –
    out in the fiercest of storms,
    harassed by wild beasts,
    keeping watch through the lonely hours of the night.
Funny really, isn't it? –
    all that over a bunch of sheep,
    for let's face it, they're stupid creatures at the best of times,
    often driving you to near distraction.
You try to help them and what do they do? –
    wander away as soon as look at you.
You try to protect them,
    but, half a chance, and they're off again,
    straight into the teeth of danger.
Infuriating!
Yet somehow a bond develops between you,
    until the time comes when, if you're worth your salt,
    you'll do anything for those sheep,
    even risk your own life to save their necks.
You think that strange?
You shouldn't,
    for we're like sheep ourselves,
    as foolish, headstrong and maddening as any of them –
    following the crowd,
    ignoring guidance,
    careering blindly towards catastrophe.
Why should anyone bother with us?
And yet the Lord does just that,
    like a shepherd,
    always there to guard us, guide us, feed us,
    seeking when we're lost,
    rejoicing when we're found,
    protecting us from evil,
    meeting our every need.
Would he risk his life for us, as I for my sheep?
It sounds ridiculous, I know,
    too fanciful for words,

and yet when I consider the extent of his love,
the care he shows each day,
I really believe that he would;
that not only would he risk his life
but, if necessary, he'd give it, freely and gladly,
willing to die for us so that we might live!

Prayer

Loving God,
    time and again we have gone astray from you.
You seek us out,
    you set us on our feet,
    and we believe next time it will be different,
    but it's not;
    still we wander from your side.
We are weak and foolish,
    undeserving of your love,
    yet still you reach out to us,
    drawing us back to your side.
We praise you for the wonder of your grace,
    for your willingness through Christ
    to lay down your life for the life of the world.
We thank you for your constant provision of all our needs.
Have mercy on our repeated failures,
    and continue to guide us, we pray,
    watching over us even when we lose sight of you.
Lead us on through the changes and chances of this life,
    and through the valley of the shadow of death,
    until we are safely gathered into your kingdom
    and the journey is done.
In the name of the shepherd of all,
    Jesus Christ our Lord.
Amen.

47
WHAT CAN I SAY, LORD?

David

Reading – Psalm 51:1-12

Have mercy on me, O God,
according to your steadfast love;
according to your abundant mercy
blot out my transgressions.
Wash me thoroughly from my iniquity,
and cleanse me from my sin.

For I know my transgressions,
and my sin is ever before me.
Against you, you alone, have I sinned,
and done what is evil in your sight,
so that you are justified in your sentence
and blameless when you pass judgement.
Indeed, I was born guilty,
a sinner when my mother conceived me.

You desire truth in the inward being;
therefore teach me wisdom in my secret heart.
Purge me with hyssop, and I shall be clean;
wash me, and I shall be whiter than snow.
Let me hear joy and gladness;
let the bones that you have crushed rejoice.
Hide your face from my sins,
and blot out all my iniquities.

Create in me a clean heart, O God,
and put a new and right spirit within me.
Do not cast me away from your presence,
and do not take your holy spirit from me.
Restore to me the joy of your salvation,
and sustain in me a willing heart.

Meditation

What can I say, Lord?
What *can* I say?
I've failed you again, haven't I?
Despite all my promises,
    all my good intentions,
    I've gone and let you down
    like so many times before.
And I'm sickened,
    crushed,
    disgusted with myself,
    ashamed I could be so pathetically weak,
    so hopelessly false.
I tried so hard, that's what gets me down.
I was determined to make up for the lapses of the past,
    to show you that I'm really serious
    about this business of discipleship,
    and to prove that the trust you've shown in me,
    your willingness to forgive and go on forgiving,
    actually means something to me,
    despite the way it may seem.
But could I do it?
No.
For a few hours,
    a few days, perhaps,
    but finally I fell as I always do,
    back into the old familiar ways.
Why, Lord?
What's wrong with me?
What am I going to do?
I can't change,
    not by myself.
I've tried it,
    and it's just no good,
    the weaknesses running too deep,
    too much a part of me,
    for me to conquer them alone.
It's in your hands, Lord,
    only you have the power to help me.
I know I don't deserve it,
    that I've no claim on your love or mercy,

but I'm begging you,
    pleading on bended knee,
    pardon my iniquities.
Deal kindly, despite my folly,
    cleanse my heart and renew my spirit.
Mould me,
    fashion me,
    forgive me,
    restore me,
    so that perhaps one day, by your grace,
    I may serve as I should.
Lord, in your mercy, hear my prayer.

Prayer

Lord,
    it is easy to go through the motions of confession;
    to claim we are sorry for our sin
    and to make promises about our desire to serve you
    without really thinking about what we are saying.
Familiarity leads us to take your grace for granted,
    and so we fail to appreciate
    the gravity of letting you down.
Yet though your nature is always to have mercy,
    you are grieved by our failings,
    not least because they deny us the fullness of life
    which you desire for all your people.
Help us, then, to see ourselves as we really are,
    the bad as well as the good,
    and give us a genuine sense of repentance
    over everything in our lives that is contrary to your will.
So may we receive the forgiveness you long to give,
    and experience your transforming, renewing power,
    through the grace of our Lord Jesus Christ.
Amen.

48

I HAD A SHOCK TODAY

Moses

Reading – Psalm 90 (attributed to Moses)

Lord, you have been our dwelling place in all the generations.
Before the mountains were brought forth,
or ever you had formed the earth and the world,
from everlasting to everlasting you are God.

You turn us back to dust,
and say, 'Turn back you mortals.'
For a thousand years in your sight
are like yesterday when it is past,
or like a watch in the night.

You sweep them away; they are like a dream,
like grass that is renewed in the morning;
in the morning it flourishes and is renewed;
in the evening it fades and withers.

For we are consumed by your anger;
by your wrath we are overwhelmed.
You have set our iniquities before you,
our secret sins in the light of your countenance.

For all our days pass away under your wrath;
our years come to an end like a sigh.
The days of our life are seventy years,
or perhaps eighty, if we are strong;
even then their span is only toil and trouble;
they are soon gone, and we fly away.

Who considers the power of your anger?
Your wrath is as great as the fear that is due you.
So teach us to count our days
that we may gain a wise heart.

Turn, O Lord! How long?
Have compassion on your servants!
Satisfy us in the morning with your steadfast love,
so that we may rejoice and be glad all our days.
Make us glad as many days as you have afflicted us,
and as many years as we have seen evil.
Let your work be manifest to your servants,
and your glorious power to their children.
Let the favour of the Lord our God be upon us
and prosper for us the work of our hands –
O prosper the work of our hands!

Meditation

I had a shock today.
I caught sight of my reflection in a pool of water,
    and I didn't recognise the man I saw there.
He looked old,
    anxious,
    weary,
    the hair thinning and flecked with grey,
    the forehead pitted with wrinkles,
    the eyes heavy, full of trouble,
    as though he bore the cares of the world on his shoulders,
    and I thought, 'What a shame . . . poor old fellow . . .
    who's he?'
Only, of course, it was me,
    those worn and jaded features
    reflecting the man I'd become,
    and I was overwhelmed suddenly
    by an awareness of my mortality,
    the fleeting nature of this brief span of ours,
    here today and gone tomorrow.
Yes, I knew it before, in theory anyway,
    but today it's hit home with a chilling intensity –
    the stark realisation that life is rushing by
    and nothing can stop it;
    that all our hopes and plans, toiling and striving,
    finally come to nothing.

It's not a pleasant thought, is it?
Yet funnily enough I can live with that, just about,
    for I know that though I may change, God does not,
    his power, his purpose, always the same.
It's not the fact of death that troubles me,
    so much as the waste of life,
    the way we fritter away the days God has given,
    each one poisoned by our folly and sinfulness.
We all do it,
    a thoughtless act here,
    a selfish deed there,
    and before we know it the ripples are everywhere,
    a multitude of lives caught in their wash –
    so surprising a result from so little a splash.
There's no escape, not by ourselves –
    we're all trapped in this vicious vortex of destruction,
    and only God can set us free.
We've no right to expect it –
    his judgement is well-deserved –
    but if we ask in true humility,
    if we acknowledge our faults
    and throw ourselves upon his grace,
    he may yet hear our prayer and have mercy.
Remember that, my friend,
    while there's still time and life beckons,
    for, though we can't change the future,
    with God's help we can still shape the present.
Turn to him, and the years we are given may yet bring us joy,
    our toil and trouble forgotten,
    gladness to last us all our days.

Prayer

Living God,
    we spend so much of our lives in ceaseless striving,
    pursuing first this, then that.
We labour, we fret, we fight, we struggle,
    all our thoughts so often focused
    on present gain and immediate satisfaction.
Yet all the goals which consume us
    bring but a moment's pleasure,
    each destined to fade away.
Teach us to set our hearts first on you,
    and to discover the fulfilment you long to give us
    in both this life and the next.
Help us to live not just in the context of this brief span
    you have given here on earth,
    but in the light of your eternal purpose
    in which, by your grace, you invite us all to share.
Amen.

49
I WANT TO SING TO THE LORD

David

Reading – Psalm 98

O sing to the Lord a new song,
for he has done marvellous things.
His right hand and his holy arm
have gotten him victory.
The Lord has made known his victory;
he has revealed his vindication in the sight of the nations.

He has remembered his steadfast love and faithfulness
to the house of Israel.
All the ends of the earth have seen
the victory of our God.

Make a joyful noise to the Lord, all the earth;
break forth into joyous song and sing praises.
Sing praises to the Lord with the lyre,
with the lyre and the sound of melody.
With trumpets and the sound of the horn
make a joyful noise before the King, the Lord.

Let the sea roar, and all that fills it;
the world and those who live in it.
Let the floods clap their hands;
let the hills sing together for joy
at the presence of the Lord, for he is coming
to judge the earth.
He will judge the world with righteousness,
and the peoples with equity.

Meditation

I want to sing to the Lord –
    to lift up my voice,
    lift up my soul,
    and sing his praises to the ends of the earth!
Yes, I know that may sound a bit clichéd,
    but I don't care, for it's true –
    the love he's shown,
    the goodness,
    the mercy,
    the faithfulness not just to me but to all his people,
    too special, too wonderful for anyone to keep silent.
I want to sing from the roof-tops,
    let rip from the highest mountain!
And not just any old song,
    but something new,
    something different –
    a song which captures a little of the joy
    bubbling up within me,
    and which expresses, could it be possible,
    the majesty of our God!
It can't be done, of course –
    no words enough,
    no music sufficient to declare his greatness –
    but I'm going to try, despite that;
    I'm going to make a joyful noise,
    I'm going to pour out my heart and mind and soul,
    and I'm going to exalt the name of the Lord my God
    for all I'm worth!
Forgive me if it's not pretty, the song I sing –
    it may well not be –
    but I can promise you this:
    it will be real,
    welling up from deep within,
    a great fountain of celebration,
    irrepressible,
    inexhaustible;
    a spontaneous outpouring of praise,
    overflowing with thanksgiving,
    for he has blessed us beyond our deserving,
    he has done marvellous things for us, too many to number,

he has heard our prayer and reached out in mercy –
what more could anyone ask?
But enough of this,
no time for talking;
come join me, my friends,
in glad and grateful worship:
sing to the Lord a new song!

Prayer

Lord,
we thank you for the gift of song;
for its ability to move, challenge and inspire us,
its power to express feelings of joy and sorrow,
hope and despair;
its capacity to sum up our feelings
in grateful hymns of praise.
Teach us when we worship
to use this gift thoughtfully,
singing to you from the heart,
and offering not just our songs
but ourselves with them.
Teach us to reflect on the words we use
so that they may speak *to* us
of all that you have done
and speak *for* us of all *we* would do for *you*.
O Lord,
open our lips,
and our mouths shall declare your praise.
Amen.

50

IT WAS OVER AT LAST

Psalmist

Reading – Psalm 133

How very good and pleasant it is
when kindred live together in unity!
It is like the precious oil on the head,
running down upon the beard,
on the beard of Aaron,
running down over the collar of his robes.
It is like the dew of Hermon,
which falls on the mountains of Zion.
For there the Lord ordained his blessing,
life for evermore.

Meditation

It was over at last,
    that foolish, futile feud,
    which had divided our family for so long,
    finally at an end,
    and what a joy it was!
We were together again,
    a family as God intended us to be,
    and the joy we felt knew no bounds.
Do you know what? –
    we hadn't spoken, some of us, for years!
Flesh and blood,
    yet we'd passed each other in the street like strangers,
    without even a glance, let alone a word.
Astonishing, isn't it!
Yet that's what it came to,
    one snub leading to another,
    insult traded for insult,
    until our pettiness bordered on the ridiculous.

Heaven knows what started it –
   we lost sight of that long ago –
   but once begun that dispute of ours took on a life of its own,
   a minor disagreement suddenly a full-blown war,
   a trivial dispute suddenly a matter of life or death.
It was pathetic,
   beyond belief,
   yet at the time we just couldn't see it,
   the whole foolish business the centre of our universe.
So day after day,
   year after year,
   we allowed it to fester on,
   until no part of life was unaffected by its poison.
What a price we paid!
When I think now of all we might have shared –
   the joys, the hopes,
   the fears, the sorrows,
   so many memories we might have built together –
   my heart aches with the tragedy of it all.
Yet there's no point brooding,
   regretting what might have been.
It's over now,
   consigned to history,
   and we're together at last,
   the past behind us,
   the future there for the taking,
   and it's a wonderful feeling,
   more special than I can ever tell you.
How good it is,
   how very, very good
   when kindred live together in unity.
If only we'd learned it sooner!

Prayer

Lord,
    it's easy to start a quarrel,
    so much harder to end it.
It's easy to see faults in others,
    far more difficult to see them in ourselves.
It's easy to destroy relationships,
    almost impossible to build them again
    once they have been broken.
Forgive us the weaknesses
    that create divisions among us,
    separating us from our fellow human beings –
    even from our own family and friends.
Help us so far as it lies with us
    to live in harmony with all,
    and when that harmony is broken
    teach us to act as peacemakers,
    healing hurts, restoring trust
    and breaking down the barriers that come between us.
In the name of Christ,
    who shall come to reconcile all things to himself.
Amen.

51

IT'S NO GOOD, LORD

David

Reading – Psalm 139:1-18

Lord, you have searched me and known me.
You know when I sit down and when I rise up;
you discern my thoughts from far away.
You search out my path and my lying down,
and are acquainted with all my ways.
Even before a word is on my tongue,
O Lord, you know it completely.
You hem me in, behind and before,
and lay your hand upon me.
Such knowledge is too wonderful for me;
it is so high that I cannot attain it.

Where can I go from your spirit?
Or where can I flee from your presence?
If I ascend to heaven, you are there;
if I make my bed in Sheol, you are there.
If I take the wings of the morning
and settle at the farthest limits of the sea,
even there your hand shall lead me,
and your right hand shall hold me fast.
If I say, 'Surely the darkness shall cover me,
and the light around me become night',
even the darkness is not dark to you;
the night is as bright as the day,
for darkness is as light to you.

It was you who formed my inward parts;
you knit me together in my mother's womb.
I praise you, for I am fearfully and wonderfully made.
Wonderful are your works;
that I know very well.
My frame was not hidden from you,
when I was being made in secret,

intricately woven in the depths of the earth.
Your eyes beheld my unformed substance.
In your book were written
all the days that were formed for me,
when none of them as yet existed.
How weighty to me are your thoughts, O God!
How vast is the sum of them!
I try to count them – they are more than the sand;
I come to the end – I am still with you.

Meditation

It's no good, Lord,
   it's too much for me,
   more than I can ever take in.
I've tried, you know that.
Day after day I've struggled
   to get my head round the wonder of who and what you are,
   but I just can't do it;
   your greatness is beyond the reach of human mind.
I've come far, no question,
   new insights and experiences adding to my sense of wonder,
   deepening my faith,
   enlarging my vision;
   yet I realise now that those were just a taste,
   a small sample of what is yet in store,
   for there is always more to learn,
   much that is hidden still to be revealed.
It's frightening, almost,
   for you overturn all our expectations,
   at work not just in the light, but in the darkness,
   not just in the good, but in the bad –
   no place outside your purpose
   no person beyond your grace,
   your love stronger, wider, greater, deeper
   than I've even begun to imagine!
Always you are there,
   one step ahead,
   waiting to take my hand

and lead me on to the next stage of my journey.
So that's it, Lord.
    enough is enough –
    no more tying myself into knots,
    no more juggling with the impossible.
I don't have all the answers
    and I never will have,
    but I've got you, here by my side,
    behind to guard me,
    ahead to lead me,
    above to bless me,
    within to feed me –
    your love always there,
    every moment,
    everywhere,
    in everything.
And, quite honestly, if I've got that,
    what else do I need to know!

Prayer

Great and mighty God,
    we thank you that you have the power
    to constantly surprise us,
    opening up each day new horizons
    and new experiences to explore.
We can never exhaust the possibilities of life
    or the mysteries of faith.
However far we may have travelled
    along the path of discipleship,
    the journey is always only just beginning,
    such is the wonder of your grace.
Teach us to keep hold of that great truth,
    so that we may never lose our sense of awe before you.
May our hearts thrill
    as the knowledge of your loving purpose
    continues to unfold,
    this day and for evermore.
Amen.

52
'THE FEAR OF THE LORD IS THE BEGINNING OF WISDOM'

Solomon

Reading – Proverbs 3:1-8

My child, do not forget my teaching,
but let your heart keep my commandments;
for length of days and years of life
and abundant welfare they will give you.

Do not let loyalty and faithfulness forsake you;
bind them around your neck,
write them on the tablet of your heart.
So you will find favour and good repute
in the sight of God and of people.

Trust in the Lord with all your heart,
and do not rely on your own insight.
In all your ways acknowledge him,
and he will make straight your paths.
Do not be wise in your own eyes;
fear the Lord, and turn away from evil.
It will be a healing for your flesh
and a refreshment for your body.

Meditation

'The fear of the Lord is the beginning of wisdom' –
    that's what my mother told me when I was just a boy,
    and I've remembered it ever since,
    a rule of thumb that's never left me.
A bit of a cliché, perhaps,
    the words in danger of tripping off the tongue
    just that bit too easily,
    but better that than for them never to stick at all.

And it can happen, believe me,
    the lesson we thought we'd learned today,
    forgotten tomorrow,
    the truth we thought we'd fathomed
    returning unexpectedly to perplex us.
Don't think you're different, for you're not.
We can all lose sight of the things that matter,
    every one of us.
Slowly but surely we start to drift,
    now this way, now that,
    drawn by hidden currents inexorably onwards
    until the shore we started from is lost to view.
I've witnessed it all too often,
    convictions quashed,
    principles compromised,
    scruples forgotten,
    as little by little the truth is eroded,
    worn down by the unrelenting tide
    of a hostile and dismissive world.
Yet it needn't be like that,
    not if you remember what really counts:
    the word of the Lord,
    the commandments he's given,
    the witness of his servants.
Make time for those,
    not just to read them but to make them part of you,
    engraved on your heart,
    inscribed in your soul,
    and you will find the way to life,
    a light to guide you every step you take,
    wholeness in body, mind and spirit.
That's what my mother taught me, all those years ago,
    and that's what I've set out to teach in turn,
    to share something of the wisdom she shared with me.
Not her wisdom, you understand,
    nor mine,
    but springing from the fear of the Lord,
    sustained and nurtured by him.
Discover that, my child,
    take that lesson to heart,
    and you will find treasure indeed,
    riches beyond price.

Prayer

Gracious God,
   you have spoken your word,
   you offer us your guidance,
   yet all too often we go astray.
Despite our desire to serve you,
   we are swayed by those around us,
   our faith undermined,
   our beliefs subtly influenced by pressures
   we are barely even aware of.
Forgive us the weakness of our commitment
   and teach us to make time for you each day
   to study your word and to reflect on your goodness.
Draw near to us
   and help us to draw near to you,
   so that you may be a part of us,
   filling us in heart and mind and soul.
In the name of Christ we ask it.
Amen.

53

THINK BEFORE YOU SPEAK

Solomon

Reading – Proverbs 12:6, 13-14a, 17-19; 13:2-3; 15:1-2, 4; 26:17-28

The words of the wicked are a deadly ambush,
but the speech of the upright delivers them.

The evil are ensnared by the transgression of their lips,
but the righteous escape from trouble.
From the fruit of the mouth one is filled with good things . . .

Whoever speaks the truth gives honest evidence,
but a false witness speaks deceitfully.
Rash words are like sword thrusts,
but the tongue of the wise brings healing.
Truthful lips endure for ever,
but a lying tongue lasts only a moment.

From the fruit of their words good persons eat good things,
but the desire of the treacherous is for wrongdoing.
Those who guard their mouths preserve their lives;
those who open wide their lips come to ruin.

A soft answer turns away wrath,
but a harsh word stirs up anger.
The tongue of the wise dispenses knowledge,
but the mouths of fools pour out folly . . .
A gentle tongue is a tree of life,
but perverseness in it breaks the spirit.

Like somebody who takes a passing dog by the ears
is one who meddles in the quarrel of another.
Like a maniac who shoots deadly firebrands and arrows,
so is one who deceives a neighbour
and says, 'I am only joking!'
For lack of wood the fire goes out,
and where there is no whisperer, quarrelling ceases.

As charcoal is to hot embers and wood to fire,
so is a quarrelsome person for kindling strife.
The words of a whisperer are like delicious morsels;
they go down to the inner parts of the body.
Like the glaze covering an earthen vessel
are smooth lips with an evil heart.
An enemy dissembles in speaking
while harbouring deceit within;
when an enemy speaks graciously, do not believe it,
for there are seven abominations concealed within;
though hatred is covered with guile,
the enemy's wickedness will be exposed in the assembly.
Whoever digs a pit will fall into it,
and a stone will come back on the one who starts it rolling.
A lying tongue hates its victims,
and a flattering mouth works ruin.

Meditation

Think before you speak.
It's simple advice, isn't it?
So obvious you'd hardly think it needs saying.
But it does, believe me,
    for though it may sound implausible,
    most of us do just the opposite,
    speaking first and thinking later.
Does that matter?
Well, consider for a moment the results –
    the mother wounded by a cruel jibe,
    the child crushed by a harsh rebuke,
    the marriage broken by thoughtless gossip,
    the family divided by a careless remark,
    each a symbol of the devastating power of words.
And there are countless more all around you, even as I speak –
    a word here, a word there,
    spat from curled lips,
    twisted by cruel tongues,
    or tossed wildly into the breeze
    with no thought of the consequences –
    sowing discord,

sparking hatred,
feeding bitterness.
Yet that's not the way it has to be,
for words are God's gift,
able to express so much beauty and achieve so much good.
It doesn't take much,
just a little thought and the result can be so different:
a word of thanks,
praise,
comfort,
encouragement,
spoken not to hurt but to heal,
not to curse but to bless;
offered with compassion and gentleness –
and instead of sorrow, there is joy,
instead of hatred, love,
instead of war, peace.
I've said enough,
yet more words added to those already spoken,
but promise me this,
next time you come to speak,
the words rising on your tongue,
stop and think before you say them.

Prayer

Lord,
>we thank you for the wonderful gift of speech,
>the ability through language
>to communicate with one another;
>to express our thoughts and feelings;
>to share information;
>to move, challenge and inspire;
>to offer ideas; to bring comfort.

Forgive us for the way we turn something so special
>into something so ugly,
>capable of causing such devastation.

Teach us to think more carefully about what we say,
>and to speak always with the intention of helping
>rather than hurting.

Help us to use words wisely,
>in the name of Jesus Christ,
>the Word made flesh.

Amen.

54
IT'S NOT FAIR, HE SAID

Solomon

Reading – Proverbs 6:6-9; 13:4; 24:30-34; 26:13-16

Go to the ant, you lazybones;
consider its ways, and be wise.
Without having any chief or officer or ruler,
it prepares its food in summer,
and gathers its sustenance in harvest.
How long will you lie there, O lazybones?
When will you rise from your sleep?

The appetite of the lazy craves, and gets nothing,
while the appetite of the diligent is richly supplied.
I passed by the field of one who was lazy,
by the vineyard of a stupid person;
and see, it was all overgrown with thorns;
the ground was covered with nettles,
and its stone wall was broken down.
Then I saw and considered it;
I looked and received instruction.
A little sleep, a little slumber,
a little folding of the hands to rest,
and poverty will come upon you like a robber,
and want, like an armed warrior.

The lazy person says, 'There is a lion in the road!
There is a lion in the streets!'
As a door turns on its hinges,
so does a lazy person in bed.
The lazy person buries a hand in the dish,
and is too tired to bring it back to the mouth.
The lazy person is wiser in self-esteem
than seven who can answer discreetly.

Meditation

It's not fair, he said,
   not right;
   how could God have let it happen?
And he really meant it.
He actually believed that life had given him a raw deal;
   that his sorry plight was a twist of fate,
   and fortune had conspired against him.
No matter that he'd rested while we worked,
   that he'd made merry while we made headway –
   such details were forgotten –
   it couldn't be his fault,
   no way!
So he stood there complaining,
   bemoaning his lot,
   shaking his fist at the world.
It's hard to believe, I know,
   for it was plain enough to everyone else –
   the situation of his own making,
   the inevitable result of idleness –
   but he just couldn't or wouldn't see it.
You won't find many like him, thank goodness,
   not many quite so foolish or indolent,
   but I wouldn't rest on your laurels if I were you,
   for there's a little of that man in all of us,
   and perhaps rather more than you might imagine.
We've all done it, haven't we,
   postponed that job we cannot face? –
   'All in good time', we say.
   'Not today!'
   'It will keep' –
   you know the kind of thing.
And once started so it goes on . . .
   and on . . .
   and on –
   another excuse,
   another reason for delay,
   another opportunity wasted.
It's a fool's game, for you gain nothing,
   the job still there,
   weighing on your mind,

and the longer you postpone it, the heavier it presses,
sapping your energy more surely
than had you faced the task.
No, take my advice and set to work,
    roll up your sleeves and get stuck in.
There'll be time to rest tomorrow,
    today's the time for action –
    it will be worth it, I assure you.

Prayer

Lord,
    you have given us a multitude of gifts and opportunities;
    forgive us that we sometimes fail to make use of them.
We don't think of ourselves as lazy,
    but time and again we avoid tasks
    which we ought to tackle,
    at cost to ourselves, to others
    and to you.
So many possibilities are wasted
    and so much peace of mind lost
    because we prefer to put off till tomorrow
    what we ought to do today.
Teach us to make the most of each moment,
    to utilise our talents to the full,
    and to tackle every task as it comes,
    for both our sakes and yours.
Amen.

55

MY ROSE WITHOUT A THORN, THAT'S HOW I SAW HER

Solomon

Reading – Song of Solomon 4:1-7

How beautiful you are, my love,
how very beautiful!
Your eyes are doves behind your veil.
Your hair is like a flock of goats,
moving down the slopes of Gilead.
Your teeth are like a flock of shorn ewes
that have come up from the washing,
all of which bear twins,
and not one among them is bereaved.
Your lips are like a crimson thread,
and your mouth is lovely.
Your cheeks are like halves of a pomegranate
behind your veil.
Your neck is like the tower of David,
built in courses;
on it hang a thousand bucklers,
all of them shields of warriors.
Your two breasts are like two fawns,
twins of a gazelle,
that feed among the lilies.
Until the day breathes and the shadows flee,
I will hasten to the mountain of myrrh
and the hill of frankincense.
You are altogether beautiful, my love;
there is no flaw in you.

Meditation

My rose without a thorn, that's how I saw her,
   beautiful beyond measure,
   lovelier than the morning dew.
I thrilled when I heard her voice,
   shivered with joy when I saw her face,
   and when I held her close,
   our limbs entwined,
   our bodies as one,
   my heart leapt within me.
She was everything a man could have wanted –
   attractive,
   sensual,
   passionate,
   her eyes as blue as topaz,
   lips sweet as honey,
   skin soft as down.
No wonder that I loved her,
   more fiercely and passionately
   than I thought myself capable of.
It changed, of course;
   well, it had to, didn't it?
She had her flaws after all, just as I do,
   and we had our moments as the years went by –
   harsh words,
   angry exchanges,
   even the occasional fall out –
   love tested to the limit.
Yet she's still special,
   as precious to me now as the day we met,
   if not more.
We've moved on, undeniably,
   slowly,
   almost imperceptibly,
   our relationship evolving –
   the flame of desire not so strong, though still burning,
   the expressions of affection not so obvious,
   yet we are closer than we've ever been,
   welded together through everything we've shared –
   a union not just of body, but also mind and spirit.
I loved her then, more than I believed possible.

I love her now, more than ever.
And I'll go on doing so, just as I promised,
     until my dying day,
     until death us do part.

Prayer

Gracious God,
     we thank you for the gift of human love
     and for the joy that this can bring.
We thank you for the love we are able to give and receive,
     and for the fulfilment that comes from a union
     of body, mind and spirit.
Reach out to all those whose love has been broken,
     those who have lost loved ones
     and those whose love has grown cold.
Restore love in these lives,
     and deepen that in our own,
     so that the love we are privileged to share
     may grow and flourish every step of our journey together.
In the name of Christ.
Amen.

56

I DARED TO DREAM ONCE

The Teacher

Reading – Ecclesiastes 1:2-11

Vanity of vanities, says the Teacher,
vanity of vanities! All is vanity.
What do people gain from all the toil
at which they toil under the sun?
A generation goes, and a generation comes,
but the earth remains for ever.
The sun rises and the sun goes down,
and hurries to the place where it rises.
The wind blows to the south,
and goes around to the north;
round and round goes the wind,
and on its circuits the wind returns.
All streams run to the sea,
but the sea is not full;
to the place where the streams flow,
there they continue to flow.
All things are wearisome;
more than one can express;
the eye is not satisfied with seeing,
or the ear filled with hearing.
What has been is what will be,
and what has been done is what will be done;
there is nothing new under the sun.
Is there a thing of which it is said,
'See, this is new'?
It has already been, in the ages before us.
The people of long ago are not remembered,
nor will there be any remembrance
of people yet to come
by those who come after them.

Meditation

I dared to dream once – can you believe that?
It may seem incredible now,
    but there was a time, not so long ago,
    when I was a hopeless, headstrong romantic,
    bursting with plans to change the world!
An angry young man, that's what they called me,
    and if one or two felt I went a bit too far,
    even branding me a rebel,
    the majority applauded my ideals,
    a welcome oasis in a parched and shrivelled land.
How things change –
    they wouldn't recognise me now!
Not that I look so different outwardly,
    but, inside, I'm a shadow of my former self,
    battered,
    bruised,
    beaten.
It's not been a conscious thing,
    principles compromised for the sake of expediency.
Quite the opposite –
    I still long to blaze with the same enthusiasm –
    to feel the pulse quicken,
    heart race,
    imagination soar –
    but I can't,
    and somehow I don't think I ever will again.
You see, I've seen people come and people go,
    life ebb and flow like the seasons;
    I've seen promises made and promises broken,
    hopes raised, then turned to dust;
    I've seen joy today become sorrow tomorrow,
    pleasure one moment bring pain the next;
    and it's finally worn me down,
    no point, no meaning, left in anything.
There *is* more, of course, I know that,
    for whether I see it or not,
    God is working in this strange old world of ours;
    and, yes, one day those long-gone dreams of mine
    will come true –
    a new beginning,

new kingdom,
new life.
But until that time comes, my advice to you is simple:
enjoy yourself by all means,
make the most of what you have,
but don't get carried away,
and, above all, don't put all your eggs in one basket,
for believe me, it's just not worth it.

Prayer

Gracious God,
we bring to you today our frustrated hopes,
our broken dreams and battered expectations.
As the years pass,
though some of our visions for the future are realised,
many are not and probably never will be.
Our ideals are replaced by a world-weary cynicism,
a sense that we've seen it all before.
We become reconciled to what is
rather than hunger for what yet might be.
Teach us to accept when such realism is necessary,
but teach us also still to believe in your purpose
and your ability to change the world.
Teach us to trust in your transforming power,
for you alone can make all things new.
Amen.

57

THEY THINK ME WISE, SOME PEOPLE

The Teacher

Reading – Ecclesiastes 11:8-12:7

Even those who live many years shall rejoice in them all; yet let them remember that the days of darkness will be many. All that comes is vanity.

Rejoice, young man, while you are young, and let your heart cheer you in the days of your youth. Follow the inclination of your heart and the desire of your eyes, but know that for all these things God will bring you into judgement.

Banish anxiety from your mind, and put away pain from body; for youth and the dawn of life are vanity.

Remember your creator in the days of your youth, before the days of trouble come, and the years draw near when you will say, 'I have no pleasure in them'; before the sun and the light and the moon and the stars are darkened and the clouds return with the rain; in the day when the guards of the house tremble, and the strong men are bent, and the women who grind cease working because they are few, and those who look through the windows see dimly; when the doors on the street are shut, and the sound of the grinding is low, and one rises up at the sound of the bird, and all the daughters of song are brought low; when one is afraid of heights, and terrors are in the road: the almond tree blossoms, the grasshopper drags itself along and desire fails; because all must go to their eternal home, and the mourners will go about the streets; before the silver cord is snapped, and the golden bowl is broken, and the pitcher is broken at the fountain, and the wheel broken at the cistern, and the dust returns to the earth as it was, and the breath returns to God who gave it. Vanity of vanities, says the Teacher; all is vanity.

Meditation

They think me wise, some people –
    can you believe that?
They actually hold me up as an example
    of insight, understanding and discernment.
Well, more fool them!

Oh, I've learned a bit *now,* I grant you;
    the harsh lessons of experience have finally sunk home,
    and if you call that wisdom, then I can't argue.
But it took me long enough, didn't it? –
    too long by half,
    so you won't catch me blowing my own trumpet,
    I can assure you!
I've been a fool, that's how I see it,
    for I've frittered away the years in an empty and futile search,
    brooding first over this, then about that:
    the injustices of life,
    the riddle of death,
    the search for joy,
    the bearing of sorrow,
    the lure of wealth,
    the plight of the poor –
    you name it, I've pondered it,
    hour upon hour,
    year after year,
    my life's work to scale the heights and plumb the depths.
Yet look where it's got me –
    disillusioned,
    disheartened,
    dismayed –
    the world, for all its beauty, meaningless,
    a chasing after the wind.
Is that the last word?
It can't be,
    for I realise now I got the balance wrong,
    too full of self,
    too short on God;
    too full of my own ideas to respond to his guidance.
I should have stopped long ago,
    made time when I was still young,
    life before me,
    to pause and listen to his voice,
    but I thought I could go it alone,
    find by myself the answers I sought.
It wasn't the searching that was wrong, don't think that –
    there's a time for that as there's a time for everything –
    but I lost my bearings,
    in my search for knowledge and understanding

letting life slip through my fingers.
I could brood about *that* now, all too easily,
    the opportunities I've missed,
    the days I've wasted,
    but not this time.
I may not be quite the man I was –
    the years have taken their toll –
    but I know now what really matters,
    and I'm going to savour the time that's left to me,
    every day,
    every moment,
    celebrating each one as the gift of my creator.
And if you would be wise, my friend,
    then you will do the same,
    not putting it off till tomorrow but starting today,
    here and now.
Do that, and you won't go far wrong!

Prayer

Eternal God,
    we spend so much of our lives seeking happiness,
    yet much of the time we are frustrated.
We turn from one thing to another,
    believing for a moment
    that it may offer the fulfilment that we crave,
    but so many pleasures are fleeting,
    here today and gone tomorrow.
There are times when life seems empty,
    when nothing seems permanent,
    not even those things most precious to us.
Help us to find the rest for our souls
    which you alone can give;
    to discover in you that inner peace which can never change
    but will go on satisfying for all eternity.
Help us to live each day in tune with you,
    rejoicing in all you have given
    and anticipating all you have yet to give.
Through Christ our Lord.
Amen.

58

DID WE KNOW GOD WOULD SAVE US?

Shadrach, Meshach and Abednego

Reading – Daniel 3:1, 3-6, 8-9, 12-14, 16-18

King Nebuchadnezzar made a golden statue whose height was sixty cubits and whose width was six cubits; he set it up on the plain of Dura in the province of Babylon.

So the satraps, the prefects, and the governors, the counsellors, the treasurers, the justices, the magistrates, and all the officials of the provinces, assembled for the dedication of the statue that King Nebuchadnezzar had set up. When they were standing before the statue that Nebuchadnezzar had set up, the herald proclaimed aloud, 'You are commanded, O peoples, nations, and languages, that when you hear the sound of the horn, pipe, lyre, trigon, harp, drum, and entire musical ensemble, you are to fall down and worship the golden statue that King Nebuchadnezzar has set up. Whoever does not fall down and worship shall immediately be thrown into a furnace of blazing fire.'

Accordingly, at this time certain Chaldeans came forward and denounced the Jews. They said to King Nebuchadnezzar, 'O king, live for ever! . . . There are certain Jews whom you have appointed over the affairs of the province of Babylon: Shadrach, Meshach, and Abednego. These pay no heed to you, O king. They do not serve your gods and they do not worship the golden statue that you have set up.'

Then Nebuchadnezzar in furious rage commanded that Shadrach, Meshach and Abednego be brought in; so they brought those men before the king. Nebuchadnezzar said to them, 'Is it true, O Shadrach, Meshach, and Abednego, that you do not serve my gods and you do not worship the golden statue that I have set up?'

Shadrach, Meshach and Abednego answered the king, 'O Nebuchadnezzar, we have no need to present a defence to you in this matter. If our God whom we serve is able to deliver us from the furnace of blazing fire and out of your hand, O king, let him deliver us. But if not, be it known to you, O king, that we will not serve your gods and we will not worship the golden statue that you have set up.'

Meditation

Did we know God would save us,
    that whatever we faced he would see us through,
    safe to the other side?
Well, no, we didn't actually,
    despite what some may tell you.
We wish we had done,
    for we'd have felt a whole lot happier,
    ready to take whatever the king might throw at us.
But there were no guarantees, no cast-iron certainties –
    we had to wait, and trust, and hope.
Of course he *could* deliver us,
    but *would* he?
Who could say?
After all, why bother with us?
We were nobody special,
    just three young men from Judah,
    and though Nebuchadnezzar had singled us out
    for special treatment,
    it didn't mean God had done the same.
We wouldn't be the first people to die for their faith, nor the last.
Yet at the time that wasn't our chief concern –
    our faith was on the line,
    our freedom, our integrity, our identity as a nation
    hanging in the balance,
    and we had the chance to tip the scales.
It wouldn't have taken much to toe the line,
    just a quick bow and it would all have been over –
    surely not too awful a pill to swallow?
But what then,
    what would happen the next time, and the time after,
    when the challenge came again?
First one compromise, then another,
    and before long there'd be nothing left,
    our lives bought at the cost of our souls.
So we stood firm,
    hoping when it came to it he'd see reason,
    respect our consciences,
    honour our principles,
    but we were wrong,
    not even a glimmer of compassion as he sent us off to our deaths.

I can't describe the heat of that furnace,
    enough to knock you over before you even got close,
    and as they thrust us towards it, our blood ran cold,
    limbs frozen in abject terror,
    as hope began to fade.
There was still time, of course,
    time for God to step in and save us –
    a last-minute reprieve,
    a stay of execution.
We knew he *could* do it, but *would* he?
And then they opened the door and hurled us in,
    guards collapsing in agony as the heat overwhelmed them,
    and we thought it was all over,
    three more martyrs, soon forgotten.
Only it wasn't three,
    there were four of us, and we were alive,
    walking unharmed in the fire,
    not even a hair on our heads singed by flames.
You think Nebuchadnezzar was puzzled by what he saw?
He wasn't the only one!
But then the truth dawned,
    as our words came back to us:
    'Our God is able to deliver us from the fiery furnace.'
That's what we'd claimed,
    that's what we hoped,
    and that's what we found.
We knew he *could* do it –
    we knew now he *had*!

Prayer

Sovereign God,
    we thank you for those who have had the courage
    to stand up for their faith
    in the face of persecution and danger,
    those whose dedication to you
    has been an inspiration and example to others.
We thank you that today we are free to worship as we please,
    without any need for fear or secrecy.
But, above all, we thank you for the assurance
    that whatever we may face,
    whatever dangers may threaten us,
    you are able to deliver us from evil.
In life and in death you are by our side,
    so that finally nothing will be able to separate us
    from the wonder of your love.
Help us, then, to offer you our heartfelt worship,
    and to honour you each day with faithful service,
    to the glory of your name.
Amen.

59

I KNEW WHAT IT MEANT IMMEDIATELY

Daniel

Reading – Daniel 5:1-9, 13a, 16b-17, 23-31

King Belshazzar made a great festival for a thousand of his lords, and he was drinking wine in the presence of the thousand. Under the influence of the wine, Belshazzar commanded that they bring in the vessels of gold and silver that his father Nebuchadnezzar had taken out of the temple in Jerusalem, so that the king and his lords, his wives, and his concubines might drink from them. So they brought in the vessels of gold and silver that had been taken out of the temple, the house of God in Jerusalem, and the king and his lords, his wives, and his concubines drank from them. They drank the wine and praised the gods of gold and silver, bronze, iron, wood and stone.

Immediately the fingers of a human hand appeared and began writing on the plaster of the wall of the royal palace, next to the lampstand. The king was watching the hand as it wrote. Then the king's face turned pale, and his thoughts terrified him. His limbs gave way, and his knees knocked together. The king cried aloud to bring in the enchanters, the Chaldeans, and the diviners; and the king said to the wise men of Babylon, 'Whoever can read this writing and tell me its interpretation shall be clothed in purple, have a chain of gold around his neck, and rank third in the kingdom.' Then all the king's wise men came in, but they could not read the writing or tell the king the interpretation. Then King Belshazzar became greatly terrified and his face turned pale, and his lords were perplexed.

Then Daniel was brought in before the king. The king said to Daniel, 'If you are able to read the writing and tell me its interpretation, you shall be clothed in purple, have a chain of gold around your neck, and rank third in the kingdom.'

Then Daniel answered in the presence of the king, 'Let your gifts be for yourself, or give your rewards to someone else. Nevertheless I will read the writing to the king and let him know the interpretation. . . . You have exalted yourself against the Lord of heaven! The vessels of his temple have been brought in before you, and you and your lords and your concubines have been drinking wine from them. You have praised the gods of silver and gold, of bronze, iron, wood, and stone, which do not see or hear or know; but the God in whose power is your very breath, and to whom you belong in all your ways, you have not honoured. So from his presence the hand was sent and this writing was inscribed. And this is the writing that was inscribed: MENE, MENE, TEKEL, and PARSIN. This is the interpretation of the matter: MENE, God has numbered the days of your kingdom and brought it to an end; TEKEL, you have been weighed on the scales and found wanting; PERES, your kingdom is divided and given to the Medes and Persians.'

Then Belshazzar gave the command, and Daniel was clothed in purple, a chain of gold was put around his neck, and a proclamation was made concerning him that he should rank third in the kingdom.

That very night Belshazzar, the Chaldean king, was killed. And Darius the Mede received the kingdom, being about sixty-two years old.

Meditation

I knew what it meant immediately,
    the moment I saw the writing on the wall,
    but could I tell it,
    dare I pronounce the fateful words?
It was a tough decision,
    for who was I,
    a mere exile from the land of Judah,
    to stand before the king of Babylon and declare God's judgement –
    the end of his reign,
    the collapse of his kingdom?
Whatever else, I would hardly be popular;
    lucky, more like, to escape with my life.
Yet when the question came there was no hesitation,
    no doubt in my mind,
    the issue confronting me suddenly crystal clear.
He'd laughed in the face of God for too long, that man,
    strutting about like some preening peacock,
    as if he were lord not just of Babylon, but the whole world.
And if that wasn't enough, worse had followed,
    not just pride but sacrilege –
    our holy vessels plundered from the temple,
    desecrated for some drunken orgy,
    all so that he could make merry with his cronies.
A huge joke, he considered it,

the most fun he'd had in ages,
    and proof conclusive that nothing and no one
    could compare with the mighty Belshazzar,
    ruler of the greatest empire the world had so far seen.
Well, he was in for a rude awakening,
    for he'd gone too far this time,
    even God's patience tested beyond the limit.
And that's what I told him, straight down the line.
No beating about the bush,
    no dressing up the truth,
    but the bare and simple facts –
    his time had come,
    the party was over,
    the day of reckoning was at hand.
It had to be said,
    and I was glad to say it,
    but I waited afterwards with bated breath,
    expecting at any moment to feel the full force of his fury.
Yet to the man's credit, it never came.
He just nodded quietly, with an air of resignation,
    almost as if he'd known what was coming,
    his worst fears confirmed,
    ready to bow at last to something higher than himself.
It wasn't the message he wanted to hear,
    hardly one to welcome,
    but he recognised it for what it was,
    the truth, pure and simple,
    and it won respect,
    a grudging admiration,
    even from him.

Prayer

Loving God,
> we claim to be seekers after truth,
> but the reality is that it sometimes scares us.

It probes too deeply into areas we prefer kept hidden;
> it challenges us in ways we would rather not face;
> it exposes issues we find hard to deal with.

Despite our fine-sounding words
> we are often less than honest with ourselves
> and with others.

Forgive us,
> and give us the courage and sensitivity we need
> both to face the truth and to speak it,
> in the name of Christ,
> the way, the truth, and the life.

Amen.

60

I KNEW IT WAS A TRAP,
THE MOMENT THEY ANNOUNCED IT

Daniel

Reading – Daniel 6:6-11

The presidents and satraps conspired and came to the king and said to him, 'O King Darius, live for ever! All the presidents of the kingdom, the prefects and the satraps, the counsellors and the governors are agreed that the king should establish an ordinance and enforce an interdict, that whoever prays to anyone, divine or human, for thirty days, except to you, O king, shall be thrown into a den of lions. Now, O king, establish the interdict and sign the document, so that it cannot be changed, according to the law of the Medes and the Persians, which cannot be revoked.' Therefore King Darius signed the document and interdict.

Although Daniel knew that the document had been signed, he continued to go to his house, which had windows in its upper room open towards Jerusalem, and to get down on his knees three times a day to pray to his God and praise him, just as he had done previously. The conspirators came and found Daniel praying and seeking mercy before his God.

Meditation

I knew it was a trap, the moment they announced it –
    I'd have been a fool not to, wouldn't I? –
    and, believe me, I was under no illusions
    as to the inevitable outcome.
It had been coming for a long time –
    jealousy turning to resentment,
    and resentment to hatred –
    so, when the news broke
    the writing, so to speak, was on the wall.
This was it:
    they were out to destroy me,
    to put paid to my faith once and for all.
Was I scared?

Of course I was –
    beside myself with terror!
It just didn't bear thinking about –
    flesh ripped to shreds,
    limb torn from limb,
    a ghastly, grisly death.
So why did I carry on regardless, I hear you ask?
Couldn't I at least have been a touch more discreet,
    a shade less provocative? –
    no one would have blamed me.
And you're right, it's what the king said himself.
Had I only gone to another room,
    or simply drawn the curtains,
    it would have saved so much unnecessary trouble.
But would it?
Even supposing my enemies had been satisfied,
    happy to have compromised my convictions,
    could that have been a happy ending?
I don't think so.
You see, it wasn't only about me,
    it was about my people –
    our freedom, our future, our faith –
    and had I given in on that one point,
    who could say what might have followed?
It could have spelt all manner of persecution for us all.
So I went up to my room as usual,
    and knelt in prayer,
    making quite certain nobody could miss me.
It was purgatory, every moment,
    the hardest prayer of my life,
    and, I have to confess,
    if I had one eye on God
    the other was on that pit of lions,
    and the picture before me was far from pretty.
Yet when the moment came
    and I was thrown among them,
    what a surprise,
    a miracle if ever there was one!
They were like kittens,
    more interested in play than prey!
The Lord had honoured my faith and closed their mouths!
You think me *brave*?

Well, perhaps a little,
    though I tell you what –
    there's a sense in which it was *easy* for me,
    for I knew what I was up against,
    the threat I was facing,
    the issues involved.
It's the unseen pressures which frighten me,
    the slow, subtle manipulation,
    the erosion of faith by stealth;
    that's what I'm not sure I could cope with, even now.
And, make no mistake, it's not just me
    who might face *that* den of lions,
    it's all of us.
May God deliver us from the time of trial!

Reading – Daniel 6:19-23

Then, at break of day, the king got up and hurried to the den of lions. When he came near the den where Daniel was, he cried out anxiously to Daniel, 'O Daniel, servant of the living God, has your God whom you faithfully serve been able to deliver you from the lions?' Daniel then said to the king, 'O king, live for ever! My God sent his angel and shut the lions' mouths so that they would not hurt me, because I was found blameless before him; and also before you, O king, I have done no wrong.' Then the king was exceedingly glad and commanded that Daniel be taken up out of the den, and no kind of harm was found on him, because he had trusted his God.

Prayer

Lord,
    we thank you for the privilege we have
    of being able to worship and witness to you freely.
We thank you that we can read your word
    and declare your name
    without fear of recrimination.
Yet save us from ever imagining because of this
    that our faith is safe from challenge.
We live in a world in which Christian values
    are constantly being undermined,
    where greed and selfishness are held up as virtues,
    where wealth and success have all too often replaced you
    as the real object of humankind's devotion.
And every day the pressure is there to conform;
    to give a little ground – first here, then there,
    until little by little our convictions are diluted
    and the distinctiveness of our faith destroyed.
Teach us to be awake to the dangers we face,
    and give us strength to resist them
    through holding fast to you.
Amen.

THE WORD OF THE LORD

61

I THOUGHT I'D HEARD WRONGLY

Amos

Reading – Amos 5:18-24

Alas for you who desire the day of the Lord!
Why do you want the day of the Lord?
It is darkness, not light;
as if someone fled from a lion,
and was met by a bear;
or went into the house and rested a hand against the wall,
and was bitten by a snake.
Is not the day of the Lord darkness, not light,
and gloom with no brightness in it?

I hate, I despise your festivals, and I take no delight in your
    solemn assemblies.
Even though you offer me your burnt offerings and grain offerings,
I will not accept them;
and the offerings of well-being of your fatted animals
I will not look upon.
Take away from me the noise of your songs;
I will not listen to the melody of your harps.
But let justice roll down like waters,
and righteousness like an everflowing stream.

Meditation

I thought I'd heard wrongly,
    my wires crossed somewhere,
    for the message was scandalous,
    too shocking even to contemplate, let alone proclaim.
Their sacrifices, meaningless?
Their worship, empty?
Their songs, noise?
Their offerings, worthless?

It seemed little short of blasphemy,
    a contradiction of everything I'd been taught since childhood,
    and for a moment my world was thrown into confusion.
Yet there was no getting away from it,
    that's what God was saying, loud and clear.
I struggled to take it in, you can imagine,
    wondering what on earth it could all mean,
    and wondering if I could dare proclaim it.
All right, so maybe they weren't Judeans,
    but then we can't all have everything, can we!
They were God's people, nonetheless,
    a devout nation just as we were,
    on the surface anyway –
    scrupulous in outward piety,
    meticulous in their attention to the Law,
    the sort of people you'd find it hard to find fault with,
    upright,
    godly,
    respectable,
    pillars of the local community.
So what was the problem?
How could God condemn them?
Only then I stopped,
    and looked not at their faith but their lives,
    not at their worship but their witness,
    and suddenly I saw it, clear as day.
It was all show –
    their piety,
    their zeal,
    their rituals,
    their prayers,
    all just an empty facade belying a hollow interior.
They praised God,
    but served self.
They preached justice,
    but practised corruption.
Their words said one thing,
    their deeds another.
And the tragedy is they couldn't see it,
    eyes blinded by the trappings of religion,
    outward observance everything,
    substance replaced by shadow.

Those have their place, don't get me wrong,
    but only as a means to an end,
    never an end in themselves.
Forget that and there is nothing so sad,
    and no one so lost;
    for while you may think you have everything,
    the reality is this:
    you have nothing at all.

Prayer

Lord,
    it's easy to go to church,
    hard to reach out to the world.
It's easy to say our prayers,
    hard to act upon them.
It's easy to offer our money,
    hard to give you our lives.
It's easy to sing your praises,
    hard to live to your glory.
Forgive us for so often taking the easy way;
    the way of outward show rather than inner faith.
Move within us,
    so that the words of our lips may show themselves
    in the thoughts of our hearts,
    and the claims of our faith be proven
    through the sincerity of our service.
Amen.

62

I NEVER REALISED HOW MUCH HE CARED

Hosea

Reading – Hosea 11:1-9

When Israel was a child, I loved him,
and out of Egypt I called my son.
The more I called them,
the more they went from me;
they kept sacrificing to the Baals,
and offering incense to idols.

Yet it was I who taught Ephraim to walk,
I took them up in my arms;
but they did not know that I healed them.
I led them with cords of human kindness,
with bands of love.
I was to them like those
who lift infants to their cheeks.
 I bent down to them and fed them.

They shall return to the land of Egypt,
and Assyria shall be their king,
because they have refused to return to me.
The sword rages in their cities,
it consumes their oracle-priests,
and devours because of their schemes.
My people are bent on turning away from me.
To the Most High they call,
but he does not raise them up at all.

How can I give you up, Ephraim?
How can I hand you over, O Israel?
How can I make you like Admah?
How can I treat you like Zeboiim?
My heart recoils within me;
my compassion grows warm and tender.
I will not execute my fierce anger;

I will not again destroy Ephraim;
for I am God and no mortal,
the Holy One in your midst,
and I will not come in wrath.

Meditation

I never realised how much he cared,
    how deeply and passionately he loved us.
He'd seemed remote up till then,
    set apart from us in splendid isolation,
    a God to approach with caution.
Not that I ever questioned his goodness –
    he'd been gracious to us from the beginning,
    calling us into being as a nation,
    delivering us time after time from oppression,
    leading us with infinite patience
    despite our refusal to follow –
    but I'd always had this picture of him as being distant,
    a God whose face we could never see,
    sovereign,
    righteous,
    holy,
    and ultimately, to be honest, a little frightening.
When we came to worship, we did so in awe,
    and as we knelt in prayer, we approached with trepidation,
    knowing he could judge as well as bless,
    punish, as well as save –
    and let's face it, after the way we'd behaved
    there was every reason for punishment,
    and none at all for mercy.
We'd worshipped false gods,
    pale reflections of our own fears and fantasies,
    instead of the Lord of heaven and earth.
We'd oppressed the poor and exploited the weak,
    let greed run riot and vice go unchecked.
We'd said one thing and done another,
    spoken of justice yet practised deceit,
    so what reason had we to expect anything other than judgement,
    due recompense for all our sins?

Only he couldn't do it!
When the moment came to reach out and punish,
    he drew back,
    heart lurching within him –
    the memories too strong,
    his compassion too great,
    love refusing to be denied.
It wasn't any merit on our part which saved us,
    don't think that,
    no hidden virtue uncovered or past deed recalled.
We'd failed him completely,
    spurning his goodness and abusing his grace,
    yet, despite it all, he refused to let us go.
And I realised then that, despite his sovereignty
    and righteousness,
    still he loved us, more than we can ever begin to imagine;
    a love which will keep on giving,
    keep on burning
    and keep on reaching out for all eternity,
    whatever it may take,
    whatever it might cost!

Prayer

Gracious God,
    we talk often about love,
    but we have little idea what it really is.
The love we show to others is invariably flawed,
    corrupted by ulterior motives and self-interest.
We can scarcely begin to fathom
    the immensity of the love you hold for us;
    a love that is inexhaustible,
    awesome in its intensity,
    devoted beyond measure.
Forgive us for losing sight
    of this one great reality at the heart of our faith
    without which all else is as nothing.
Forgive us for portraying you
    as a God of vengeance and justice
    when, above all, you are a God of love;

a God who, despite our repeated disobedience,
    refuses to let us go.
Teach us to open our hearts to all you so freely give,
    and so may we love you and others
    with something of that same total commitment
    you unfailingly show.
In the name of Christ.
Amen.

63

I KNEW IT WOULD HAPPEN, DIDN'T I?

Jonah

Reading – Jonah 1:1-3; 3:1-3a, 5; 3:10-4:4, 11

Now the word of the Lord came to Jonah son of Amittai, saying, 'Go at once to Nineveh, that great city, and cry out against it; for their wickedness has come up before me.' But Jonah set out to flee to Tarshish from the presence of the Lord. He went down to Joppa and found a ship going to Tarshish; so he paid his fare and went on board, to go with them to Tarshish, away from the presence of the Lord. . . .

The word of the Lord came to Jonah a second time, saying, 'Get up, go to Nineveh, that great city, and proclaim to it the message that I tell you.' So Jonah set out and went to Nineveh, according to the word of the Lord. . . . And the people of Nineveh believed God; they proclaimed a fast, and everyone, great and small, put on sackcloth.

When God saw what they did, how they turned from their evil ways, God changed his mind about the calamity that he had said he would bring upon them; and he did not do it. But this was very displeasing to Jonah, and he became angry. He prayed to the Lord and said, 'O Lord! Is this not what I said while I was still in my own country? That is why I fled to Tarshish at the beginning; for I knew that you are a gracious God and merciful, slow to anger, and abounding in steadfast love, and ready to relent from punishing. And now, O Lord, please take my life from me, for it is better for me to die than to live.' And the Lord said, 'Is it right for you to be angry? . . . Should I not be concerned about Nineveh, that great city, in which there are more than a hundred and twenty thousand persons who do not know their right hand from their left, and also many animals?'

Meditation

I knew it would happen, didn't I?
I knew those wretched Ninevites would go and repent
   if God gave them half a chance.
And that's precisely what they've done –
   covered themselves in sackcloth and ashes,
   grovelled in abject submission,

and begged him for mercy.
Can't he see through them?
Apparently not,
   only too ready, it seems, to let bygones be bygones
   and embrace them with open arms.
Isn't that just typical of him,
   always ready to turn a blind eye
   the moment anyone claims to be sorry?
It's nauseating!
Honestly, can you blame me for running away like that
   the moment he called me?
I knew immediately what his game was –
   I've seen it happen all too often –
   this God of ours is too soft by half.
Why waste time pussy-footing around,
   that's what I'd like to know?
There were no excuses for Nineveh.
They must have known all along
   that what they were doing was wrong,
   the very name of the place synonymous with corruption,
   so why not just have done with it
   and wipe them off the face of the earth,
   put an end to it once and for all?
That's what I'd have done, and taken pleasure in it,
   but not God, oh no.
He has to send muggins, here, doesn't he,
   to give them a warning,
   knowing full well the moment they hear it
   they'll be fawning on him like lovesick fools.
   Oh yes, it's his right, I accept that –
   if he reckons they're worth saving
   then it's his business and no else's –
   but why did he have to choose me? –
   that's what I find hard to stomach.
He knows my feelings on the matter,
   what I'd do to those Ninevites given half the chance,
   so surely he could have chosen someone more suited to the task?
I can't understand him, I really can't;
   you'd almost think he wants to teach me a lesson
   as much as them.
Gracious me, what am I saying?
Whatever next!

Prayer

Lord,
  it's easy to talk about loving others,
  much harder to mean it.
It's one thing to talk about forgiveness,
  quite another to put it into practice.
If we are honest,
  there are some people we find it hard to love
  and impossible to forgive.
We want people to suffer for the things they've done,
  to pay the price for their actions,
  and the thought of them getting off scot-free
  is one we find hard to accept.
Yet if you dealt with us according to our deserving,
  none of us could hope to escape punishment,
  for we have all failed you in ways too many to number.
Help us to recognise that your grace is greater
  than we can ever begin to imagine,
  and may we rejoice in the wonder of your love
  which embraces all.
Amen.

64
COULD IT BE TRUE?

Isaiah

Reading – Isaiah 6:1-8

In the year that King Uzziah died, I saw the Lord sitting on a throne, high and lofty; and the hem of his robe filled the temple. Seraphs were in attendance above him; each had six wings; with two they covered their faces, and with two they covered their feet, and with two they flew. And one called to another and said: 'Holy, holy, holy is the Lord of hosts; the whole earth is full of his glory.'

The pivots on the thresholds shook at the voices of those who called, and the house filled with smoke. And I said: 'Woe is me! I am lost, for I am a man of unclean lips, and I live among a people of unclean lips; yet my eyes have seen the King, the Lord of hosts!'

Then one of the seraphs flew to me, holding a live coal that had been taken from the altar with a pair of tongs. The seraph touched my mouth with it and said: 'Now that this has touched your lips, your guilt has departed and your sin is blotted out.' Then I heard the voice of the Lord saying, 'Whom shall I send, and who will go for us?' And I said, 'Here am I; send me!'

Meditation

Could it be true?
Could God, in his mercy, forgive even me?
It seemed incredible,
    too implausible for words,
    for there was so much in my life not as it should be,
    so many ways I daily let him down.
Does that surprise you,
    me being a prophet and all that?
It shouldn't do,
    for I was under no illusions as to my own importance,
    not for a moment.
If God ever wanted to use me
    it would be despite who I was, not because of it,
    that's what I'd always imagined.

My faults were all too apparent to me,
   and all too painful to contemplate.
I wanted to be different, don't get me wrong –
   there was nothing I'd have liked better
   than to offer faithful, unblemished service –
   but there was no escaping reality:
   I was as weak as the next man,
   unable to resist temptation,
   quick to go astray.
What reason was there to think I could change?
So when God appeared to me that day in the temple,
   I hate to say it, but I panicked,
   consumed by a sense of my own unworthiness.
It was only a vision, I know,
   but it brought home the shocking contrast
   between his purity and my sin,
   his strength and my weakness.
How could I ever bridge that gap?
There was no way I could even begin to,
   but the next moment I felt God reach out and touch me,
   summoning me to service,
   taking away my guilt,
   making me whole.
Me, Isaiah, a prophet?
Could it be true?
Could God really make me new?
It seemed beyond belief,
   childish, romantic nonsense!
Yet that's what he promised,
   and that's what he proved,
   not just to me but countless others across the years.
He called me to proclaim forgiveness,
   a new start for all,
   freedom from our sins.
And I've discovered, beyond all doubt,
   the wonderful, astonishing truth of that message –
   the simple, stupendous fact that whoever you are,
   whatever you've done,
   it doesn't matter;
   God is always ready to forgive what *has* been
   and take what *is*,
   shaping it by his grace to transform what's yet to be.

Reading – Isaiah 1:16-18

Wash yourselves; make yourselves clean; remove the evil of your doings from before my eyes; cease to do evil, learn to do good; seek justice, rescue the oppressed, defend the orphan, plead for the widow. Come now, let us argue it out, says the Lord; though your sins are like scarlet, they shall be white as snow; though they are red like crimson, they shall become like wool.

Prayer

Gracious God,
    we have no claim on your goodness,
    no reason to ever expect mercy.
Despite our best intentions, time and again we fail you,
    preferring our way to yours.
We say one thing, yet do another;
    we claim to love you, yet openly flout your will.
Forgive us, for, try as we might,
    we cannot seem to help ourselves.
Come to us, we pray,
    and blot out our faults.
Renew us through your Holy Spirit,
    redeem us through the grace of Christ,
    and remake us through your great love
    so that we may live and work for you,
    to the glory of your name.
Amen.

65

Does this sound daft to you

Isaiah

Reading – Isaiah 11:1-9

A shoot shall come out from the stump of Jesse,
and a branch shall grow out of his roots.
The spirit of the Lord shall rest on him,
the spirit of wisdom and understanding,
the spirit of counsel and might,
the spirit of knowledge and the fear of the Lord.
His delight shall be in the fear of the Lord.

He shall not judge by what his eyes see,
or decide by what his ears hear;
but with righteousness he shall judge the poor
and decide with equity for the meek of the earth;
he shall strike the earth with the rod of his mouth,
and with the breath of his lips he shall kill the wicked.
Righteousness shall be the belt around his waist,
and faithfulness the belt around his loins.

The wolf shall live with the lamb,
the leopard shall lie down with the kid,
the calf and the lion and the fatling together,
and a little child shall lead them.
The cow and the bear shall graze,
their young shall lie down together;
and the lion shall eat straw like the ox.
The nursing child shall play over the hole of the asp,
and the weaned child shall put its hand on the adder's den.
They will not hurt or destroy on all my holy mountain;
for the earth will be full of the knowledge of the Lord
as the waters cover the sea.

Meditation

Does this sound daft to you –
   a wolf living with a lamb,
   a lion grazing with an ox,
   a child playing happily with a snake?
It does to me, I have to admit it,
   now that I've had time to consider the implications.
But it didn't at the time,
   not when the idea first caught hold of me.
You see, I had this picture of a different kind of world,
   a society where barriers are broken down,
   where all the petty disputes that so often divide us
   are a thing of the past.
Imagine it –
   no more violence,
   no more fear,
   no more hatred,
   no more suffering;
   a world at one with itself,
   all creatures living together in harmony,
   nation existing peaceably alongside nation,
   people set free to be themselves –
   valued,
   loved,
   respected,
   not for what we can get out of them,
   but simply for what they are.
Is that so daft?
Well yes, it probably is,
   because nine times out of ten,
   ninety-nine times out of a hundred,
   for most of us, when the pressure's on,
   it's number one who comes first,
   a question of 'I'm all right and never mind the rest'.
We'd like it to be different, obviously,
   but even when we're not simply paying lip-service to high ideals,
   we can't finally change ourselves, try as we might.
Yet give me one thing –
   it's a wonderful idea, isn't it,
   this world of peace and justice? –
   a beautiful picture –

worth striving for, I'd say,
even worth dying for.
And who knows, one day,
just maybe,
somebody might actually come along
with the faith and courage not just to dream about it,
but to bring it about;
not simply to share the vision,
but to live in such a way that it becomes real –
God's kingdom, here on earth.

Prayer

Gracious God,
sometimes we look at this world of ours
and we despair.
We see its greed, corruption, hatred and violence,
and we ask, 'How can it ever change?'
The heady dreams of youth are worn down
on the treadmill of experience
until a world-weary cynicism takes over.
Although we still make the right noises,
in our hearts we have given up expecting any real change.
Forgive us that sense of despair, Lord.
Forgive us for losing sight of all you are able to do.
Move within us, rekindling faith and hope,
and so help us not just to believe change can happen
but to play our part in ensuring it does.
Amen.

66

BETHLEHEM – NOT MUCH OF A PLACE, IS IT?

Micah

Reading – Micah 5:2-5a

But you, O Bethlehem of Ephrathah,
who are one of the little clans of Judah,
from you shall come forth for me
one who is to rule in Israel,
whose origin is from of old, from ancient days.
Therefore he shall give them up until the time
when she who is in labour has brought forth;
then the rest of his kindred shall return
to the people of Israel.
And he shall stand and feed his flock in the strength of the Lord,
in the majesty of the name of the Lord his God.
And they shall live secure, for now he shall be great
to the ends of the earth;
and he shall be the one of peace.

Meditation

Bethlehem – not much of a place, is it?
I can't pretend otherwise.
Nothing special about it, or unusual,
    just your typical Judean town really,
    a sleepy provincial backwater
    quietly going about its own business.
And why not?
Don't think I'm knocking it –
    quite the opposite –
    it just isn't the sort of place you'd expect
    to hit the headlines,
    still less to set the world on fire.
Yet you know what,
    ever since I passed through last week

I've had this strange feeling
that God has put his finger on that town,
singled it out for a particular purpose,
a special honour that will give it a place in history for ever.
Yes, ridiculous, I know –
I've told myself that time and time again these last few days –
but it makes no difference,
I just can't get the idea out of my head.
It's raised a few eyebrows, there's no denying it –
a right one we've got here,
that's what people are thinking when I tell them.
And who can blame them?
'Prove it!' they tell me.
'Show us the evidence!'
And of course I can't, for there isn't any;
just this hunch that God was speaking to me.
Yet before you write the idea off completely,
stop and think for a minute,
for is it really as way out as it first sounds?
Wouldn't it actually be typical of the way God so often works –
confounding our expectations,
turning our view of the world upside down,
using the little to accomplish the great,
the insignificant to achieve the spectacular,
the humble to astonish the proud?
Remember Moses! Joshua! David!
Remember Egypt! Jericho! Goliath!
Time and again it's been the same story –
where God is concerned, small is beautiful.
I may, of course, be wrong this time, I accept that.
It could simply be some crazy bee in my bonnet.
But I don't think so.
In fact the more I think about it
the more certain I feel it's the way God will choose –
surprising us not simply through his coming
but through the very way he comes.
You may think different, it's up to you –
keep on looking to Jerusalem if you want to.
But me?
I'm looking to Bethlehem,
the last place you'd expect, admittedly,
but in God's eyes, last but not least!

Prayer

Sovereign God,
     time and again you have overturned human expectations,
     using the most unlikely of people
     in yet more unlikely surroundings.
You have shown beyond doubt that no situation or person
     is outside the scope of your purpose –
     that each one can be used by you.
Teach us, then, to be open
     to everything you would do through those around us,
     and to recognise also all you can do through us,
     working in ways we would never dare to contemplate
     and can scarcely imagine.
Sovereign God,
     you recognise the potential of everyone and everything –
     help us to do the same.
Amen.

67

DO YOU EVER STOP AND WONDER ABOUT THE FAIRNESS OF LIFE?

Nahum

Reading – Nahum 1:2-10

A jealous and avenging God is the Lord,
the Lord is avenging and wrathful;
the Lord takes vengeance on his adversaries
and rages against his enemies.
The Lord is slow to anger but great in power,
and the Lord will by no means clear the guilty.

His way is in whirlwind and storm,
and the clouds are the dust of his feet.
He rebukes the sea and makes it dry,
and he dries up all the rivers;
Bashan and Carmel wither,
and the bloom of Lebanon fades.
The mountains quake before him,
and the hills melt;
the earth heaves before him,
the world and all who live in it.

Who can stand before his indignation?
Who can endure the heat of his anger?
His wrath is poured out like fire,
and by him the rocks are broken in pieces.
The Lord is good,
a stronghold in a day of trouble;
he protects those who take refuge in him,
even in a rushing flood.
He will make a full end of his adversaries,
and will pursue his enemies into darkness.
Why do you plot against the Lord?
He will make an end;
no adversary will rise up twice.
Like thorns they are entangled,

like drunkards they are drunk;
they are consumed like dry straw.

Meditation

Do you ever stop and wonder about the fairness of life?
I do, or at least I used to.
It's hard not to, isn't it,
    when all around you see evil going unpunished
    and good trampled underfoot?
And for years that's precisely what we *did* see,
    a regime as corrupt and cruel
    as any you might care to imagine,
    greed, envy, wickedness rampant within it,
    rotten to the core.
We'd suffered it all as best we could,
    but faith had worn thin and hope run dry.
'Where was God?' we couldn't help asking.
'How could he sit back and allow an empire like that to hold sway,
    lording it over the nations?
It made a nonsense of everything –
    our convictions,
    our teaching,
    our faith in God's eternal purpose –
    everything ultimately called into question.
It was impossible not to doubt,
    and there were many all too willing to voice their feelings,
    such was their anger and frustration
    at the seeming injustice of it all.
I was the same for a time,
    as confused and bitter as any;
    but not any more,
    for suddenly the tables have been turned,
    the boot now firmly on the other foot,
    and with it my faith has been restored.
It's wrong to gloat, I know,
    but wouldn't you feel the same
    if you'd been through what we faced –
    your land pillaged,
    your people humiliated,
    your God usurped by worthless idols?

We'd had no choice but to listen to their jibes,
   pander to their wishes,
   but now it's different –
   at long last they must reap what they've sown,
   stand up and give account for their crimes,
   and you won't catch me shedding any tears.
Let them pay, that's what I say,
   no sentence too harsh,
   no punishment too severe.
You think me heartless?
You're probably right.
But it's good at last to see evil conquered and truth prevail,
   to see hatred and violence put in their place,
   pride heading for a fall.
I'm not saying it answers everything, not by a long way,
   for there'll be others to step into their shoes just as evil;
   yet I know now, with a certainty nothing can destroy,
   whatever we may face,
   however hopeless it may seem,
   God's will shall triumph
   and right will prevail!

Prayer

Lord,
   we can't help wondering sometimes what life is all about.
When we see the good suffer and the wicked prosper
   our faith is shaken,
   and we inevitably start to question.
There is so much we cannot understand,
   so much that seems to contradict
   everything we believe about you.
Teach us that, despite all this, you are there,
   striving against everything which frustrates your will
   and denies your love.
Teach us to hold on to those moments in life
   when we see wrongs righted and justice done at last.
Above all, teach us to look at the cross of Christ,
   and to draw strength from the victory of love
   over what had seemed to be the triumph of evil.
Amen.

68
'DOES IT MATTER?' THEY SAID

Zephaniah

Reading – Zephaniah 1:7a, 10-16; 3:9-13

Be silent before the Lord God!
For the day of the Lord is at hand.

On that day, says the Lord,
a cry will be heard from the Fish Gate,
a wail from the Second Quarter,
a loud crash from the hills.
The inhabitants of the Mortar wail,
for all the traders have perished;
all who weigh out silver are cut off.
At that time I will search Jerusalem with lamps,
and I will punish the people
who rest complacently on their dregs,
those who say in their hearts,
'The Lord will not do good, nor will he do harm.'
Their wealth shall be plundered,
and their houses laid waste.
Though they shall build houses,
they shall not inhabit them;
though they plant vineyards,
they shall not drink wine from them.

The great day of the Lord is near,
near and hastening fast;
the sound of the day of the Lord is bitter,
the warrior cries aloud there.
That day will be a day of wrath,
a day of distress and anguish,
a day of ruin and devastation,
a day of clouds and thick darkness,
a day of trumpet blast and battle cry
against the fortified cities
and against the lofty battlements.

At that time I will change the speech of the peoples
to a pure speech,
that all of them may call on the name of the Lord
and serve him with one accord.
From beyond the rivers of Ethiopia
my suppliants, my scattered ones,
shall bring my offering.
On that day you shall not be put to shame
because of all the deeds by which you have rebelled against me;
for then I will remove from your midst
your proudly exultant ones,
and you shall no longer be haughty
in my holy mountain.
For I will leave in the midst of you
a people humble and lowly.
They shall seek refuge in the name of the Lord –
the remnant of Israel;
they shall do no wrong and utter no lies,
nor shall a deceitful tongue
be found in their mouths.
Then they will pasture and lie down,
and no one shall make them afraid.

Meditation

'Does it matter?' they said.
'Does it make a scrap of difference –
   the way we act,
   the way we think –
   to the course our lives will take?'
They'd believed so once, no question,
   each one of them convinced that one step out of line
   and God would be down on them
   like a ton of bricks,
   a rod of iron,
   swift to exact revenge.
A God of justice, that's how they'd seen him,
   rewarding good and punishing evil.
But that was then,
   and this is now.
They'd seen the way of the world since then –

how the strong crush the weak and the rich fleece the poor,
   how virtue goes unrewarded and evil seems to thrive.
'What had God done to stop it?' they wanted to know.
'When had he ever stepped in
   to tip the scales and set things right?'
Well, if he had, it wasn't in their lifetime –
   the theory said one thing,
   the facts said another –
   so look to yourself, they told me,
   for no one else will:
   not God,
   not man,
   not anyone.
Is that how you see it?
I hope not,
   for they couldn't be more wrong.
There may not be a thunderbolt from on high,
   instant punishment to fit the crime,
   but did anyone say there would be? –
   if that's how God works then heaven help the lot of us.
Yet if they really believe he doesn't care,
   that he's twiddling his thumbs in divine indifference,
   they're in for a rude awakening.
Perhaps not today,
   perhaps not tomorrow,
   but the reckoning *will* come –
   a time when each will reap what they have sown,
   finally called to account for their actions.
Make no mistake, it will happen,
   corruption caught at last in its own web,
   evil poisoned by its own venom,
   and when it does all flesh will know that he is God,
   sovereign in judgement,
   ruler over all.
Ignore me if you like,
   it's up to you –
   it's your future we're talking about,
   you who must face the consequences.
Only remember this:
   when the party's over and the inquest begins,
   when the court sits and the verdict is given,
   don't say I didn't warn you.

Prayer

Sovereign God,
    we cannot help wondering sometimes
    about the justice of life.
We see so much that is wrong,
    so much we cannot make sense of,
    and we ask ourselves why you stand by and let it happen.
Day after day we watch helplessly
    as truth is trodden underfoot,
    love exploited,
    and the innocent suffer,
    while those who least deserve it seem to flourish.
Help us, confronted by such enigmas, not to lose heart.
Teach us to recognise that loving you brings its own rewards,
    greater than any this world can offer,
    and remind us also that the time will come
    when everyone will answer to you,
    and justice will prevail.
Amen.

69
WHAT'S GOING ON?

Habakkuk

Reading – Habakkuk 1:2-4

O Lord, how long shall I cry for help,
and you will not listen?
Or cry to you, 'Violence!'
and you will not save?
Why do you make me see wrongdoing
and look at trouble?
Destruction and violence are before me;
strife and contention arise.
So the law becomes slack
and justice never prevails.
The wicked surround the righteous –
therefore judgement comes forth perverted.

Meditation

What's going on?
Can anyone tell me?
I thought this God of ours was meant to be good,
    on the side of justice, love, righteousness;
    a God who rewards the faithful and punishes the wicked.
Well, it's a nice thought,
    but you could have fooled me!
I look around and see just the opposite,
    greed, hatred, violence everywhere;
    corruption carrying off the spoils
    while the weak go to the wall.
It's the law of the jungle out there,
    every man for himself,
    and it seems to me God is doing nothing about it,
    turning a blind eye to the whole sorry business.

I'm sorry if that shocks you,
   but that's the way it feels sometimes,
   and I'm fed up pretending otherwise.
Oh, the time will come when the tables are turned,
   don't misunderstand me;
   one day we'll see right prevail and love emerge victorious –
   I hold on to that conviction with all my being,
   the one thing that makes sense of this mystifying world of ours.
But don't tell me it works like that here and now,
   that the good will prosper,
   the upright be vindicated,
   for quite clearly it isn't so.
I've watched the innocent suffer, the blameless abused.
I've seen the weak exploited, the poor crushed.
I've witnessed naked greed,
   wanton desire,
   brazen deceit,
   each vying for power,
   and each achieving their ends.
Don't think I doubt God,
   I don't,
   but I question the way we dress him up,
   and I question a faith which claims sin brings suffering
   and obedience reward,
   for it's just not that simple,
   not that simple at all.
It's up to you, of course,
   you may disagree,
   call me a heretic,
   a blasphemer –
   it's your right.
But next time life rears up and bites you,
   ask yourself this:
   is it God's doing? –
   his wrath? –
   his punishment? –
   or is he suffering there with you,
   sharing your anger,
   voicing your pain,
   and longing for that day
   when not just *your* questions, but *his*,
   will finally receive their answer?

Reading – Habakkuk 3:17-19

Though the fig tree does not blossom,
and no fruit is on the vines;
though the produce of the olives fails,
and the fields yield no food;
though the flock is cut off from the fold,
and there is no herd in the stalls,
yet I will rejoice in the Lord;
I will exult in the God of my salvation.
God, the Lord, is my strength;
he makes my feet like the feet of a deer,
and makes me tread upon the heights.

Prayer

Lord,
    we can't make sense of life sometimes,
    and it is foolish even to try,
    for we know that this world is not as you want it to be.
We pray day by day,
    'Your kingdom come, your will be done',
    and in that prayer we recognise
    that your purpose is constantly being frustrated,
    your will repeatedly blocked.
Save us, then, when life is a mystery,
    from blaming you.
Deliver us from a naïve faith
    which assumes that if we follow you
    material blessing and worldly satisfaction will surely follow.
Help us, despite everything which conspires against you,
    to hold on to the conviction
    that in the fullness of time
    good will conquer evil,
    and your love triumph over all.
Amen.

70

IT WAS THE LAST THING I EXPECTED

Jeremiah

Reading – Jeremiah 1:4-10; 20:7-9

Now the word of the Lord came to me saying, 'Before I formed you in the womb I knew you, and before you were born I consecrated you; I appointed you a prophet to the nations.' Then I said, 'Ah, Lord God! Truly I do not know how to speak, for I am only a boy.' But the Lord said to me, 'Do not say, "I am only a boy"; for you shall go to all whom I send you, and you shall speak whatever I command you. Do not be afraid of them, for I am with you to deliver you, says the Lord.' Then the Lord put out his hand and touched my mouth; and the Lord said to me, 'Now I have put my words in your mouth. See, today I appoint you over nations and over kingdoms, to pluck up and to pull down, to destroy and to overthrow, to build and to plant.'

(The fears expressed by Jeremiah in the above passage from Chapter 1 are shown, in the following verses from Chapter 20, to have been well founded, but so also is God's promise to put his words in Jeremiah's mouth.)

Lord, you have enticed me,
and I was enticed;
you have overpowered me,
and you have prevailed.
I have become a laughingstock all day long;
everyone mocks me.
For whenever I speak, I must cry out,
I must shout, 'Violence and destruction!'
For the word of the Lord has become for me
a reproach and derision all day long.
If I say, 'I will not mention him,
or speak any more in his name,'
then within me there is something like burning fire
shut up in my bones;
I am weary of holding it in,
and I cannot.

Meditation

It was the last thing I expected,
   the last thing I wanted –
   me, Jeremiah, a prophet?
Ridiculous!
I was just a boy,
   still learning the ways of the world,
   no experience of life at all,
   the very idea of speaking in public purgatory to me.
So I told him straight:
   'Sorry, Lord, but no thank you.
   Ask someone else, not me!'
Blunt perhaps,
   but there was no point beating around the bush, was there?
I knew my strengths and limitations, as well as anyone,
   and this was beyond me, I had no doubt of it.
Only he wouldn't take no for an answer.
Don't look at yourself, he said,
   look at me!
It's not *your* gifts, *your* wisdom, *your* words that matter,
   but *mine*,
   and you can rest assured that I will be with you
   whenever you need me,
   ready to speak,
   ready to strengthen,
   ready to save.
What could I say?
There was no escape.
I suppose I could have argued,
   but I wasn't rebellious by nature
   and if God thought he could use me, fine –
   only I honestly didn't think he could.
There were so many others more gifted than me,
   more qualified for the job;
   teachers, preachers, leaders,
   each one of them naturals,
   capable of captivating the crowds with their gift of oratory,
   holding them spellbound through their subtle way with words.
Me? – I went weak at the knees at the very thought.
Yet God, apparently, could see something in me I couldn't,
   qualities I never knew existed,

and he's used them since then in a way that has left me staggered.
No, I can't say I've enjoyed being a prophet,
    quite the contrary –
    it's been costly,
    demanding,
    and at times downright dangerous,
    precious few welcoming the message I've brought,
    and plenty being positively hostile.
But the words had to be spoken,
    the message delivered,
    and despite the way I sometimes felt,
    I was the one to do it,
    no way I could keep silent,
    much though I often longed to.
Call me mad if you like –
    plenty have –
    but I haven't finished yet, not by a long way,
    and I don't think I ever will,
    for it's my countrymen we're talking about here,
    foolish, stubborn, sinful perhaps,
    yet still my people and still God's,
    so as long as there's the chance of even one person listening,
    one person's life being turned around,
    I'll go on proclaiming the message
    until I draw my final breath.

Prayer

Lord God,
   there are times when we wish you'd never called us
   to discipleship.
When the demands made upon us are too many
   and the cost seems too great,
   when you ask of us more than we feel capable of,
   we can't help wondering if we've made a mistake
   in committing ourselves to your service.
Yet you see in us gifts
   which we have not even begun to recognise,
   and you are able to supply what is lacking
   to use us in ways we would never dream possible.
Teach us then to look at life with your eyes,
   seeing not the obstacles but the possibilities,
   and so may we respond in faith,
   offering our all to you
   in confident expectation and joyful praise.
Amen.

71

YOU'RE WASTING YOUR TIME, THEY TELL ME

Jeremiah

Reading – Jeremiah 31:31-34

The days are surely coming, says the Lord, when I will make a new covenant with the house of Israel and the house of Judah. It will not be like the covenant that I made with their ancestors when I took them by the hand to bring them out of the land of Egypt – a covenant that they broke, though I was their husband, says the Lord. But this is the covenant that I will make with the house of Israel after those days, says the Lord: I will put my law within them, and I will write it on their hearts; and I will be their God, and they shall be my people. No longer shall they teach one another, or say to each other, 'Know the Lord,' for they shall all know me, from the least of them to the greatest, says the Lord; for I will forgive their iniquity, and remember their sin no more.

Meditation

You're wasting your time, they tell me,
    chasing an impossible dream –
    one they'd like to believe in, could it possibly come true,
    but hopelessly unrealistic,
    naïve to the point of folly.
And to be honest, I can't say I blame them,
    for when you look at our record,
    our history as a nation,
    there seems as much chance of us mending our ways
    as a leopard changing its spots.
We've tried to be different, heaven knows,
    striven body and soul to turn over a new leaf,
    but somehow we always end up
    making the same mistakes we've always made,
    the spirit willing but the flesh weak.
So, yes, when they hear me speaking of new beginnings,
    a fresh start,

it's hardly surprising they nod their heads knowingly
    with a wry smile and surreptitious wink.
They've seen it all before, too many times –
    promises made only to be broken,
    good intentions flourishing for a moment
    only to come to nothing –
    what reason to think it should be any different now?
Yet it can be, I'm sure of it,
    not because of anything *we* might do
    but because of what *God* will do for us,
    working within,
    moulding,
    shaping,
    like a potter fashioning his clay,
    until his love flows through our hearts
    and his grace floods our whole being.
It sounds far-fetched, I know,
    a wild and foolish fantasy,
    and whether I'll see it in my lifetime, who can say?
But I honestly believe that one day the time will come –
    a day when God breaks down the barriers which keep us apart,
    when through his great mercy we become a new creation,
    healed,
    restored,
    forgiven –
    and in that hope I will continue to serve him,
    speaking the word he has given,
    confident that in the fullness of time it shall be fulfilled!

Prayer

Gracious God,
    you know how much we want to serve you.
We have resolved so many times
    to live more faithfully as your people
    that we have lost count,
    yet, somehow, when the moment of challenge comes
    we are found wanting.
Despite the good which we long to do,
    we fall victim yet again to the same old weaknesses,

unable to conquer the feebleness of our sinful nature.
Have mercy, O God,
  and renew us through your Holy Spirit.
Cleanse us through the love of Christ,
  and put a new heart and a right spirit within us.
Dwell within us and fill our souls
  so that truly you may be our God
  and we shall be your people.
Amen.

72

I THOUGHT I WAS AN EXPERT

Ezekiel

Reading – Ezekiel 1:1, 4-5a, 13, 15, 16b, 22, 26, 28

In the thirtieth year, in the fourth month, on the fifth day of the month, as I was among the exiles by the river Chebar, the heavens were opened, and I saw visions of God.

As I looked, a stormy wind came out of the north: a great cloud with brightness around it and fire flashing forth continually, and in the middle of the fire something like gleaming amber. In the middle of it was something like four living creatures. . . . In the middle of the living creatures there was something that looked like burning coals of fire, like torches moving to and fro among the living creatures; the fire was bright, and lightning issued from the fire.

As I looked at the living creatures, I saw a wheel on the earth beside the living creatures, one for each of the four of them . . . their construction being something like a wheel within a wheel.

Over the heads of the living creatures there was something like a dome, shining like crystal, spread out above their heads. . . . And above the dome over their heads there was something like a throne, in appearance like sapphire; and seated above the likeness of a throne was something that seemed like a human form.

Like the bow in a cloud on a rainy day, such was the appearance of the splendour all around. This was the appearance of the likeness of the glory of the Lord.

When I saw it, I fell on my face, and I heard the voice of someone speaking.

Meditation

I thought I was an expert;
    that I, more than any, had glimpsed the wonder of God –
    his majesty,
    his power,
    his splendour.

I was a priest, you see,
   the temple my second home,
   and I'd worshipped there,
   sacrificed there,
   year after year,
   for as long as I could remember.
Surely I, of all people, should have understood his greatness?
Yet that day, by the river Chebar, I realised otherwise.
It was the last thing I expected,
   and the last place I'd have expected it;
   not Jerusalem,
   not even Judah,
   but a strange and distant country,
   land of foreign idols –
   Babylon!
Could God meet us there –
   his hand, his love, extend that far?
It seemed impossible,
   a vain and foolish dream,
   and I'd given it up long ago,
   dismissing it as so much fantasy.
He was holy, righteous,
   and we were steeped in sin,
   having wantonly and wilfully flouted his purpose;
   how then could he ever draw near,
   even had he wished to?
But suddenly, out of the blue, as I stood gazing homewards,
   I saw this vision,
   awesome,
   mysterious,
   God enthroned in glory,
   sovereign over all.
I can't quite describe it,
   not as I want to,
   for there are no words sufficient,
   no pictures able to capture the wonder of that moment.
But there were tongues of fire and flashes of lightning,
   peals of thunder, rushing of wind,
   wheels within wheels, and wings touching wings,
   a rainbow of colour, whirlwind of sound.
And above it all, on a living chariot,
   moving now this way, now that,

mighty, glorious, omnipotent,
   the Lord of hosts, ruler of heaven and earth,
   hidden in splendour.
It was staggering,
   incredible,
   and I fell down in homage,
   tears of joy filling my eyes;
   for he was *here*, seeking us out,
   as much God *here* in Babylon as anywhere else!
He had come to redeem us,
   to lead us home,
   no empire able to withstand his power,
   no people able to thwart his will.
Though *we* had failed him time and again,
   weak and foolish in so much,
   still he would not fail *us*.
I thought I was an expert,
   one who knew everything about God there was to know,
   but I'll never think that again, not for a moment,
   for I caught a glimpse of his greatness,
   just the merest glimmer, nothing more;
   and I'm still struggling to take even that in –
   that fleeting revelation –
   let alone to grasp the whole!

Prayer

Gracious God,
   you are above all, beneath all,
   beyond all, within all.
You are God of past, present and future,
   of space and time, heaven and earth,
   all people, all creatures, all creation.
Forgive us that we lose sight of those awesome realities,
   settling instead for a fragmented picture of who you are
   shaped by our own narrow horizons,
   our flawed and limited understanding.
Save us from comfortable discipleship,
   from a faith which insulates us from your challenge

rather than exposes us to your call.
Stir our imaginations,
    and help us to open our lives a little more each day
    to your great glory
    which is constantly waiting to surprise us.
In the name of Christ we pray.
Amen.

73

AM I MEANT TO FEEL SORRY FOR THEM?

Obadiah

Reading – Obadiah 1-4, 12, 15b

The vision of Obadiah.
Thus says the Lord God concerning Edom:
We have heard a report from the Lord,
and a messenger has been sent among the nations:
'Rise up! Let us rise against it for battle!'
I will surely make you least among the nations;
you shall be utterly despised.
Your proud heart has deceived you,
you that live in the clefts of the rock,
whose dwelling is in the heights.
You say in your heart,
'Who will bring me down to the ground?'
Though you soar aloft like the eagle,
though your nest is set among the stars,
from there I will bring you down, says the Lord.
You should not have gloated over your brother
on the day of his misfortune;
you should not have rejoiced over the people of Judah
on the day of their ruin;
you should not have boasted on the day of distress.
As you have done, it shall be done to you;
your deeds shall return on your own head.

Meditation

Am I meant to feel sorry for them?
You think I should, don't you?
But I don't,
    and I won't –
    not even the merest hint of pity.
They've got it coming to them, that's how I see it,

high time someone clipped their wings,
    for they've lorded it over their neighbours for too long,
    sneering at their misfortune,
    gloating over their downfall,
    gathering like vultures to pick greedily over the bones.
We know, for we've been there,
    suffering their looting and pillage for ourselves,
    violated in our hour of need.
Well, now it's their turn,
    and in my book they deserve whatever they get,
    no fate too harsh for them.
Yes, I know that seems hard,
    and there'll be plenty to condemn me for it, no doubt.
Show a bit of compassion, that's what they'll tell me;
    try seeing things from their point of view,
    forgive and forget.
Yet it's not that simple,
    for these people simply won't learn.
Day after day, year after year,
    they've rubbed our noses in the dust,
    sneering at our misfortune,
    and, to be frank, we've had our fill,
    fed up to the back teeth with their constant crowing.
So now that they're the ones facing humiliation,
    can you honestly blame us for feeling a touch smug?
They've been happy to dish it out;
    now the joke's on them,
    and we can scarcely stop ourselves laughing.
Yes, we should know better, I don't dispute it,
    but remember this:
    it wasn't us who set them up for a fall;
    it was them –
    their own pride,
    their own greed,
    their own stupidity –
    so when the moment comes and they're brought low,
    don't be surprised when no one comes running to help them,
    least of all us –
    they've only themselves to blame.

Prayer

Gracious God,
  you tell us that as we forgive
  so we shall be forgiven,
  and the thought of that is frightening,
  for we find forgiving others so very difficult.
When we are hurt, insulted, let down,
  our natural inclination is to want revenge,
  and we allow that thirst to fester within us
  until it grows out of all proportion
  to the wrong we have suffered.
Teach us to leave vengeance to you,
  knowing that in your own time justice will be done.
Save us from that sense of bitterness within
  which finally will destroy *us* more than anyone.
Amen.

74

I THOUGHT I KNEW HIM BETTER THAN MOST

Isaiah

Reading – Isaiah 55:6-11

Seek the Lord while he may be found,
call upon him while he is near;
let the wicked forsake their way,
and the unrighteous their thoughts;
let them return to the Lord, that he may have mercy on them,
and to our God, for he will abundantly pardon.
For my thoughts are not your thoughts,
nor are your ways my ways, says the Lord.
For as the heavens are higher than the earth,
so are my ways higher than your ways
and my thoughts than your thoughts.
For as the rain and the snow come down from heaven,
and do not return there until they have fed and watered the earth,
making it bring forth and sprout,
giving seed to the sower and bread to the eater,
so shall my word be that goes out from my mouth;
it shall not return to me empty,
but it shall accomplish that which I purpose,
and succeed in the thing for which I sent it.

Meditation

I thought I knew him better than most,
    that over the years I'd come to understand him
    as few have even begun to.
And I suppose I had – to a point –
    for I'd glimpsed the wonder of his presence,
    I'd heard the sound of his voice,
    and, by his grace, I'd declared his purpose
    and made known his love:
    good news for all the world.

Impressed?
You shouldn't be –
    for it was nothing,
    just the merest glimmer of light,
    a tiny window on to an indescribable world of mystery.
Oh it was special, don't get me wrong,
    every moment of my ministry a privilege
    which I shall always treasure,
    shaping *my* life and that of countless others.
I spoke of love, and my heart thrilled within me,
    leaping like a deer sensing streams of life-giving water.
I spoke of forgiveness,
    a fresh start,
    new beginnings for us all,
    and my spirit sang for joy,
    dancing in exultation.
I spoke of light shining in the darkness,
    reaching out into the gloom,
    reviving, renewing, restoring,
    and my mouth gave praise to God,
    a song on my lips and his word on my tongue.
Yes, it was magical, no question,
    enough to set my soul on fire and my heart ablaze,
    yet it was a fraction of the whole,
    a speck of flotsam in the vast and unfathomable ocean
    that is God.
Whatever I'd glimpsed, far more lay hidden;
    whatever I'd grasped, far more had yet to be revealed,
    whatever I thought I'd understood,
    there was more always out of reach,
    too awesome even to contemplate,
    for we were different,
    he before all and over all, sovereign over space and time,
    and me? –
    a fleeting breath,
    a passing shadow,
    like the flower of the field, here today and gone tomorrow.
I thought I knew him, better than any,
    and to be fair, I did,
    my knowledge of him growing each day –
    new insights,
    new discoveries,

new wonders beyond imagining,
but I recognise now that, however far I've come,
there's further still to go,
more yet to learn –
for all my travelling, the journey's only just begun!

Prayer

Sovereign God,
  all too often we have lost sight of your greatness,
  settling instead for a picture of you we feel comfortable with.
We have frustrated your will
  through the smallness of our vision.
We have missed opportunities to serve you
  through the narrowness of our horizons.
We have denied ourselves your mercy
  through the confines we place upon your grace.
Time and again we have presumed
  that your ways are *our* ways
  and your thoughts *our* thoughts,
  forgetting that you are beyond words
  or human understanding.
Forgive us,
  and teach us never to underestimate
  the awesomeness of your being
  or the extent of your love.
Amen.

75

I COULD HARDLY BELIEVE WHAT I WAS SEEING

Haggai

Reading – Haggai 1:1-9

In the second year of King Darius, in the sixth month, on the first day of the month, the word of the Lord came by the prophet Haggai to Zerubbabel son of Shealtiel, governor of Judah, and to Joshua son of Jehozadak, the high priest. Thus says the Lord of hosts: These people say the time has not yet come to rebuild the Lord's house. Then the word of the Lord came by the prophet Haggai, saying: Is it a time for you yourselves to live in panelled houses, while this house lies in ruins? Now therefore thus says the Lord of hosts: Consider how you have fared. You have sown much, and harvested little; you eat, but you never have enough; you drink, but you never have your fill; you clothe yourselves, but no one is warm; and you that earn wages earn wages to put them into a bag with holes.

Thus says the Lord of hosts: Consider how you have fared. Go up to the hills and bring wood and build the house, so that I may take pleasure in it and be honoured, says the Lord. You have looked for much, and, lo, it came to little; and when you brought it home, I blew it away. Why? says the Lord of hosts. Because my house lies in ruins, while all of you hurry off to your own houses.

Meditation

I could hardly believe what I was seeing;
    quite honestly, it left me speechless!
After all we'd been through,
    everything God had done for us,
    to ignore him so brazenly –
    it was beyond belief.
Yet there they were,
    building bigger and better homes for themselves each day,
    and not a thought for the house of God
    lying in ruins just a few yards from their door.
You'd have thought they'd have learned their lesson, wouldn't you? –

those interminable years in Babylon
enough to bring anyone to their senses –
but not them, I'm afraid;
it was just like it had always been,
self first
God second.
Only they didn't seem to realise it, that's the strange thing;
they honestly felt hard done by,
cheated, somehow, as their dreams turned to ashes,
and their hopes lay trodden in the dust.
'What's happened?' they asked me.
'Why has God brought us back, only to withhold his blessing?'
Incredible, I know, yet true!
Couldn't they see it was their own fault,
the result of their own folly?
Apparently not.
Yet it should have been clear to anyone
that a society based on greed –
on looking after number one and never mind the rest –
could only end one way,
in utter rack and ruin.
It grieved me to see it,
but it grieved God far more,
for once again he saw his people frittering away
the riches he'd given,
squandering his precious gift of life.
Would it all end in tears, once more?
It nearly did,
but, thankfully, this time when he spoke,
they were ready to listen,
ready to learn,
and ready to change.
If only you could see us now,
what a difference it's made!
We're not just a country again,
a group of exiles restored to our homeland –
we're a community,
a nation,
a people united in faith.
I'm not saying everything's perfect, our troubles over,
for I've no doubt there will be more mistakes
and more trials to face,

but we realise now that there's more to life
than our own interests,
more to this world than self;
and the irony is, in giving God his rightful place,
we've discovered our own worth too,
and the worth of everyone, and everything, around us.

Prayer

Lord,
   you have given to us without counting the cost.
Forgive us that we find it so hard to give back to you.
We intend to respond,
   but we are enslaved to self,
   our own interests constantly thrusting themselves forward
   until they blot out all else.
Teach us to recognise the road to true fulfilment,
   to understand that unless we are willing
   to lose everything we have,
   we will never finally find anything worth having.
Teach us to let go of self
   and, in serving you and others,
   to discover the life you freely offer us,
   brimming over beyond measure.
Amen.

76
WAS IT WORTH CONTINUING?

Zechariah

Reading – Zechariah 14:1, 6-9

See, a day is coming for the Lord, when the plunder taken from you will be divided in your midst.

On that day there shall not be either cold or frost. And there shall be continuous day (it is known to the Lord), not day and not night, for at evening time there shall be light.

On that day living waters shall flow out from Jerusalem, half of them to the eastern sea and half of them to the western sea; it shall continue in summer as in winter.

And the Lord will become king over all the earth; on that day the Lord will be one and his name one.

Meditation

Was it worth continuing?
Could we go on any longer closing our eyes to the truth?
It was hard not to ask that,
    as, once more, our hopes came to nothing.
We thought we'd turned the corner
    after the traumas and turmoil of exile –
    a new beginning to blot away the memory
    of those interminable years,
    so hard to bear, so bitter to remember.
Not that we were treated badly there, we could never say that,
    but there was always a sense of emptiness,
    the knowledge that we were far from home;
    far from the land of our fathers and the city of God.
We could never forget that, try though we might,
    so when the chance came to return,
    you can imagine, we grasped it,
    beside ourselves with joy,
    looking forward with eager expectation

to a bright new era,
God's kingdom, here on earth.
Only it didn't happen that way.
After the initial euphoria came the harsh reality –
the magnitude of the challenge before us,
and the feebleness of our resources to meet it.
We did our best, of course –
little by little restoring the temple –
but it soon became clear to everyone,
even the most optimistic,
that we could never regain past glories,
let alone surpass them.
It was a question of making do,
getting by as best we could –
the sooner we reconciled ourselves to second best,
the better for everyone.
I thought the same until today, I have to admit it,
my despair and disillusionment as keen as anyone's.
But not any more,
for God granted me last night an astonishing vision,
a picture of a glorious new kingdom
unlike any I've seen before.
I saw a new dawn, bathing the world in light,
the sun rising ever higher, warm upon my face,
shimmering across streams of living water,
sparkling upon fields wet with dew.
I saw a new creation at one with itself,
a land reflecting God's love and mercy,
with him there at the centre,
ruling in splendour,
all in all.
I saw a kingdom of justice and truth,
sorrow a thing of the past,
despair consigned to history,
our cup running over with good things.
And my spirit leapt,
dancing in joyful celebration!
We're not there yet, not by a long way,
but God has given us a glimpse of things to come,
a taste of paradise;
and we're resolved now to keep going,
however long it may take us,

whatever the setbacks,
until the day we enter that kingdom,
and see his glory,
more wonderful than we can ever imagine!

Prayer

Sovereign God,
  you have promised that the time will come
  when your kingdom will be established,
  your people rejoice in the wonder of your love
  and all creation celebrate your goodness.
It is this prospect
  which inspires us to new endeavours of faith
  and which gives us strength in times of adversity,
  yet there are times, if we are honest,
  when the vision starts to fade.
Confronted by the harsh realities of life,
  we wonder sometimes if it makes sense
  to keep on believing.
Assure us in such moments that, despite appearances,
  you are there
  and that, in the fullness of time,
  your will shall triumph and our hope be vindicated.
Amen.

77

I DIDN'T HAVE MUCH TO OFFER

Ezra

Reading – Ezra 7:6-10

Ezra went up from Babylonia. He was a scribe skilled in the law of Moses that the Lord the God of Israel had given; and the king granted him all that he asked, for the hand of the Lord his God was upon him.

Some of the people of Israel, and some of the priests and Levites, the singers and gatekeepers, and the temple servants also went up to Jerusalem, in the seventh year of King Artaxerxes. They came to Jerusalem in the fifth month, which was in the seventh year of the king. On the first day of the first month the journey up from Babylon was begun, and on the first day of the fifth month he came to Jerusalem, for the gracious hand of his God was upon him. For Ezra had set his heart to study the law of the Lord, and to do it, and to teach the statutes and ordinances in Israel.

Meditation

I didn't have much to offer, I knew that –
    no extravagant gifts,
    no stunning insights –
    just a love of God
    and a desire to serve him as best I could.
So I made it my goal to study his word,
    to read sentence by sentence the book of the law.
    so that I might know his will
    and help rebuild our nation.
Nothing dramatic, true – still less glamorous –
    but it was something I could do,
    and a job that needed doing.
Why?
Because I'd seen for myself
    what forgetting God could lead to,
    the tragic results of flouting his will
    and ignoring his commandments.

I'd been there in Babylon, remember,
    sharing my people's exile,
    enduring the frustration and heartache
    of being far from the land of our fathers,
    cut off from the city of God;
    and if there was one thing I'd resolved during that time,
    it was this:
    never, never again!
So I read, and kept on reading,
    hour after hour,
    day after day,
    until my head throbbed and my eyes ached,
    no detail too small,
    no point too trivial,
    everything noted and stored carefully away.
It was an obsession, I admit it,
    but, you see, this was to be a fresh start for our people,
    a bright new chapter in our history,
    and I was determined we shouldn't waste it.
We'd paid the price for past mistakes,
    but had we learned our lesson?
There was only one way to be sure.
Did I take it too far?
Some would say so,
    and, yes, they're probably right,
    for anything can be abused, even God's word,
    and through my emphasis on the fine print
    I fear I may have obscured the whole picture.
It's not the words that matter but the message,
    the spirit rather than letter of the law,
    and if you get that wrong, then better not to read at all.
But that's finally down to you, not me.
I've given the tools, as best I can;
    it's up to you to use them.

Prayer

Living God,
    you have given us your word in the Scriptures,
    but all too often we fail to read them.
We dip in casually as the mood takes us,
    selecting those bits which suit us best
    and ignoring the passages
    which might prove difficult or demanding.
Even the little we read is rarely applied to our lives
    in a way that really touches them.
Despite the claims we make for it,
    the reality is that much of the Bible is a closed book to us.
Forgive us,
    and help us make time and space in our lives
    to study your word,
    to hear you speaking,
    and to respond in faith.
Amen.

78

I KNEW THINGS HAD BEEN BAD BACK IN JERUSALEM

Nehemiah

Reading – Nehemiah 1:1-7

The words of Nehemiah son of Hacaliah. In the month of Chislev, in the twentieth year, while I was in Susa the capital, one of my brothers, Hanani, came with certain men from Judah; and I asked them about the Jews that survived, those who had escaped the captivity, and about Jerusalem. They replied, 'The survivors there in the province who escaped captivity are in great trouble and shame; the wall of Jerusalem is broken down, and its gates have been destroyed by fire.'

When I heard these words I sat down and wept, and mourned for days, fasting and praying before the God of heaven. I said, 'O Lord God of heaven, the great and awesome God who keeps covenant and steadfast love with those who love him and keep his commandments; let your ear be attentive and your eyes open to hear the prayer of your servant that I now pray before you day and night for your servants, the people of Israel, confessing the sins of the people of Israel, which we have sinned against you. Both I and my family have sinned. We have offended you deeply, failing to keep the commandments, the statutes, and the ordinances that you commanded your servant Moses.'

Meditation

I knew things had been bad back in Jerusalem,
    we all did, every man, woman and child.
Never mind that we'd never been there –
    we'd heard the stories too many times to be in any doubt:
    how the soldiers had marched in,
    demolishing the walls and torching the city,
    looting, raping and pillaging,
    before carrying off the cream of the nation into exile
    while the rest were left to fend for themselves.
Our hearts had bled for them at first,

the dreadful images those stories conjured up
haunting us day and night,
and we were resolved never to forget
nor forgive those dreadful deeds.
But it was long ago now,
and as the dust had settled, so we had settled with it,
the strange land of Babylon not so dreadful after all,
offering to those with the wit to take them, rich rewards
and swift advancement;
good homes,
good jobs,
good prospects.
We still *believed* we cared,
still even called Jerusalem 'home'
in a romantic sort of way,
but for most of us it had become just a name,
promising much,
signifying little.
I was as guilty as any, I'm afraid,
for life had worked out well for me –
a trusted position at court,
the king's own cup-bearer –
what reason was there to rock the boat?
Only, then, my brother turned up, fresh from Jerusalem,
and suddenly the whole sorry picture was laid bare before me –
the squalor,
the suffering,
the misery of a once-proud people in a once-proud city
brought to abject ruin,
an object of ridicule to all around them.
How did I feel?
I was overcome – there's no other word for it –
not just with sorrow, but shame,
for in my own way I was as responsible as any,
their hopelessness, at least in part, down to me.
Ostensibly a victim, I had become one of the victors,
ensconced in my comfortable home,
secure and respected,
the needs of those outside, even my own people,
quietly swept under the carpet.
It hadn't been done consciously,
still less planned,

but it had happened nonetheless,
  and the truth hurt, more than I can tell.
What did I do?
I went back, of course,
  using my influence, as God surely intended I should,
  to secure safe passage home,
  and the resources needed to help them start afresh.
You should see it now,
  it's a different place –
  the walls rebuilt,
  the city restored,
  the future beckoning;
  but I'm haunted once again,
  unable to forget that dreadful moment
  when our failure was exposed –
  a moment which taught me that it's one thing to think you care;
  to believe someone, somewhere, matters;
  quite another when it comes to proving it.

Prayer

Living God,
  we talk of being a light to the nations,
  of reaching out with your love to the ends of the earth,
  but sometimes we do not even get
  as far as those on our own doorstep.
For all our high ideals,
  we fail to recognise the great family to which we belong,
  our concern more for ourselves or our own immediate circle
  than the wider world.
Forgive us for the many times we have failed you
  through the narrowness of our vision,
  and give us sensitivity
  to the needs of our brothers and sisters in Christ,
  and a willingness to respond to people everywhere.
In his name we pray.
Amen.

79

IT HAD BEEN A HARD TIME BY ANYONE'S STANDARDS

Joel

Reading – Joel 2:12-14, 26-32

Even now, says the Lord,
return to me with all your heart,
with fasting, with weeping, and with mourning;
rend your hearts and not your clothing.
Return to the Lord, your God,
for he is gracious and merciful,
slow to anger, and abounding in steadfast love,
and relents from punishing.
Who knows whether he will turn and relent,
and leave a blessing behind him,
a grain offering and a drink offering
for the Lord, your God?
You shall eat in plenty and be satisfied,
and praise the name of the Lord your God,
who has dealt wondrously with you.
And my people shall never again be put to shame.
You shall know that I am in the midst of Israel,
and that I, the Lord, am your God and there is no other.
And my people shall never again be put to shame.
Then afterwards I will pour out my spirit on all flesh;
your sons and your daughters shall prophesy,
your old men shall dream dreams,
and your young men shall see visions.
Even on the male and female slaves,
in those days, I will pour out my spirit.
I will show portents in the heavens and on the earth,
blood and fire and columns of smoke.
The sun shall be turned to darkness,
and the moon to blood,
before the great and terrible day of the Lord comes.
Then everyone who calls on the name of the Lord
shall be saved;

for in Mount Zion and in Jerusalem
there shall be those who escape, as the Lord has said,
and among the survivors shall be those whom the Lord calls.

Meditation

It had been a hard time by anyone's standards –
    a famine like no other we'd known before,
    cruel,
    savage,
    merciless;
    sapping our strength,
    gnawing at our bellies –
    enough to test the faith of the most devoted.
We felt close to breaking, each one of us,
    such hunger hard to bear,
    yet strangely it was a different emptiness
    that should have concerned us –
    not the hollowness in our stomachs
    but a far greater void:
    the barrenness of our faith,
    the aridity of our lives,
    spirits emaciated by lack of sustenance.
Here was the true threat to our future.
We understood those pangs in our stomach,
    knew them for what they were,
    but that dull ache deep within,
    that remorseless craving;
    it left us tortured,
    bewildered,
    conscious of our need yet at a loss how to meet it.
If anything showed the measure of our fall, that was it;
    for all the time God was there,
    prompting,
    pleading,
    longing to fill our stricken souls;
    only we would not or could not see it.
And that's how it might have ended were it not for his grace,
    had he, in his mercy, not decreed otherwise.

But in love he kept on calling,
   speaking his word,
   offering his promise –
   a new era,
   a new kingdom which he would bring to pass.
Not just food and plenty, though that was gift enough,
   but his spirit deep within!
And not just for some, the chosen few,
   but all –
   young and old,
   man and woman,
   slave and free,
   rich and poor!
It was unheard of,
   unthinkable,
   a picture exceeding all our expectations –
   surely too good to be true?
Yet that's what he told us,
   the time coming when our sons and daughters will prophesy,
   our old men dream dreams and the young see visions,
   when all flesh will know the indwelling of his presence.
Can it be true?
I still wonder sometimes,
   for can he really touch not just one life but so many,
   transforming what *is* into what he would have it be?
It seems impossible,
   only I've tasted his power for myself,
   experienced the renewal his spirit brings,
   and I know now that not only *can* it be –
   it *has* to be –
   for then, and only then, can we find the nourishment we need
   and the fulfilment we crave –
   food to feed our souls!

Prayer

Gracious God,
    we thank you that whoever we are,
    whatever our age, sex, colour or background,
    we can know you for ourselves
    through the living presence of your Holy Spirit.
We thank you that you meet our innermost needs,
    filling our empty souls to overflowing
    through that Spirit's power.
Come to us now,
    and help us to dream dreams and see visions.
Help us to catch a new sense of all you have done,
    all you are doing, and all you have yet to do.
In the name of Christ.
Amen.

80
NOT LONG NOW, THEY TELL ME

Malachi

Reading – Malachi 2:17–3:3a, 5

You have wearied the Lord with your words. Yet you say, 'How have we wearied him?' By saying, 'All who do evil are good in the sight of the Lord, and he delights in them.' Or by asking, 'Where is the God of justice?'

See, I am sending my messenger to prepare the way before me, and the Lord whom you seek will suddenly come to his temple. The messenger of the covenant in whom you delight – indeed, he is coming, says the Lord of hosts. But who can endure the day of his coming, and who can stand when he appears?

For he is like a refiner's fire and like fullers' soap; he will sit as a refiner and purifier of silver, and he will purify the descendants of Levi. I will draw near to you for judgement; I will be swift to bear witness against the sorcerers, against the adulterers, against those who swear falsely, against those who oppress the hired workers in their wages, the widow and the orphan, against those who thrust aside the alien, and do not fear me, says the Lord of hosts.

Meditation

Not long now, they tell me –
    just a little longer and the day will come,
    the Messiah arrive –
    a new era,
    the dawn of a wonderful new age,
    God's kingdom here on earth,
    with us, his chosen people, right at the centre of it!
No more suffering,
    no more smarting under the yoke of occupation,
    but freedom,
    prosperity,
    blessings too many to number!
That's what they tell me, anyway –

what they're all expecting.
If only they knew!
If only they could see themselves as they really are,
    perhaps then they'd change their tune.
For I tell you this, they've got it horribly wrong,
    each way off the mark and heading for a terrible let-down.
Oh he's coming all right, the Messiah, no doubt about that –
    maybe not in my lifetime,
    maybe not in theirs –
    but he's coming, just as they say.
Only it won't be the party some seem to imagine –
    not a bit of it.
Why?
Do you really have to ask?
Just look around at the mess we're in,
    the state of our society,
    the shallowness of our lifestyles.
Can you see the Messiah giving us a pat on the back
    when he sees it all?
I can't.
He'll be shocked, more likely,
    dismayed at the way we've failed so miserably
    to prepare for his coming,
    and I can't see him turning a blind eye,
    no matter who we are.
I wish I could say different.
Truly, I'd love to believe I'm mistaken,
    that we're ready and waiting for his coming.
But we're nowhere near it,
    nowhere near it at all.
Let them look forward if they want to.
Let them pray for the day of the Lord.
I only hope, before he answers us,
    that God gives us time to take a long hard look at ourselves,
    get our house in order
    and ask just who it is we're expecting,
    for otherwise,
    when the day finally arrives,
    I have this grim foreboding
    that many crying out now to see him come,
    will end up doing all they can to see him gone.

Prayer

Lord,
    you call us to test ourselves
    and ensure that we are still in the faith.
Help us to take that challenge seriously,
    for it is all too easy to imagine everything is well
    when in fact we've lost our way.
We may still follow you outwardly,
    but in our hearts be far from you,
    our love grown cold.
Save us, we pray,
    from the ever-present danger of complacency.
Draw us closer to you, day by day,
    so that our faith may always be as real and as fresh
    as the day we first believed.
Prepare us for your coming again in Christ,
    so that we may be ready to receive him
    and found faithful in his service.
In his name we pray.
Amen.

PART TWO

SERVICES

1
IN THE BEGINNING

Introduction 'In the beginning when God created the heavens and the earth, the earth was a formless void and darkness covered the face of the deep, while a wind from God swept over the face of the waters . . . God saw everything that he had made, and indeed, it was very good' (Genesis 1:1-2, 31a). Words from the opening chapter of Genesis expressing God's satisfaction in his creation. Yet within just a few pages, a very different picture emerges – a saga of human disobedience and rebellion in which the participants find themselves estranged from both God and each other. And in all this is a powerful portrayal of our human condition today: our potential for good, our penchant for evil. So what went wrong? Where did God's plans come adrift, and why? How is it that at one moment we can scale the heights and the very next plumb the depths? It is questions such as these which we will explore today as we turn again to the pages of Scripture and reflect on some of the events recorded there 'in the beginning'.

Silence or Hymn *Morning has broken*
Jesus is Lord! Creation's voice proclaims it

Prayer Sovereign God,
    above all,
    before all,
    beyond all,
    within all,
    we praise you for your gift of life
    and for the wonder of creation;
    for everything in this world that has the power
    to move, fascinate and inspire us.
Forgive us for abusing what you have given,
    squandering, exploiting,
    desecrating and destroying

the many treasures of our planet.
Forgive us for abusing you,
    turning our backs on your love
    and ignoring your will.
Through your grace, have mercy
    and remake us in your likeness,
    so that we may be the people
    you would have us be,
    and live each day for your glory,
    through Jesus Christ our Lord.
Amen.

Comment   There can be few passages of Scripture which have created such heated debate as the opening chapters of Genesis. While some, even today, argue for a strictly literal interpretation of the text, others maintain it refers to humankind in general, its aim being to communicate fundamental theological truths. No doubt debate will continue, but, however you approach them, the creation narratives, and the account of the 'Fall' in particular, graphically illustrate key aspects of human nature. In one sense, at least, Adam and Eve represent us all: in their instinctive attempts to shift blame for their actions on to someone or something other than themselves. And the irony is that, more often than not, we, like Adam, are unaware of doing so.

Reading   Genesis 3:1-13

Meditation 1   *Don't blame me, it wasn't my fault! – Adam*

Comment   How can any of us begin to understand what was in the mind of God as he set about the business of creation? The answer, of course, is that we can't; the ways and thoughts of God are totally beyond our comprehension. The more we try to make sense of his purposes, the more aware we become of our inability to do so, for with God, as in so much of life, we are repeatedly confronted by unfathomable mysteries. Yet although grappling with such issues can be unsettling, it can also be immensely rewarding, for it reminds us that God is not remote and detached from his creation, but intimately involved with its future. Despite all the mistakes we make, our future not only matters to him, it is his overwhelming concern!

Reading Genesis 3:14-19, 22-24

Meditation 2 *What have I done?* – God

Silence or Hymn *Dear Lord and Father of mankind*
Just as I am, without one plea

Comment There's an old saying, 'When anger arises, think of the consequences' – a variation of 'Stop, and count to ten'. But while the advice may be familiar, and the sense behind it plain to see, when the moment comes we all too easily forget. The trouble with anger is that it clouds our vision, making even the most mild-mannered of people act entirely out of character. The consequences can be disastrous for all concerned. In the story of Cain and Abel we find not only anger let loose, but envy also – another basic yet enormously destructive human emotion. The resultant cocktail proves lethal!

Reading Genesis 4:2b-10

Meditation 3 *If only I'd listened* – Cain

Comment There are few of us who like to stand out from the crowd. The occasional foible is one thing, eccentricity quite another. No one likes to be thought odd. Yet when Noah set to work building an ark in the middle of the wilderness he must have looked exactly that – a strange character if ever there was one. It is hard to imagine the ridicule he must have been subjected to day after day as he laboured on his extraordinary enterprise with no sign of rain let alone flood. Given all that he must have faced, it is tempting to suggest he may have had the last laugh, but laughter was probably the last thing on his mind after the tragedy which followed. The story of Noah is not about saying 'I told you so' to a cynical and hostile world. It is rather about having the courage to be different in the hope that someone, somewhere, may perhaps take notice.

Reading   Genesis 6:11-22

Meditation 4   *'A right one we've got here!'* – Noah

Prayer   Almighty God,
   there is so much in our world
   that fills us with sadness –
   so much pain and suffering,
   sorrow and despair,
   hatred and division,
   evil and injustice.
We look at the greed, corruption,
   violence and exploitation,
   and we wonder what hope there can possibly be,
   our hearts heavy within us.
Almighty God,
   there is so much in our world
   that fills *you* with sorrow too –
   so much hurt and distress,
   misery, discord and wickedness,
   and, like us, *your* heart aches within you,
   agonising over your fallen creation.
But, *unlike* us, *you* never give up,
   your love giving everything,
   even your only Son,
   to redeem, restore and renew.
Though all else conspires against you,
   still you will carry on working
   until the end of time,
   healing our wounds
   and drawing all things to yourself.
Come, then, and create us anew.
Teach us to respond to your love,
   and so to play our part
   in working for your kingdom,
   until all things are reconciled to you in Christ,

and we are one with you and him,
now and for evermore.
Amen.

Silence or Hymn *Now thank we all our God*
O Lord of every shining constellation

Blessing

2
AMAZING GRACE

Introduction Consider this for a character reference: greedy, ruthless, deceitful, utterly selfish, cunning and corrupt. What place do you think such a person would have in the purpose of God? Our innate sense of justice tells us none, but stop and think again, for the character we are focusing on today was all of those and more, and yet was to become the founding father of Israel, revered and respected even today as an example of faith. He is, if you haven't guessed it, Jacob, the man who was ready to deceive and exploit his own family to secure his own ends, and finally to grapple with God himself until he had secured his blessing. How do we make sense of this puzzle? The answer, of course, is summed up in one word which takes us not only to the heart of his remarkable story but to the heart of the gospel itself – the word 'grace'. In the chequered tale of Jacob is a graphic reminder that God deals with us not according to what we deserve, but according to his gracious mercy which reaches out in love, as much despite us as because of us. Yet there is a reminder, too, that we must be willing to seek, to set our hearts on God's blessing, if we are to receive the gifts he so freely offers.

Hymn *Great is your faithfulness*
Love divine, all loves excelling

Prayer Almighty God,
  you are greater than our minds can imagine,
  sovereign over history,
  the creator of the ends of the earth,
  and yet you have time for each one of us.
You are all good,
  all true,
  all holy,
  all righteous,
  and yet you accept us with our many imperfections.

You are the source of love,
   the fount of knowledge,
   the giver of life,
   the one who gives meaning to our universe,
   and yet you delight in our companionship.
Almighty God,
   such things are too wonderful for us,
   too awesome to take in,
   but we marvel at your grace,
   we rejoice in your goodness,
   and we offer now our worship.
Help us through all we do and think and say
   to grow closer to you this day, and every day,
   through Jesus Christ our Lord.
Amen.

Comment   There are some stories which leave a bitter taste in the mouth, seeming to contradict everything we believe about right and wrong. The epic saga of Esau and Jacob is one such example. It features a man who, not once but twice, was to take advantage of his gullible brother and steal blessings which were rightfully his. Yet if the outcome for Jacob was a happy one, for Esau it was anything but. Swindled out of his birthright through little apparent fault of his own, he was left to make the best of a thoroughly bad job. Those seeking reassuring spiritual truths from this story should beware, for they will find instead a concoction of treachery, self-interest and opportunism on a breathtaking scale. We sanitise these away at our peril. Esau was by no means perfect, but morally speaking, compared with Jacob, he comes across as an angel. Yet it was Jacob who finally ran away with the spoils. Lessons certainly can be learned from these narratives but, like it or not, we are dealing here finally with the grace of God which confounds all our expectations. To face up to that truth is a profoundly disturbing experience.

Reading   Genesis 25:29-30; 27:30-38

Meditation 7   *Let's face it, I was a complete fool* – Esau

Comment   It's a sad fact of life that few things live up to our expectations. We can spend years striving to reach some goal which we think will answer all our problems, only to find, no sooner do we achieve it, that we are overwhelmed by a sense of anticlimax. There is something of this truth in the celebrated story of Jacob's dream at Bethel. For years he had plotted and schemed to swindle his brother Esau out of his rightful inheritance and, at last, with the connivance of his mother, the opportunity presented itself. Yet after the initial flush of success, the inevitable questions surfaced. Exactly what went through his mind we can never know but perhaps it was along the lines: Was it all worth it? Surely there is more to life than material gain? In the vision which came to him that night, Jacob was to realise there is indeed more – far more than he'd ever begun to contemplate.

Reading   Genesis 28:10-17

Meditation 8   *Have you ever been brought down to earth with a bump?* – Jacob

Silence or Hymn   *To God be the glory! Great things he has done! Immortal, invisible, God only wise*

Comment   How many of us, when we hear the expression 'grappling with God', picture in our minds an actual physical wrestling contest? Probably few, if any. It's a strange idea, isn't it? Completely different from the more traditional picture of humble and obedient acceptance. Yet that is what we find in surely one of the most dramatic if enigmatic incidents recorded anywhere in the Bible. The imagery is crude, if not to say shocking – a mysterious stranger who accosts Jacob by the ford at Jabbok turning out to be none other than God himself. More puzzling still, so tenaciously does Jacob cling hold during the ensuing test of strength that God is unable to extricate himself without first granting a blessing. It all gets, as Alice might have said, 'curiouser and curiouser'. Yet it is the very primitiveness of this encounter which makes it so compelling. There is no false piety here, no alabaster saint far removed from our human condition. Here is an individual like any one of us, warts and all, struggling to come to terms with the complex realities of life and faith. Who knows quite what Jacob wrestled with in the darkness of that night? Doubt, fear, pride, guilt – you name it and it was probably there! Symbolic the whole story may be – its power remains undiminished, giving hope and encouragement to all those who grapple with God in their turn.

Reading   Genesis 32:9-12, 22-31

Meditation 10   *There was no way I deserved it* – Jacob

Comment   According to traditional wisdom, 'you can't bury the past'. For Jacob the truth of those words must have seemed all too real when his sons returned from the fields one day with the shattering news that his son Joseph was dead! Illogical though it may be, there seems to be an instinctive human tendency to interpret any kind of misfortune in terms of divine retribution, and perhaps Jacob did much the same, his mind instinctively harking back to his all too murky past. Yet while such a view of God undoubtedly finds a place in the Old Testament, so also does a very different picture: the portrayal of a God always willing to forgive and forget, ready to put the past behind us, however little we may deserve it, and help us to begin again. This is the God, fortunately for Jacob, who emerges time and again in his story – a God of whom we can truly sing 'Amazing grace! How sweet the sound that saved a wretch like me!'

Reading   Genesis 37:3-4, 12-13a, 14, 17b-20, 22-24a, 26-28, 31-35

Meditation 11   *Was it a punishment for those mistakes long ago?* – Jacob

Prayer   Mighty God,
        we praise you for the wonder of your love.

Though we merit little, you give us much.
Though we deserve judgement, you show us grace.
Though we deal falsely, you always stay true.
Day by day you grant us your blessing
   despite our repeated disobedience
   and our many faults,
     your goodness going beyond our expectations
     and defying human reason.
Receive, then, our joyful worship
   and our heartfelt thanksgiving,
     and help us to respond in faithful service,
     to the glory of your name.
Amen.

Silence or Hymn   *Amazing grace!*
       And can it be?

Blessing

3

MOSES – THE MAN AND THE MISSION

Introduction   If we are looking for memorable stories in the Old Testament we could do no better than turn to the saga of Moses. Hidden as a baby in the bulrushes; fleeing for his life after killing an Egyptian taskmaster in a fit of rage; confronted by God in a burning bush on Mount Sinai; demanding the release of his people from Egypt; leading them to safety through the waters of the Red Sea; returning to Sinai to receive the ten commandments – the list is truly astonishing, enough to fill a book in itself! Today we have time to consider only a few of those episodes. We look not just at the events themselves but at the human weaknesses and problems which were part of them and to which we can so easily relate. Yet we look also at the guiding hand of God which, through triumph and adversity, was always there, offering help in time of need and inexorably bringing his purpose to fulfilment. We ask what we can learn about the man and his mission, and, more important, what we can learn about God's purpose for us today.

Hymn   *Be still, for the presence of the Lord*
For the might of your arm we bless you

Prayer   Gracious God,
we thank you for enabling us to know you,
for calling us, by your grace,
to share in your sovereign purpose.
Though that call brings challenge as well as fulfilment,
trials as well as blessing,
you are always by our side,
offering us the strength and encouragement
we need
to continue our journey.
For all the ways you have led us thus far,
and for the guidance you shall yet give,
receive our praise.

Help us to trust in your will,
    to respond to your summons,
    and to work always for your glory,
    this day and for evermore.
Amen.

Comment   When were we last confronted with a challenge which seemed completely beyond us but which somehow we had to face? Anyone who has been in such a situation will have at least some insight into how Moses must have felt when God unexpectedly called him to go before Pharaoh in Egypt and demand the release of his people. It was a lot to ask of anyone, but for someone like Moses, nervous and hesitant in speech, it was little short of purgatory. This was one request he could do without! The trouble was, God apparently couldn't do without him! And so began one of the most astonishing conversations between God and man recorded in Scripture. On the one hand we have the sheer humanity of Moses, coming up with reason after reason why he was the least suitable candidate for the job, and on the other we have God countering every argument Moses could muster with an unanswerable riposte. It's hard not to feel sorry for Moses as finally he is almost browbeaten into submission. But it is impossible equally not to be inspired by the God who provides all the resources needed, and more besides, to face the challenge he brings.

Reading   Exodus 3:1-15

Meditation 15   *I can't do it, Lord* – Moses

Comment   How good are we at bouncing back after disappointments? It is a rare gift to be able to take setbacks in our stride and continue undaunted, yet that is precisely what we see in the story of Moses. Called to seek an audience with Pharaoh and to demand the release of his fellow Israelites from slavery, he was to suffer repeated frustrations as his requests were either turned down flat or granted for a moment only to be denied later. It would have been hard enough for Moses to continue undeterred had he naturally warmed to the task in hand, but when we remember that every moment was an ordeal for him, so much so that his brother Aaron was enlisted for support, we realise the full extent of his dedication. No one could have blamed him had he washed his hands of the whole venture after the first few attempts; in fact, that's probably what most of us would have done in his place! Yet, with incredible resilience, he battled on until at last he achieved success. In his story is not just a memorable picture of human perseverance, but a glimpse of the God who reaches out with equal devotion to his people in every place and time, determined to set them free from all that holds them captive.

Reading   Exodus 11:1, 4-10

Meditation 16   *I was ready to call it a day* – Moses

Silence or Hymn   *Moses, I know you're the man*
We are marching in the light of God

Comment   We talk sometimes of experiencing a roller-coaster of emotions, and if ever that phrase was appropriate, it must surely be in describing the story of the crossing of the Red Sea. Imagine if you can the astonishing sequence of feelings those involved must have gone through. First suspense and excitement as, after so many disappointments, they left Egypt and headed out into an unknown but exciting future. But then dread, dismay and despondency as it became apparent that Pharaoh had changed his mind and was in hot pursuit of them. After this, sheer amazement at the sight of the waters opening before them, and finally, having crossed safely to the other side, an overwhelming sense of relief and exultation. There is a lesson for us here. Life does not always go smoothly, no matter how great our faith may be. It brings its fair share of challenges, even times when the future looks hopeless, but, come what may, God is with us, in both the good and the bad, the ups and the downs. We should remember that next time trouble strikes. Whatever the obstacle confronting us, God is able to lead us safely through.

Reading   Exodus 14:8-14, 21-28

Meditation 17   *It was the worst moment of my life* – Moses

Comment   Faith, we are told, is one of the great qualities of the Christian life; an essential ingredient of genuine discipleship. But living with faith is far from easy, for most of us prefer cast-iron certainties to promises we must accept on trust. Nowhere is this more so than when it comes to the fact of death and our hope of eternal life. We believe in the resurrection and the kingdom of heaven, but we can't help wishing we knew a bit more about it. Where will it be? How will we get there? When will it come? What will it be like? These and a host of other questions all too easily play on our minds, insidiously undermining our confidence. 'If only we knew,' we tell ourselves. 'If only we could see, then it would all be so much easier.' But the fact is that we do not need to see anything more than God has already revealed, for true faith should be based on what we experience today as much as what we're promised tomorrow. When God is an ever-present reality in our lives we need no proofs as to the future. It is this that was the secret of Moses, a man, we are told, who, like Abraham before him, walked with God. There's no way, of course, that Moses would have thought in terms of the kingdom of heaven or eternal life, for such beliefs did not take shape until many years afterwards, but there has surely never been a finer example of the trust we need to have in God's purpose for the future; a future that begins here and now.

Reading   Deuteronomy 34:1-5

Meditation 19   *I've seen it!* – Moses

Prayer   Living God,
you met with Moses on the mountain-top –
meet with us now;
you called him to a lifetime of service –
speak to us now;
you equipped him to honour that calling –
work in us now;
you led him safely through adversity –
go with us now.
Living God,
Lord of heaven and earth, space and time,
hear us now,
through Jesus Christ our Lord.
Amen.

Hymn   *'Forward!' be our watchword*
The journey of life may be easy, may be hard

Blessing

4

THE PAINFUL TRUTH

Introduction 'Be truthful, now – what do you think?' How many times have we been asked a question like that? And the chances are, when it came, our heart sank, for we knew full well that the judgement we were being asked to give was likely to cause upset, if not outright offence. As the old saying has it, 'truth hurts'. Few of us find it easy to be honest in awkward situations like those and fewer still relish having the truth spoken to them. Yet sometimes we need people with the courage to do just that if we are to see ourselves as we really are and so find the spur we need to rectify our faults. To quote another saying, this time the words of the Greek philosopher Socrates: 'Think not those faithful who praise all thy words and actions, but those who kindly reprove thy faults.' Have we the courage to speak the painful truth to others? And, more important still, are we willing to hear it spoken to us in turn?

Prayer Gracious God,
    you are always true,
    always faithful,
    your promises unshakeable,
    your word a sure foundation
    on which we can depend.
We know we can trust you utterly,
    for there is no falsehood in you,
    no way in which you can be deceived,
    and yet you reach out to all in love.
Forgive us that we are so often the opposite,
    fickle,
    faithless,
    economical with the truth
    in our dealings with others
    and reluctant to be honest with ourselves.
Speak to us today
and show us the secret

of speaking the truth in love.
Help us to open our lives to your searching gaze
    and so open our hearts to your redeeming love,
    through Jesus Christ our Lord.
Amen.

Hymn   *When the Church of Jesus shuts its outer door*
Speak, Lord, in the stillness

Comment   Every so often in our lives we face a straight choice between what we believe to be right and wrong. We know well enough the choice we ought to make, but making it is another matter. It may conflict with our personal preferences, entail costly self-sacrifice, or perhaps risk unpopularity. For Balaam, summoned by Balak, king of the Moabites to pronounce a curse on the Israelites, it meant all those things and more – the very real possibility that he might incur not simply his patron's wrath but also his revenge at being slighted. What makes the story all the more remarkable is that Balaam had no axe to grind, being neither a worshipper of the God of Israel nor having any reason to favour them as a nation. To go against Balak's instructions in the way he did was inviting trouble, but Balaam had encountered God in a way he had never begun to before. After that, there could be only one result.

Reading   Numbers 22:1-8, 12; 23:7a, 8-12

Meditation 22   *Poor old Balak, you should have seen his face* – Balaam

Comment   Putting Christian principles into practice can be a complicated affair. For example, on the one hand, we are told not to judge in case we should be judged in turn, and in consequence we make allowances for the faults of those around us, all too aware we are far from perfect ourselves. Yet, on the other hand, we are told to judge wisely, to discern between good and evil, and to stand up for what is right. So where does that leave us? It was just such a quandary which the prophet Nathan found himself facing when God called him to speak out against David concerning his part in the death of Uriah, and his subsequent marriage to Bathsheba. Few could envy Nathan his mission. To speak out against anyone is hard enough, but to denounce a king to his face must have taken some doing. How much easier to plead 'Who am I to judge?', and so leave the matter to someone else to sort out. But, king or no king, David had to be called to account for his actions, and Nathan realised that he was the man to do it. This is not to say we have a right to judge, still less to condemn, for none of us can ever know the whole story behind any one person or action. But, equally, evil needs to be exposed as such, however painful the process. Fail to do that, and everyone finally will suffer the consequences.

Reading   2 Samuel 12:1-7

Meditation 33   *Should I have kept quiet? –* Nathan

Silence or Hymn   *Lord, speak to me, that I may speak*
The Church of Christ in every age

Comment   The truth, the whole truth and nothing but the truth. It sounds good, doesn't it? – what all of us, in theory, would like to strive for. But while such truth may be the ultimate goal of the law, in the daily business of human relationships it is often something we shy away from for fear of hurting others or reflecting badly on ourselves. To tell somebody what they would rather not hear takes courage, especially when the result is to place us firmly in the firing line. A little white lie can seem far the most attractive option for all concerned. Yet where would we be today without those who have had the courage to speak out in the cause of truth, regardless of the consequences? The thought scarcely bears thinking about. Possibly there are some situations when honesty needs to be tempered with sensitivity, but we must beware of using this as an excuse for shirking important issues – moral cowardice can easily become a habit. Truth may sometimes be painful; we all nevertheless need to face it.

Reading   Daniel 5:1-9, 13a, 16b-17, 23-31

Meditation 59   *I knew what it meant immediately* – Daniel

Comment   It is a rare gift to be able to speak frankly to others in such a way as to couple honesty with sensitivity, but the person we can depend on for a candid answer, come what may, is a priceless treasure indeed. Amos was such a person. The message God gave him to speak was not an easy one, almost certain to receive a hostile reception, and the fact he was a Judean daring to poke his nose in the affairs of neighbouring Israel only added insult to injury. Yet Amos knew that the words needed saying and he did not flinch from saying them. No doubt few enjoyed what they heard, but those who were willing to act on it would have found their faith immeasurably enriched through doing so. What of us? Have we the courage to hear Amos' voice today? It may well be a disturbing experience, but it will be worth it!

Reading   Amos 5:18-24

Meditation 61   *I thought I'd heard wrongly* – Amos

Prayer   Lord,
    it isn't easy to face the truth
    for there is much we prefer to hide
    from ourselves as well as others.
We are ashamed of our many failings –
    the way we so easily succumb to temptation
    and so often fail to honour you.
We talk of strength,
    but show weakness.
We speak of serving others,
    but have time only for ourselves.
We preach forgiveness,
    but in practice are swift to judge.
Though we have caught a glimpse of what life
    could be,

the reality is that we fall pathetically short,
yet we keep up a facade for the world
rather than admit the facts.
Lord, you see us as we are,
for there can be nothing hidden from you,
and yet still you love us.
Give us courage, then, to face ourselves honestly,
and to acknowledge our faults,
so that we may know the forgiveness you offer
and rejoice in renewal of life,
through Jesus Christ our Lord.
Amen.

Hymn   *Master, speak! Your servant's listening*
Who is on the Lord's side?

Blessing

5
A FRIEND IN NEED

Introduction   What kind of friend are we? The sort who can be depended on in a crisis, or the fair-weather variety, swift to vanish into the night the moment there is any suggestion that commitment might cost something? Naturally we all like to think we're the former – true, loyal, trustworthy – but we should ask ouselves honestly: how many people would we be willing to make sacrifices for? For the Christian, not only should friendships possess a special quality; the very concept of friendship has been widened by Jesus to include those both near and far, those we are close to and those who will always be strangers. To demonstrate such friendship is hard indeed and few will get anywhere near it, but today we hear the stories of four people who, centuries before Christ, showed themselves to be a friend in need. What is God saying to us about our service to others through their example?

Silence or Hymn   *Come, all who look to Christ today*
Blest be the tie that binds

Prayer   Gracious God,
    you do not call us servants or slaves
    but friends.
You want us to enjoy a personal relationship with you
    through Jesus Christ,
    a daily experience of your love.
Teach us what that means and help us to accept it.
You tell us that there is no greater love we can show
    than this: to lay down our life for our friends.
You want us to serve others,
    to love our neighbours as ourselves,
    to display a special quality of love
    in all our relationships.
Teach us what *that* means, and help us to fulfil it.
Teach us today the meaning of friendship,

both with you and one another,
through Jesus Christ our Lord.
Amen.

Comment   There can surely be few more memorable stories in the Old Testament than that found in the book of Ruth; a tale of love, loyalty and friendship at its best. At its centre stands a young woman whose family has been overwhelmed by disaster, to the point that she is finally encouraged by her mother-in-law to return to her home country of Moab where perhaps she might pick up the pieces of her life. An opportunity many of us might have grasped, but for Ruth the ties of family and friendship came first. She knew it might prove costly, but she was willing to pay whatever price was asked. Her unforgettable words of selfless devotion and commitment give us not simply a summary of the quality of love which should characterise Christian fellowship, but a glimpse of God's love for all, expressed most wonderfully through his living and dying amongst us in Christ.

Reading   Ruth 1:8-17

Meditation 25   *Was I making a mistake staying with her like that?* – Ruth

Comment   Blood is thicker than water, so they say, and certainly family ties can be more powerful than any other. Occasionally, however, life throws up situations where that special bond is challenged. So it was for Jonathan, son of Saul, king of Israel. Loyal to his father to the point, ultimately, of dying with him in battle, the time came, nonetheless, when the father-son relationship was to be tested by the conflicting demands of friendship. There were many complicating factors, not least Saul's increasingly unbalanced state of mind, but the question Jonathan had to answer, though painful, was simple enough. To whom did his first allegiance lie? In all of this, we can, of course, draw allusions to Christian discipleship and our relationship with God, but the lessons here concerning human relationships are equally important and should not be spiritualised away. Jonathan took that most painful of steps of putting friend before family. Are we ready to show that same depth of commitment to those we count our friends today?

Reading 1 Samuel 20:1-3, 12-17

Meditation 30 *Do you know how it felt? – Jonathan*

Silence or Hymn *I've found a friend, O such a friend*
Let there be love shared among us

Comment We move next to the story of Esther, a woman who to this day is revered within Judaism, not simply as a model of courage but above all as an example of faith. Hers was an example of selfless devotion, freely putting the safety of others before her own, never mind the consequences. We should not be deceived by the absence of religious terminology from the narrative. Esther, as much as any other in the Old Testament, was called to grapple with God. It is the very fact that she saw this not as some great act of piety but as a simple expression of solidarity with her people, which accounts for the respect accorded to her. Faith and life went hand in hand for her, each indissolubly linked, the one a natural outworking of the other. Can the same be said of us?

Reading Esther 3:8-10; 4:1, 5, 9-16

Meditation 40 *Could I honestly make a difference? – Esther*

Comment We turn finally to Nehemiah, one of the lesser-known figures in the Old Testament and, at first reading, understandably so. The book named after him is not an easy one to read, displaying an antipathy towards so-called 'foreigners' which borders on the xenophobic, coupled with a chilling level of religious intolerance. Yet when we recall the persecution the Jews had already suffered countless times in their history up to this point, we can begin to understand the reasoning behind this apparent paranoia. To this we must add Nehemiah's concern over the steady dilution of his people's faith which had resulted from exposure to outside influences; a slow but inexorable compromise of principles and convictions. In our modern-day cosmopolitan and multi-faith society, we can well understand such tensions. But though all this troubled Nehemiah there was one thing which troubled him still more; namely a crushing sense of guilt as the sufferings of his fellow countrymen back in Israel became known to him. His swift response to their plight provides a powerful challenge concerning our response to the many social needs around us and, above all, to the sufferings of the wider world which today cannot be ignored, however much we try to escape them.

Reading   Nehemiah 1:1-7

Meditation 78   *I knew things had been bad back in Jerusalem* – Nehemiah

Prayer   Loving God,
we thank you
that you are a God we can depend on,
always there in times of need,
our truest friend.
Whatever we may face,
however sorely we may test your love,
still you stand by us.
Help us to show such friendship
in our relationships with others:
to offer support in times of crisis,
encouragement in times of fear,
comfort in times of sorrow
and hope in times of despair.
And, as you have been faithful to us,
help us to be faithful to you,
ready to serve you whatever the cost may be,
giving our all in the cause of Christ,
for his name's sake.
Amen.

Silence or Hymn   *Brother, sister, let me serve you*
Put peace into each other's hands

Blessing

6

THE DARK NIGHT OF THE SOUL

Introduction Joy, light, peace, faith – these are the sort of words most of us would associate with the Christian faith and which we hear repeated week after week as we gather together to worship God. And, of course, there is every reason that we should, for it was to make possible gifts such as these that Christ came and died among us. Yet though most of us, most of the time, would happily describe Christian discipleship in such terms, there are occasions when we find that more difficult; occasions when life brings sorrow rather than joy, darkness rather than light, upheaval rather than peace, and doubt rather than faith. For some this may stem from tragedy, for others from disappointment, while for others still it may represent a sudden crisis of belief for which they can find no rhyme or reason, but for all it represents a time of desperate pain and loneliness. Not only is there the sense of isolation from God; there are also feelings of guilt and failure at daring to question what once seemed so certain. Mercifully, such times are usually short, no more than a brief interlude before conviction returns, but, just occasionally, it can lead to what has been termed 'the dark night of the soul', an experience of desolation and despair when there seems to be no one to turn to and nothing to hope for. There are no easy answers for those facing such a time, but it is good to remind ourselves that many have been there before us and finally emerged from the darkness to find light shining again, realising in the process that God has been with them all along, even in the bleakest moments. Today we think of some of those for whom the way has been hard and faith has been tested, and we ask not only what they learned through their trials but what can we learn in turn.

Hymn *Through the love of God our Saviour*
When your confidence is shaken

Prayer   Eternal God,
                mighty and mysterious,
                sovereign over all,
                it is beyond the power of human words
                to express your greatness,
                for you are higher
                than we can ever begin to imagine.
        We praise you for that truth,
                yet we acknowledge, also,
                that it can be hard to live with,
                for it can make you seem beyond us
                in a different way –
                remote,
                distant,
                detached from our situation,
                oblivious to our need.
        We thank you that such times are rare,
                but they *do* come for many
                and *can* come to all –
                times when you seem so mysterious,
                so far removed from our human situation,
                that we question whether you are there at all.
        Help us to understand that moments like these
                are as much a part of our pilgrimage as any other,
                that doubt can be a stepping stone to faith
                and darkness a pathway into light.
        Speak to us now,
                and may your word be a lamp to our path.
        Come to us now,
                and may your radiance shine in our hearts.
        Lighten our darkness, Lord, we pray,
                in Jesus' name.
        Amen.

Comment   Of all the things that test our faith, there is surely
                none greater than the problem of suffering. Quite
                simply, why does God allow it? Why doesn't he step
                in and put an end to the pain and misery which seems
                to dog so many lives? The question has perplexed
                individual believers, clergy, philosophers and theo-
                logians alike across the centuries. It is all too easy
                to come up with pat answers and trite assumptions

which serve only to confuse the issue and add to the heartache of those wrestling with inexplicable suffering. The book of Job was written precisely to counter such simplistic responses, flatly contradicting the received wisdom of his day that suffering was God's punishment for sin and that a godly life goes hand in hand with health, happiness and prosperity. No alternative theory, however, is offered in its place. To do that would be to risk repeating the mistake. What Job offers instead is the conviction that even when we cannot begin to understand, and even when life flies in the face of all we believe, God is there.

Reading   Job 23:2-17

Meditation 41   *What did I do wrong, can you tell me? –* Job

Comment   The opening words of Psalm 22 must surely be some of the most familiar in all Scripture. Most likely, however, we recognise them not as part of this Psalm, but as the anguished cry of Jesus from the cross. It is inevitable that we will interpret the words in this light, the association imbuing them with special meaning, but we should never forget that centuries before Christ they were uttered in another poignant cry of dereliction. Just what lay behind them we shall never know, but it is clear that something happened to David to bring him to the depths of despair. Life, it seems, had lost its meaning for him. So it has been across the years for countless others; an unseen multitude who, their lives already in turmoil, have endured the added anguish of even God seeming to be absent. No one would wish such moments on anybody, but we should take heart that even those closest to God can be tested like this, and take more heart still from the fact that very often it has been precisely during those times that God has been supremely at work.

Reading   Psalm 22:1-2, 7-11, 16b-19, 23-24

Meditation 45   *I felt alone –* David

Silence or Hymn   *Will your anchor hold in the storms of life?*
Guide me, O thou great Jehovah

Comment   Few books in the Bible come as more of a surprise than the book of Ecclesiastes. The opening few words, after introductory preliminaries, unequivocally set the scene for all that is to follow: 'Vanity of vanities, says the Teacher, vanity of vanities! All is vanity.' Quite simply, this isn't the sort of message you expect to find in the pages of Scripture, but as you read on, it gets worse! How about this, for example: 'What do mortals get from all the toil and strain with which they toil under the sun? For all their days are full of pain, and their work is a vexation; even at night their minds do not rest. This also is vanity.' And so it goes on, in similar vein, page after page. There are some who find this apparent world-weariness a little shocking, unsure what to make of it; but others find here a refreshing honesty about life in the Teacher's willingness to voice inner frustrations and deeply held feelings which most of us are reluctant to acknowledge, let alone tackle. Perhaps the note of cynicism finally goes too far, but the issues raised nonetheless need to be faced. Tackle them squarely, and our faith will grow stronger, able to face the vicissitudes of life and make sense of the purposes of God within them.

Reading   Ecclesiastes 1:2-11

Meditation 56   *I dared to dream once* – The Teacher

Comment   If the book of Job does not offer an answer to the problem of suffering, this does not mean it is devoid of hope. On the contrary, despite everything he experienced, Job ultimately found his faith deepened and enriched. The journey was undeniably painful but he was to emerge stronger and wiser for it. And there are many, having wrestled with deep suffering themselves, who can testify to something similar. Not that any welcomed what they faced, still less that they saw it as inflicted by God, but rather the experience led them on to deeper insights into the ultimate realities of life. The mystery is not fully resolved, yet some sense is made of it: out of darkness God brings light; out of evil, something good; out of despair, hope. Not only is this one of the great lessons of this unforgettable book; it is also a promise to hold on to if ever *we* face such times of testing. Though *we* lose sight of God, *he* will not lose sight of us.

Reading   Job 29:1-6; 30:16-23

Meditation 42   *I used to laugh once, long ago* – Job

Reading   Job 38:1-2; 40:7-9; 42:1-6

Prayer   Loving God,
       we thank you that you are with us
       not just in the good times but in the bad,
       for, with you, even the darkness is as light.
   When life is hard and joys are few,
       when faith is tested and hope seems lost,
       even then you are by our side,
       your arms beneath us,
       your hand upon us,
       your love around us.
   Though we may not see it,
       you are there,
       leading us through the night of doubt and sorrow.
   Reach out then, now, to all in darkness,
       and hold them close.
   Support them through your grace
       until the night is passed,
       the dawn breaks,
       and they rejoice again
       in the sunshine of your love,
       through Jesus Christ our Lord.
   Amen.

Silence or Hymn   *Through the night of doubt and sorrow*
Through all the changing scenes of life

Blessing

7
STRENGTH IN WEAKNESS

Introduction   What does it mean to talk about strength in weakness? The idea sounds nonsensical, a complete contradiction in terms, and, wrongly understood, it is precisely that. If we imagine that every frailty is in fact a source of power, every Achilles' heel the secret of some Herculean endowment, then we are in for a rude surprise. No weakness in itself is something to be proud of. It is how we deal with weakness that matters – whether we persist nonetheless in attempting to prove ourselves or whether we recognise our ultimate dependence on divine grace. God, and God alone, is able to turn weakness into strength. The more we understand that, the more he is able to work within us.

Silence or Hymn   *I lift my eyes to the quiet hills*
O Lord of the kingdom, where losing is winning

Prayer   Mighty God,
　　　enthroned in splendour,
　　　crowned with glory,
　　　ruler over all,
　　　we owe our life to you.
Receive our praise.

Eternal God
　　　moving throughout history,
　　　giving your word,
　　　calling your people,
　　　we owe our hope to you.
Receive our praise.

Living God,
　　　full of love,
　　　full of kindness,
　　　full of compassion,
　　　we owe our joy to you.
Receive our praise.

Gentle God,
    speaking through your Spirit,
    through the quietness,
    through your still, small voice,
    we owe our peace to you.
Receive our praise.

Gracious God,
    abounding in love,
    slow to anger,
    rich in mercy,
    we owe our all to you.
Receive our praise.

Lord of all,
    our strength and shield,
    our rock and our fortress,
    our God and our Redeemer,
    we owe our worship to you.
Receive our praise.

Through Jesus Christ our Lord.
Amen.

Comment When were we last confronted with a challenge which seemed completely beyond us but which somehow we had to face? Anyone who has been in such a situation will have at least some insight into how Moses must have felt when God unexpectedly called him to go before Pharaoh in Egypt and demand the release of his people. It was a lot to ask of anyone, but for someone like Moses, nervous and hesitant in speech, it was little short of purgatory. This was one request he could do without! The trouble was, God apparently couldn't do without him! And so began one of the most astonishing conversations between God and man recorded in Scripture. On the one hand we have the sheer humanity of Moses, coming up with reason after reason why he was the least suitable candidate for the job, and on the other we have God countering each argument with an unanswerable riposte. It's hard not to feel sorry for

Moses as finally he is almost browbeaten into submission. But it is impossible equally not to be inspired by the God who provides all the resources needed, and more besides, to face the challenge he brings.

Reading Exodus 3:1-15

Meditation 15 *I can't do it, Lord* – Moses

Comment Of all the strong men in history, Samson must surely rank among the most famous. Yet, paradoxically, he is remembered equally as one of the weak men of history, a man who allowed himself to be duped not only into betraying the secret of his strength but, more important, into betraying his principles as well. Physically powerful, he was spiritually puny, despite his vow, as a nazirite, of service to God. He learned the hard way where true strength lies. Don't let the same be true of us.

Reading Judges 16:4-22

Meditation 24 *Do you know what they told me? Love is blind!* – Samson

Silence or Hymn *A sovereign protector I have*
God is our strength and refuge

Comment There can be few stories better loved or better known than the timeless tale of David and Goliath, a story retold by countless generations across the years. So what is the secret of its popularity? Part of it, no doubt, is the unforgettable portrayal of that message we instinctively warm to – the victory of good over evil. But there is more to it than this. What appeals most is the massive gulf between the two main characters: on the one hand, Goliath, a seasoned warrior and imposing giant of a man; on the other, David, little more than a boy. Their celebrated encounter represents a classic example of the underdog coming out on top, triumphing against all the odds. There can be few plots more extensively used by writers throughout the centuries. The difference is that the story of David and Goliath is not fiction but fact – an enduring testimony to the way God is able to use what seems weak to conquer the strong.

Reading   1 Samuel 17:4, 8, 32, 38-40, 42-45, 48-49

Meditation 29   *You should have seen their faces as I walked out there –* David

Comment   It's always pleasing, isn't it, when a midget turns the tables on a giant? Whether it be a non-league football team defeating its premier league relations, a village store fighting off competition from an out-of-town supermarket, or a local pressure group resisting the plans of a multinational company, our hearts warm to tales of the underdog come good. Partly it's because we enjoy seeing the powerful and influential brought down a peg or two, but more important is the conviction such stories give us that unpromising beginnings need not be a barrier to success. This theme, as we have seen, runs throughout the Old Testament, from Moses taking on the might of Egypt to David killing Goliath, from Elijah triumphing over the prophets of Baal to Daniel facing up to the terrors of the lions' den. The prophet Micah adds one more unforgettable picture to the list in the little town of Bethlehem so beloved of Christmas carols. It is hard today to appreciate how extraordinary it must have seemed at the time to hear God's promised Messiah associated with this insignificant and out-of-the-way town, notwithstanding its associations with King David. Jerusalem, surely, was the natural choice for such a ruler – the only place fitting for someone of such stature! In human terms, this may have been true, but not in God's. As so often before and since, God proves himself to be a God of the unexpected. In his kingdom the first invariably find themselves last, and the last first.

Reading   Micah 5:2-5a

Meditation 66   *Bethlehem – not much of a place, is it? –* Micah

Prayer   Sovereign God,
>you came to our world in Christ
>and you lowered yourself,
>taking the form of a servant,
>enduring suffering and humiliation,
>even finally death on a cross.

Yet through that sacrifice
>you won the greatest of all victories,
>triumphing over evil,
>scattering darkness,
>defeating death itself.

What appeared to be weakness
>was shown as strength.

What seemed like disaster
>was revealed as triumph.

What the world deemed failure
>proved to be glorious success.

Teach us to recognise that now, as then,
>you turn life upside down,
>working in the most unexpected of ways
>through the most unexpected of people.

Teach us that you can work in *our* lives too,
>taking our frail faith and feeble commitment,
>and using our very weakness
>to demonstrate your glory.

Take us and use us for your kingdom,
>through Jesus Christ,
>the Lord yet servant of all.

Amen.

Silence or Hymn   *I need you every hour, most gracious Lord*
Meekness and majesty

Blessing

8
FOOD FOR THOUGHT

Introduction What is the secret of wisdom? That is a question which has occupied the minds of muses and sages across the centuries. For some of us the answer lies in academic study, immersing ourselves in books and learning. For others it is to be found in the university of life, experience helping us to become worldly wise. For others still the solution is to let go of the world and lose oneself in mystical speculation. But for the writer of the book of Proverbs the answer was much more simple: 'The fear of the Lord is the beginning of wisdom.' Trust in God, seek his will, respect his guidance, and we shall discover the true meaning of life. The range of topics which the book of Proverbs goes on to cover may, at times, appear to be surprisingly down to earth, yet we should not confuse the advice given there with the worldly wisdom mentioned earlier. Faith is concerned with the daily stuff of life, yes, and thank God for that, but it brings to it a new dimension, a different perspective, which ultimately stands accepted wisdom on its head.

Silence or Hymn *Speak, Lord, in the stillness*
Our Father God, thy name we praise

Prayer Sovereign God,
  we are here to worship you,
  having made a space in our lives
  to pause and reflect.
We come to listen to your word,
  and to ponder in the silence
  what you would say to us.
We come to hear your voice,
  and in the stillness to receive your guidance.
Open our eyes to your presence,
  our hearts to your love
  and our minds to your will.
Direct our thoughts,

enlarge our understanding,
and shape our lives,
so that we may live and work for you,
to the glory of your name.
Amen.

Comment There can be few more effective ways of getting across an important message than through the use of proverbs. Just a handful of words can sum up the most profound of truths, not only encapsulating their essence but simultaneously provoking reflection about the issues these raise. A pithy saying lives on in the memory long after facts, which we have laboriously struggled to absorb, have been forgotten. No doubt this is why King Solomon similarly set such store by proverbs. He found in them a simple yet effective method of communicating the wisdom for which he was rightly famous; and in his astonishing collection which comprises the bulk of the book of Proverbs, we find an apophthegm to address just about every facet of life and faith. There is more, of course, to wisdom than simply being able to repeat such sayings parrot fashion. We need to consider what each is saying and, above all, to make them a part of our lives. Could we but begin to do that, we would start to rival Solomon himself in terms of our insight into, and understanding of, the complex realities of daily life.

Reading Proverbs 3:1-8

Meditation 52 *'The fear of the Lord is the beginning of wisdom'* – Solomon

Comment If you need a job doing, ask a busy person. Words which have become a bit of a cliché, yet they are true nonetheless. For some people the very thought of hard work makes them go weak at the knees, to the point that they keep on putting it off, *ad infinitum*. Others simply get stuck in, and in no time at all the job gets done. Most of us are probably somewhere in between. We do what's expected of us – most of the time anyway – and perhaps just occasionally, if we're feeling especially virtuous, we do that little bit extra; yet somehow there's always something left undone, just enough to niggle away in the back of the mind and disturb our peace. We know we've got to do it, but we just can't summon up the enthusiasm. We know it will have to be done eventually, yet we invariably succeed in putting it off one more day. Is it worth it? We may buy ourselves a little time – an evening together away from the children, a morning lie-in, an afternoon on the beach, but the thought of that job is always there, haunting us like some tantalising spectre. The longer we leave it, the worse the prospect becomes and the less we feel inclined to do it. If we are not careful, we slip into a self-perpetuating downward spiral, achieving ever less as we prevaricate all the more. The warnings of Solomon in the proverbs which follow may seem over the top in terms of our own lives, but beware: the danger may be more real than we think!

Reading   Proverbs 6:6-9; 13:4; 24:30-34; 26:13-16

Meditation 54   *It's not fair, he said* – Solomon

Silence or Hymn   *Grant us thy light, that we may know*
Lord, your word shall guide us

Comment   Anyone who has been in an argument (and that probably means *all* of us) will be well aware of the power of the tongue. As positions polarise, so words become more heated, hurled at each other in anger rather than exchanged in thoughtful debate. Tempers flare, and words give way to abuse, much said which may be regretted long afterwards. No wonder, then, that many of the proverbs of Solomon warn against the dangers of the tongue. Yet if words can be used for evil, they can equally be employed for good. Like so many of God's gifts, they are a two-edged sword, capable of being used or abused. The choice sounds straightforward enough, but the reality is very different, for words have a tendency to run away with us, developing a life of their own. Unless we learn to watch our tongues, we may well find that they become our master instead of us theirs.

Reading   Proverbs 12:6, 13-14a, 17-19; 13:2-3; 15:1-2, 4; 26:17-28

Meditation 53   *Think before you speak* – Solomon

Silence

Comment   We have listened to words of wisdom concerning the things we say, the things we do and the things we think, and also about wisdom itself. But how often do we take time to reflect upon such words? Reading the Bible today is something we take for granted, all too literally. We have a bewildering variety of translations to choose from, and a host of material designed to help us understand what we are reading, yet how often do we make time to study God's word? In all too many households the Bible is left to gather dust, serving more as a talisman than a source of instruction. Our last reading and meditation explores such a danger, calling us to consider the reaction of Josiah, king of Judah, when, early in his reign, the book of the Law was unexpectedly discovered in the temple, where it had been stored away and forgotten for many years. A regrettable oversight, some might have called it, but not Josiah. For him it was a calamity which had to be addressed immediately, for in his eyes this neglect of God's word was tantamount to throwing one of his most precious gifts back in his face. Are we guilty of doing the same today? A Bible sitting on the shelf helps no one; it's reading it that counts!

Reading   2 Chronicles 34:14–21

Meditation 39   *Do you know what we found today?* – Josiah

Prayer   Living God,
   you have spoken to us in so many ways,
   offering a light for our path
   and food for our souls.

Forgive us that all too often
  we squander the resources you have given,
  neglecting your Word
  and failing to make time to hear your voice.
Help us to make time for you
  not just today but every day,
  so that we may receive your guidance
  and understand your will.
Teach us the secret of true wisdom,
  in knowing and serving you,
  through Jesus Christ our Lord.
Amen.

Silence or Hymn   *We limit not the truth of God*
Open our eyes, Lord

Blessing

9

COUNTING OUR BLESSINGS

Introduction   When were we last told to 'count our blessings'? Probably not so long ago. It's an expression that is often used yet rarely thought about, for how many of us have ever taken it literally and made a point of adding up all the good things in life? The fact is that most of us are too busy even to try, for the list, were we to start, would be virtually endless, there being so much in this world to celebrate and so many reasons to give thanks. Sadly, though, it is part of our nature to lose sight of that truth. What fills us with joy today leaves us cold tomorrow. What appears awesome one moment seems commonplace the next. Instead of rejoicing in God's goodness, we take it for granted to the point that we can even consider ourselves short-changed by him. We all need, sometimes, to stop and take stock, recognising afresh how lucky we really are. If we start counting our blessings, though we may not finish, we will discover life taking on a new meaning, brimming over with joy again, full to overflowing!

Silence or Hymn   *For the beauty of the earth*
Now thank we all our God

Prayer   Gracious God,
   you have shown us such love
   that we ought to worship you constantly,
   but sometimes we forget you are even there.
You have granted such blessings
   that we ought to celebrate always,
   but we don't,
   more often than not
   feeling sorry for ourselves instead.
You have given us such a wonderful world
   that we ought to marvel unceasingly,
   but that's not what happens,
   familiarity, on the contrary, breeding contempt.

You have displayed such mercy
   that we ought to thank you continually,
   but we rarely thank you at all,
   your grace seen as ours by right
   rather than a gift we can never deserve.
Forgive us, we pray,
   and help us to appreciate your great goodness.
Remind us today of all we have received
   from your loving hand,
   and help us to respond through joyful praise
   and grateful service,
   to the glory of your name.
Amen.

Comment   'Sing a new song to the Lord'. What better way to express our gratitude for all the good things God has given us? For David and the other writers of the Psalms there seems to have been an almost irresistible impulse to burst into song in glad and grateful praise whenever they thought of God. Time and again we find a similar refrain: 'Make a joyful noise to the Lord'; 'Let everything that has breath praise the Lord'; 'Sing to God, O kingdoms of the earth; sing praises to the Lord.' And so we could go on. Do we feel that same sense of joy bubbling up within us, that same desire to express our gratitude for God's goodness? If not, it may be worth asking ourselves whether we have lost sight of the many reasons we have to give thanks; whether we have become so preoccupied with the pressures and problems of daily life that all else has become obscured, our perspective seriously distorted. Let us pause then today, and for a few moments think about all the blessings we have received, all the reasons why we should join with the psalmist in singing a new song to the Lord.

Reading   Psalm 98

Meditation 49   *I want to sing to the Lord* – David

Comment   Few books of the Bible would appear to offer less fertile ground for exploring the theme of 'counting our blessings' than the book of Ecclesiastes. At first sight, its contents seem to comprise a message of almost total negativity. Yet, if we look more closely, there is perhaps a glimmer of light at the end of the tunnel. Not, it must be said, a sudden about-face, nor indeed any indication that the Teacher has moderated his views about the futility of life, but an acknowledgement that one thing at least can make sense of it all, and that is God. The end of the matter, he tells us, is this: 'Fear God, and keep his commandments; for that is the whole duty of everyone.' Hardly an outpouring of praise, still less suggesting any sense of celebration, but in these sombre, even stern, words of conclusion, we are offered, after all the apparent hopelessness that has gone before, reason to hope. Exactly what went through the Teacher's mind as he summed up his arguments we cannot know, but it's nice to believe that he discovered a new sense of purpose, a renewed awareness of God which breathed unexpected joy into his life. Of course, this is only speculation, and unfounded speculation at that; not so much a reading between the lines as a rewriting of the script. Yet there is just something about the note on which the book ends to suggest that alongside the cynicism of all that goes before there is a wry smile, a shrug of the shoulders and a spark of anticipation spluttering back into life.

Reading   Ecclesiastes 11:8–12:7

Meditation 57   *They think me wise, some people* – The Teacher

Silence or Hymn   *All creatures of our God and King*
Praise, my soul, the King of heaven

Comment   Which of us hasn't at some time gazed up at the night sky and marvelled at the wonder of creation. We live in a world of incredible beauty and a universe of awesome splendour – so much to rejoice in, so many reasons to thank God. More wonderful still is the fact that, as the words of Psalm 8 remind us, God has a special place for us within that creation;

despite our insignificance in terms of space and time, each of us is precious in his sight. Yet alongside the joy, that truth also brings challenge for it means that we have a unique role in stewarding what God has given. Today, with growing pressures on our environment and the very real threat of global warming, the words of Psalm 8 take on particular significance. We have plundered this world's resources too freely, with little thought for our long-term responsibilities. As Christians we need to add our voice to the mounting calls for a sensible stewardship of creation. To fail in that is to betray the trust God has placed in our hands and to wantonly fritter away his blessings.

Reading   Psalm 8

Meditation 43   *Is it possible?* – David

Comment   Just occasionally in life something happens to remind us of the special things we need to celebrate; those blessings, those gifts which really matter. Sadly such moments are all too rare. More often than not we lurch from one demand, one crisis, one responsibility to another, scarcely finding time to draw breath and reflect on the reasons we have to give thanks. We find ourselves complaining of our lot, resenting the pressures put upon us, viewing life from a distorted angle and jaundiced perspective. It is a vicious circle which feeds on itself – the more sorry for ourselves we feel, the more cause there seems for such feelings. Yet if we stop and truly consider – if we make time, in the words of the old saying mentioned earlier, to 'count our blessings' – life seems very different. There is so much that is not only good but indescribably wonderful, beautiful beyond words. Make time in your life to consider such things and you may well find yourself echoing the words of David: 'The boundary lines have fallen for me in pleasant places; I have a goodly heritage'.

Reading   Psalm 16

Meditation 44   *I'm a lucky man* – David

Prayer   Loving God,
we have so much to thank you for,
but all too often we forget it.
Instead of remembering what we *have* got,
we think of what we *haven't*.
Instead of rejoicing in the good things of life,
we dwell on the bad.
Instead of celebrating the present,
we brood on the past or worry about the future.
You have showered blessings upon us,
too many to number,
yet we have not had eyes to see it.
Forgive us our failure to recognise your goodness,
the ingratitude which constantly looks for more
rather than rejoices in what is given,
and the shallowness which blinds us
to the things that really matter.
Open our hearts to the wonder of your love
and the richness of your provision,
so that we may give you the thanks you deserve,
and delight in life as you desire.
Through Jesus Christ our Lord.
Amen.

Silence or Hymn   *O Lord my God, when I in awesome wonder*
For beauty of meadows, for grandeur of trees

Blessing

10
A FRESH START

Introduction Wouldn't it be nice sometimes to have a second bite at the cherry? When we've made some foolish mistake, when we've missed a golden opportunity, when we've taken a wrong decision, wouldn't it be good to go back and, with the benefit of hindsight, to get things right second time round? Sadly, that's not the way life works, and sometimes we have to live with the frustration of making the best of a bad job. Yet that's only half the truth, for though we can't undo the past, with God's help we can shape the future. He is always working to make us new, always waiting for the opportunity to give us a fresh start. We have only to acknowledge our faults to find forgiveness and begin again. If we doubt that, let us listen now to the stories of David, Naaman and Isaiah for each was to discover in a wonderful way the transforming power of God within their lives.

Silence or Hymn *Dear Master, in whose life I see*
Lord, I was blind, I could not see

Prayer Lord,
  this is the day that you have made,
  and we praise you for it.
We thank you not just for today but every day,
  each one brimming over with promise,
  rich in opportunities to know and serve you better.
Help us to recognise each moment as your gift,
  to be received with gratitude
  and lived to the full.
And help us to understand that with you,
  every moment can be a new beginning,
  the past put behind us,
  the future waiting,
  and the present ours to rejoice and be glad in.
Lord, this is the day that you have made,
  and we praise you for it.

Receive our worship
  speak your word,
  and touch our hearts,
    through Jesus Christ our Lord.
Amen.

Comment   It is often said, with some justification, that love is
blind. Yet love is not alone in exhibiting such a
weakness. Greed, envy, lust and ambition, not to
mention the thirst for drugs or alcohol, can equally
close our eyes to everything other than the object of
our desire – with devastating consequences. So it
was to prove for David, faced suddenly with the
alluring prospect of Bathsheba taking a bath on the
rooftop of her house. A great and devout king he
may have been; it counted for nothing – like a moth
drawn towards a candle he was unable to resist the
pull of temptation. We cannot excuse David's actions,
but we can understand them, for, if we are honest,
which of us can confidently say we could never fall?
Before we cast the first stone in any situation, however dreadful it may seem, we do well to remind
ourselves that 'there, but for the grace of God, go I'.

Reading   2 Samuel 11:2-6, 14-17, 26-27

Meditation 32   *I'm ashamed now, looking back* – David

Comment   The words of the Psalms are surely some of the most
astonishing personal testimonies ever given. Written
over three thousand years ago, they are able to speak
today as if the words are fresh on the page. None more
so than Psalm 51. Its cry of frustration is one which
finds echoes in the experience of every Christian,
calling instantly to mind the anguished cry of the
Apostle Paul years later: 'Wretched man that I am!
Who will rescue me from this body of death?'
(Romans 7:24). Time and again we attempt to amend
our ways, to conquer a particular failing, to follow
Christ more closely, to live more faithfully as his
disciples. Yet time and again the story is the same,

the old weaknesses rear their ugly heads and we find ourselves back where we started. The fact is we cannot change ourselves, however much we may wish to; we are dependent upon the grace of God and his transforming power at work within us. That truth may be self-evident today in the light of Jesus; the wonder of this Psalm is that David recognised it well over a thousand years before his coming!

Reading   Psalm 51:1-12

Meditation 47   *What can I say, Lord? –* David

Silence or Hymn   *There's a wideness in God's mercy*
Great God of wonders, all thy ways

Comment   The higher we rise, the harder we fall – so, at least, conventional wisdom tells us. But there is another side to that observation, for we could equally say we must be brought low before we can rise high. In the story of Naaman both of these truths are well demonstrated. Asked to bathe in the muddy waters of the Jordan, he storms off in a fit of pique, the idea of so demeaning himself complete anathema. It is only the gentle coaxing of his entourage which makes him see reason – what does a dent to his pride matter if it leads finally to personal wholeness? We can hardly miss the absurdity of Naaman's initial reaction, yet do we recognise with equal clarity the same foolishness in ourselves? How often do we allow a misplaced sense of our own importance to blind us to the right way forward? How many times have we deprived ourselves of the opportunity for a fresh start rather than admit our dependence on God? It is a natural human tendency to believe we can go it alone – the story of Naaman reminds us that we can't.

Reading   2 Kings 5:1-5, 9-15

Meditation 37   *Who did he take me for? –* Naaman

Comment   One of the tragedies of the Church is that it has acquired a reputation for being smug, self-righteous, holier than thou. How this has happened I do not know, for while some Christians are more than ready to sit in judgement, by far the majority are all too aware of their own faults to point the accusing finger at others. At its heart, the Christian message is about forgiveness rather than judgement; about the God who is ready to accept us as we are rather than as we should be. Of course, this involves a desire to change, but it begins and ends with God rather than ourselves. While the truth of this is most clearly demonstrated through Christ, it was discovered centuries before by countless others. So it was that a young man, worshipping in the temple of Jerusalem, suddenly found himself faced by the call of God. Hopelessly inadequate though he felt, burdened by a profound sense of unworthiness, Isaiah discovered that God is always ready to take the initiative in breaking down the barriers which keep us from him. He learned, as many had found before and many have discovered since, that ours is a God of new beginnings, a God always ready to offer us a fresh start!

Reading   Isaiah 6:1-8

Meditation 64   *Could it be true? –* Isaiah

Prayer   Gracious God,
　　in shame and sorrow we come before you;
　　hear now our prayer.

We pray for ourselves,
　　for we have failed you in so much.
We have fallen short of our calling,
　　we have lost sight of your love,
　　we have been weak, selfish, thoughtless and foolish.
Gracious God,
　　have mercy.

We pray for the Church,
  our own fellowship
  and the wider body to which we belong.
Instead of unity, so often there has been division,
  instead of reaching out,
  there has been looking inwards,
  instead of faith, there have been empty words.
Gracious God,
  have mercy.

We pray for the world,
  our fellow human beings both near and far.
Instead of all having enough, millions still go hungry,
    instead of love and peace, there is war and hatred,
    instead of careful stewardship of this precious
      planet,
  its finite resources have been ruthlessly exploited.
Gracious God,
  have mercy.

Come now and help us to start again.
Forgive us the weakness and folly
  that separates us from you and one another.
Work within us and within all,
    bringing a new creation out of the old,
    light out of darkness,
    hope out of despair.
Gracious God,
  have mercy.
In the name of Christ.
Amen.

Silence or Hymn   *Spirit of the living God*
Lord, you have given yourself for our healing

Blessing

11

A LOVE THAT WILL NOT LET US GO

Introduction   Pick up a book, watch a film, listen to a pop song, and the chances are that one theme will scream out at you: love. From tales of romance to raunchy lyrics, from tear-jerking affairs of the heart to eye-popping affairs of the bedroom, love is served up in a bewildering variety of guises. Yet how many of these portrayals give us a glimpse of the real thing? Will the love they speak of stand the test of time, or will it be here today and gone tomorrow? Will it be able to cope with adversity and come out the stronger, or will it fizzle out at the first challenge it faces? True love is a rare thing indeed, something we are capable of feeling for only a very few people and, even then, it probably has its breaking point. But, as we shall be reminded today, the love of God is something that nothing can destroy. It goes on reaching out day after day, despite everything that conspires against it, refusing to give up on us, come what may.

Silence or Hymn   *Love divine, all loves excelling*
God is love

Prayer   God of truth,
    God of justice,
    God of power,
    we praise you that you are also a God of love.
Though we disobey your commandments,
    though we lose sight of your goodness,
    though we fail to love one another
    and are forgetful of you,
    still you love us.
Though we reject your guidance,
    betray our convictions,
    deny our calling,
    still you care.
Always you are there,
    watching over us,

> calling us back,
> welcoming us home.
> Day after day we receive new blessings,
> new mercy,
> new strength,
> from your loving hands.
> God of truth,
> God of justice,
> God of power,
> we praise you that you are also a God of love.
> Receive our thanks,
> in the name of Christ.
> Amen.

Comment There can be few texts in the Old Testament better loved than the twenty-third Psalm. It has brought comfort and inspiration to untold generations across the centuries. The memorable picture it paints has a timeless quality with a power to move people in a way words rarely begin to, touching us at a level deep within and speaking to our innermost needs. Perhaps the key to its power is the fact that David himself in his youth was a shepherd, so, when he wrote 'The Lord is my shepherd', he knew what he was talking about, the words rich with personal associations. Here was no sentimental comparison. It was rather the testimony of someone who understood the commitment and devotion shepherding requires, and who, in an outpouring of wonder, realised that here was an illustration of the astonishing love God has for us and all his people.

Reading Psalm 23

Meditation 46 *I met him out on the hills* – David

Comment We have looked already at one well-loved Psalm, and we look now at another equally as memorable – the words of Psalm 139. Its verses resonate with a sense of awe as David strives to give expression to his experience of God; an experience which quite clearly had been evolving over many years, culminating in this spontaneous outpouring of praise. It is hard to imagine any testimony which could more eloquently sum up the wonder of God, yet, according to David his words are woefully inadequate, the realities they attempt to describe ultimately beyond understanding, too wonderful for words! Do we feel a similar sense of awe before God? We may have done once, but familiarity can make us complacent, the flames which fired our faith losing something of their intensity as the years pass. David calls us to meet again with the living God whose love surrounds us, whose goodness sustains us, whose mercy astounds us and whose greatness is beyond all expression.

Reading   Psalm 139:1-18

Meditation 51   *It's no good, Lord* – David

Silence or Hymn   *Love is his word, love is his way*
O perfect love, all human thought transcending

Comment   Many of the characters in the Old Testament seem almost too good to be true. We can feel daunted by the depth of their piety, devotion and commitment. But not with Jonah. One of the most appealing things about this little book is the raw humanity of the reluctant prophet at its heart – a man with all the endearing qualities of our modern-day Victor Meldrew! Irascible, cold-hearted and petulant, he is just about the last person you would expect God to call into his service; his faults, if only he could see them, equally as great as the faults of those he was called to preach to. But that is the beauty of this story, for it vividly portrays God's amazing grace in action. No one in the narrative remotely deserves his blessing, yet all end up receiving it. The same holds true for us. We may pray 'forgive us our trespasses as we forgive those who trespass against us', but thankfully God is willing to go a good deal further than that. The consequences, if he wasn't, don't bear thinking about!

Reading   Jonah 1:1-3; 3:1-3a, 5; 3:10-4:4

Meditation 63   *I knew it would happen, didn't I? –* Jonah

Comment   One of the aspects of the Old Testament which puts many people off is the portrayal of God we tend to find there. In contrast to the picture revealed in Christ, we see instead a stern and vengeful God, uncompromising in his anger and ready, where necessary, to punish without any apparent compunction. There can be no denying that such a portrayal of God is present, and we should beware of dismissing it too lightly for we lose a sense of awe and reverence at our peril. Yet there is another portrait just as often painted, and nowhere is that more beautifully seen than in the book of the prophet Hosea. Taking as a model his own traumatic experience of a broken marriage, with all the heartbreak that must have entailed, he offers an insight into the anguish suffered by God at the repeated rejection and betrayal of his people. Here is an unforgettable glimpse into a love which refuses to let go despite everything that is thrown against it. There may be a few pictures in the New Testament to rival this passage; there are few to better it.

Reading   Hosea 11:1-9

Meditation 62   *I never realised how much he cared –* Hosea

Prayer   Gracious God,
    for all our talk of love we rarely actually show it.
We profess devotion,
    as long as nothing too much is asked of us.
We show affection, provided affection is returned.
Almost always, our love is conditional,
    as much about us as its intended object,
    dependent on *our* criteria,
    tied to *our* expectations.
Your love is so very different,
    constantly flowing out despite our unworthiness,
    despite everything about us that is unlovable.
You stay true though we reject you.
You continue to care for us

though we care nothing for you.
Your love is qualified by no conditions,
   being entirely about us rather than you,
   our welfare,
   our joy.
Gracious God,
   you don't just talk about love,
   you show it day after day,
   for quite simply you *are* love!
To you be praise and glory,
   now and for ever.
Amen.

Silence or Hymn   *O Love, that will not let me go*
Come, let us sing of a wonderful love

Blessing

12

A DAY OF RECKONING

Introduction   'Why do the wicked live on, reach old age, and grow mighty in power?' – words from the book of Job, which echo the modern-day saying, 'Why do the good die young?' And it's hard, isn't it, not to feel like that sometimes, for there seems to be little justice in this world of ours. So how do we respond to such an observation? For some, it can lead to a crisis of faith, everything they believe about God's purpose and final victory suddenly thrown into confusion. For others, it reinforces their lack of faith, sure proof that a God of love cannot possibly exist. But for others again, it simply deepens their conviction that one day, somehow, somewhere, God will act to right wrongs and establish justice. Today we shall see something of each of those responses as we listen to, and reflect on, words of the prophets concerning judgement. The tone of their message may at times seem brutal, but their message is one we do well to consider: a day of reckoning will come.

Silence or Hymn   *Restore, O Lord, the honour of your name*
At the name of Jesus

Prayer   Sovereign God,
   you are the beginning *and* the end,
   Alpha *and* Omega.
Forgive us for sometimes focusing more on the first
   than the second,
   rejoicing in your creation,
   celebrating your gift of life,
   but forgetting that this brings responsibility
   as well as privilege,
   and that one day we will be called to account
   for the way we have lived and acted.
Teach us, then, to live wisely,
   responding to your guidance
   and doing your will,

even though, in this life,
    everything may seem to count against it.
Help us to be faithful to you,
    as you are faithful to us,
    through Jesus Christ our Lord.
Amen.

Comment   The book of Nahum has much in common with that of Obadiah which we shall be looking at later, its theme one of undisguised glee at a catastrophe about to befall the enemies of Judah. The parallel goes further, for this pending disaster is interpreted by the prophet as proof that, despite appearances to the contrary, God will ensure that justice is finally done. That must have taken some believing, since for generations the people of Judah had suffered under the yoke of the mighty Assyrian empire. Yet sure enough, within a few years this seemingly impregnable dynasty was to collapse, as a new super-power, Babylon, emerged to take centre stage in the ancient world. In recent years we have seen events just as remarkable in the destruction of the Berlin Wall, the end of the Cold War, the removal of apartheid, and the successive overthrow of dictatorial regimes the world over. All this is not to say that everything in this life works out as it should, for there are times when it manifestly does not. Yet at the heart of our faith is the conviction that God is actively involved in human history, striving to establish his kingdom despite everything which conspires to frustrate his purpose.

Reading   Nahum 1:2-10

Meditation 67   *Do you ever stop and wonder about the fairness of life? –* Nahum

Comment   The older one gets, the more one comes to recognise that life isn't fair. The heady idealism of youth gives way to the hard-headed realism of middle age, as the truth slowly dawns that, in this life at least, people don't always get what they deserve. Honesty may be the best policy when it comes to peace of mind, but it is rarely the most lucrative option. The unpleasant truth is that all too often cheats *do* prosper. Coming to terms with facts like these is a painful business and one which can test faith to the limit, just as it did in the time of Zephaniah. There were many in his day who, faced by the apparent injustices of life, concluded that God was either disinterested in human affairs or powerless to intervene. It was an understandable mistake, but one which the prophet had no time for. In God's time, he warned, justice will be done, and be seen to be done by all. We lose sight of that truth at our peril.

Reading   Zephaniah 1:7a, 10-16; 3:9-13

Meditation 68   *'Does it matter?' they said* – Zephaniah

Silence or Hymn   *Father, let thy kingdom come*
Your kingdom come, O God

Comment   There's no getting away from it: within the Old Testament there is much which is positively vindictive. We can do our best to sanitise the message by putting on it the best possible spiritual gloss, but the fact remains that we are dealing here with raw human emotion. It may not be pretty, but it is real and, above all, it is human. Perhaps that's why passages like these make us feel uncomfortable; they hit a bit too close to home, reminding us of aspects of our own characters which we prefer to forget. Yet it is this very humanness which is one of the great strengths of the Old Testament, for it reminds us that God is able to speak through us despite our numerous flaws. So it is that Obadiah on the one hand displays a petty, if understandable, thirst for vengeance as he gleefully looks forward to the anticipated destruction of Edom, while, on the other hand, he proclaims the enduring message of God's judgement on all those who fall victim to a misplaced sense of their own importance. It is worth pausing to reflect on both the man and the message, for there is probably a bit of Obadiah and Edom in each of us.

Reading   Obadiah 1-4, 12, 15b

Meditation 73   *Am I meant to feel sorry for them? – Obadiah*

Comment   Ask somebody to name the last book of the Old Testament and the chances are they may well come up with the correct answer: the book of Malachi. Ask them to tell you what the book is about, and you will almost certainly find a response less forthcoming. Like the other so-called 'minor prophets', we may recognise the name but the book remains firmly closed. Yet anyone who has ever listened to Handel's great choral masterpiece *Messiah* will have heard at least something of this prophet's words, for there we find, set to music, Malachi's chilling challenge concerning the Messiah's coming. The words make sobering reading, not least because those they were first addressed to were convinced they were more than ready for that moment, and assured of divine approval when it finally arrived. From Malachi came the call to think again – to examine their consciences, assess their lifestyles, and ask themselves whether everything was quite as it should be. Many were in for quite a shock. The same could equally be true for us today if we allow ourselves to become complacent or stale in our faith. Malachi reminds us that a day of reckoning will come, and urges us to live each day in that perspective. Will we be ready when the day of the Lord finally comes?

Reading   Malachi 2:17-3:3a, 5

Meditation 80   *Not long now, they tell me – Malachi*

Prayer   Lord,
    we have spoken the words often enough:
    'Your kingdom come,
    your will be done,
    on earth as it is in heaven.'
We mean what we say,
    and we try to believe it will happen,
    but it is hard sometimes to hold on to that faith

when faced by the stark realities of this world.
We see so much evil, pain and hurt,
    the innocent exploited,
    the weak oppressed,
    the poor crushed,
    and we can't help wondering
    whether our talk of good conquering evil
    and right prevailing
    is all a naïve illusion.
We are not the first to question,
    nor will we be the last,
    but you call us, nevertheless,
    to hold on to our convictions
    despite everything that seems to deny your
        purpose.
Though we do not know when or how,
    one day your kingdom *shall* come,
    your will shall be done,
    and the power and glory will be yours,
    now and for evermore.
Amen.

Silence or Hymn   *O day of God, draw near*
                       The law of Christ alone can make us free

Blessing

13

A GLIMPSE OF GLORY

Introduction When were we last moved to a sense of awe in the presence of God? How long is it since we caught our breath in wonder as we offered him our worship? Hopefully such times still come, but for most of us, as life progresses, they grow fewer and farther between. Partly that's because we simply don't find time to worship as often as we should, but it's also because over-familiarity dulls our senses. See anything breathtakingly beautiful once and we gaze in amazement. See it several times and the chances are we'll pass it by without a second look. It can take a fresh pair of eyes to stir our imaginations once more and help us recapture that first-time sense of wonderment. The same can be true when it comes to God, our initial feelings of awe in his presence blunted over the years. Today, then, we look through the eyes of Aaron, Elijah, Ezekiel and Isaiah, asking what we can learn from their misconceptions and their insights into God's nature. Perhaps, through them, we may again catch a glimpse of glory.

Silence or Hymn *Worship the Lord in the beauty of holiness*
Give to our God immortal praise

Prayer Almighty God,
>   we will never grasp the whole truth about you,
>   nor even a fraction of it,
>   but what we do see, when we take time to look,
>   is enough still to fill us with awe and wonder.
> You are the Lord of all,
>   the creator of the ends of the earth,
>   the giver and sustainer of life.
> You are all good,
>   all loving,
>   all merciful,
>   involved in every moment of every day.
> Forgive us that we sometimes take that for granted,

our hearts no longer thrilling as they once did
   to the majesty of your presence.
Forgive us for growing so accustomed to you
   that we become casual, almost blasé,
   losing our sense of reverence
   as we come to worship you.
Open our eyes afresh to your greatness,
   your power,
   your sovereignty over all.
Give us again a glimpse of your glory,
   through Jesus Christ our Lord.
Amen.

Comment   Of all the mistakes it is possible to make, few are censured more frequently in the Old Testament than the worship of idols. Throughout its pages a succession of leaders and prophets pour scorn on anybody foolish enough to pay homage to an inanimate object fashioned by human hands, and, reading their scathing condemnations, it is tempting to imagine we could never make a similar mistake, the very idea laughable. Yet such self-righteousness is ill-advised, for though we would never consciously consider worshipping a man-made idol, there are insidious ways in which we do just that. The idols of our time are not carved in wood or moulded in metal, but they are no less real – money, success, power, sex, these are just a few of the modern-day 'gods' which hold sway today. And though we may not realise it, *we* may figure more prominently among their devotees than we care to admit. All too easily we shape our understanding of God to fit with what we want to believe. The result may seem more comfortable to live with, but in the final analysis it offers nothing, for, quite simply, we are left with no God at all.

Reading   Exodus 24:12-13, 18; 32:1-8, 19-20, 35

Meditation 18   *What on earth was I thinking of?* – Aaron

Comment   The story of Elijah's encounter with God on the slopes of Mount Horeb is one of the best-known and best-loved passages of the Old Testament. It has inspired countless sermons, innumerable prayers, not to mention the celebrated hymn, 'Dear Lord and Father of mankind, forgive our foolish ways.' But what is it all about, and what, in particular, is the significance of the 'still small voice' in contrast to the earthquake, wind and fire? There are probably several answers to those questions, but surely one of them must be that this experience of Elijah reminds us how easy it is to underestimate the sovereignty of God when life is not going according to plan. The prophet had lost his sense of vision and purpose, faith itself starting to reel. But there on the mountain-top all that was to change as God made himself known in a way which was to reveal a new side to his nature and offer new insights into his glory. Do we too need to think again about what the glory of God means for us today?

Reading   1 Kings 19:9-13

Meditation 35   *Was it worth carrying on? – Elijah*

Silence or Hymn   *Be still and know that I am God*
Lord, you sometimes speak in wonders

Comment   The more established we become in our faith, the more fixed our picture of God tends to become. It's not that we consciously let this happen; rather it's the old story of settling into a rut as the years go by. And the deeper we sink, so the harder we find it to escape, assuming indeed we even want to. Ideas which challenge our comfortable complacency are swiftly brushed aside, and before long a self-perpetuating cycle is established. Yet just occasionally something happens which throws everything, including our understanding of God, into the melting-pot. So it was for the prophet Ezekiel, faced suddenly with the painful prospect of exile into Babylon. Separated from his homeland, and with Jerusalem and the temple all too clearly heading for destruction, here was a crisis not just for him personally but for all his fellow-citizens taken into exile with him. How could God allow it to happen? How could faith come to terms with such a catastrophe? The experience was deeply disturbing, but the divine encounter which resulted from it was to change Ezekiel's life for ever. God, he realised, was far greater than he had ever dared imagine; more wonderful than the mind can begin to fathom!

Reading   Ezekiel 1:1, 4-5a, 13, 15, 16b, 22, 26, 28

Meditation 72   *I thought I was an expert* – Ezekiel

Comment   If there is one passage of Scripture which sums up the wonder and glory of God, it is, perhaps, Isaiah 55:6-11. Why it so special? Simply because, on the one hand, it makes the difference between God and humankind crystal clear yet, on the other, it stresses the astonishing fact that God has time for each and every one of us. We are confronted here by a God who is wholly other; more powerful, more awesome than our minds can ever begin to imagine. Any attempt to equate his thoughts or his ways with ours are doomed to failure, for the two are poles apart, as separate as the heavens are higher than the earth – yet this is the God we are called to seek while he may be found, in the confidence that he is ready to have mercy and abundantly pardon. Wholly different we may be, but God is always looking to break down the barriers which keep us apart and establish a meaningful relationship with us. These, then, are verses which call us to a humble acknowledgement of our flawed knowledge of God, yet which speak simultaneously of the wonderful adventure of faith in which we are all invited to share; an adventure which this side of eternity can never end.

Reading   Isaiah 55:6-11

Meditation 74   *I thought I knew him better than most* – Isaiah

Prayer   Sovereign God,
              no one has ever beheld the fullness of your glory,

for it is beyond human comprehension to take in.
Yet we thank you that, through Christ,
    you have made yourself known,
    revealing in him the full extent of your love,
    the wonder of your purpose,
    the awesomeness of your grace
    and the beauty of your truth.
Dwell in us now, through the Spirit of Christ,
    so that we may grow closer to him
    and closer to you.
Teach us to recognise your glory
    not just here but everywhere,
    not just today but every day,
    our hearts overwhelmed by your splendour
    and our souls giving you the glory,
    now and for evermore.
Amen.

Silence or Hymn *Holy, holy, holy, Lord God almighty*
                     Day is dying in the west

Blessing

14
THE DISTURBING CALL

Introduction What would we give to have the faith of Moses or Samuel, Elijah or Isaiah? How much easier it would be to serve God then. How much clearer our path would be. Have you ever felt like that? If so, think again, for when we read the biblical accounts of God calling people to service, almost always the initial response is the same: not delight but dismay, not pleasure but panic, not thanksgiving but fear. Look closer, and it's hardly surprising, for, as we shall see later, the things God called people to do were onerous to say the least, nine times out of ten guaranteeing a less than enthusiastic reception. Few if any of those called considered themselves suited for the job, and most would have ducked it given the chance. Yet God was to equip each one to meet the task set before them. We too may find ourselves facing challenges we believe beyond us, God's call proving a disturbing experience rather than the joyride we might have hoped for. But, if we are ready to respond, then we, like those before us, will discover that when God asks us to do something he gives us the resources we need to finish the job.

Silence or Hymn *We are called to be God's people*
The Church of Christ in every age

Prayer Sovereign God,
  you spoke and the universe was created,
  the heavens and the earth,
  the night and day,
  the sea and dry land,
  life in all its bewildering variety and beauty.
You spoke again,
  and your people heard your voice –
  Abraham, Isaac, Jacob,
  Moses, Joshua, Elijah,
  kings, priests, judges, prophets –

an ever-growing succession of those
who listened to your word
and responded to your call.
You spoke in Christ,
   your call coming once more –
   to shepherds,
   wise men,
   women,
   disciples,
   prostitutes,
   tax collectors,
   outcasts,
   sinners –
   your word bringing light and hope,
   joy and life.
You speak still –
   to us,
   to all –
   offering your mercy, wholeness and renewal,
   but calling also to loving service and bold witness.
Help us, like those before us, to respond in faith,
   ready to follow where you may lead,
   and work for the growth of your kingdom;
   to the glory of your name.
Amen.

Comment   What are you most scared of? Spiders? Snakes? The dark? Possibly even all of these? Most of us have at least one secret phobia about something. But according to those who claim to know, there is one thing probably all of us are scared of still more, and that, quite simply, is the unknown. Familiarity may breed contempt, but it also brings a sense of security; the thought of venturing out into uncharted waters is a daunting challenge which most of us prefer to avoid. It can be traumatic enough moving to a new house or starting a new job – any change more radical than that can be bewildering indeed. Yet this was the challenge faced by Abram, later to be called Abraham. Comfortably settled in the town of Haran, he suddenly felt a call to move on. The destination was unclear, as were any details as to what he might find when he got there. This was to be a step into the unknown, a journey of faith. No wonder that Abraham has been held up as a paradigm of faith ever since.

Reading Genesis 12:1-5a

Meditation 5 *Hang on a minute, I said* – Abram

Comment Anyone who has ever been hill-walking will know the experience of thinking you are nearing the summit, only to find, when you get closer, that there is another stretch to climb . . . and another . . . and another! However far we progress, there is always that little bit further to go. So it proved, in a rather different sense, for Joshua and the people of Israel following the death of Moses. After years of wandering in the wilderness they had finally arrived at the border of the promised land, their long journey at last over. Or was it? A closer inspection revealed that this new land pledged to them had already been claimed by others. The task of making it their own had only just begun. No wonder that Joshua, the newly chosen leader of Israel, felt overwhelmed by the sudden responsibility thrust upon him. His was the onerous challenge of rallying a people reeling from disappointment and inspiring them to new levels of enthusiasm and endeavour. Alone, he couldn't have done it; but, as he was to learn, he wasn't alone, for God was to honour his promise to be with him wherever he went. He goes on making that promise to us today – to anyone and everyone willing to serve him.

Reading Joshua 1:1-9

Meditation 20 *Be strong, he said* – Joshua

Silence or Hymn *The God of Abraham praise*
Just as I am

Comment For some reason, the call of Samuel has been a

favourite story for use in Sunday schools and among children in general. That is strange, for it is actually a pretty sobering tale. What attracts people, perhaps, is the innocent confusion of Samuel when he hears God's call, and his automatic assumption that it must be Eli rather than God speaking. We can all relate to uncertainty as to whether we are hearing God's voice or someone else's. The problem here, though, is that we tend to stop reading this story half-way through. Read on, and we discover what God had to say to Samuel and, through him, to Eli: a stern pronouncement of rebuke and judgement. Would we have liked to deliver that message? Probably not. And neither did Samuel, the truth finally having to be cajoled out of him. It's not easy to hear what we'd rather not hear, still less to share it with others. Have we the faith to do it?

Reading   1 Samuel 3:4-18

Meditation 27   *Three times he called me* – Samuel

Comment   Wouldn't it be wonderful if God spoke to us in a clear and unmistakable way? Have you ever thought that? It's hard not to, isn't it, and yet how would we feel if it actually happened? Would God's call be as welcome as we like to think? The experience of Jeremiah, like that of Moses, Samuel, and so many others before him, suggests it might be anything but. There was no doubting the call when it came, but, in a way reminiscent of Moses long before him, Jeremiah did his level best to resist what God was asking. 'I'm too young,' he retorted, 'too raw, too inexperienced.' No doubt he had a point, yet, reading between the lines, it is clear that the soon-to-be-prophet did not relish the task put to him. It was an ambivalence which was to remain with him through-out his ministry. And in that formative encounter is a powerful reminder once again that the call of God isn't always the easy thing we might imagine. On the contrary, it can demand of us more than we feel able to give, bringing joy, undoubtedly, but potentially sorrow in equal measure. All we can say with assurance is that whatever God asks us to do, he will give us the strength to complete, not finally through any special qualities on our part, although he may well use these, but through his sheer grace which, in the celebrated words of the Apostle Paul, 'is able to accomplish abundantly far more than all we can ask or imagine'.

Reading   Jeremiah 1:4-10; 20:7-9

Meditation 70   *It was the last thing I expected* – Jeremiah

Prayer   Gracious God,
     we thank you
     that you have spoken throughout history,
     calling people to your service.
 And we thank you for those
     who have had the courage to respond,
     even when that call has involved unpopularity,
     ridicule, and persecution.
 We thank you
     that they were ordinary everyday people,
     just like us,
     hesitant,
     fearful,
     uncertain of their ability
     to do what you asked of them.
 And, above all, we thank you that, time and again,
     you gave them the strength they needed
     when they needed it.
 Gracious God, you call us still today
     to challenging areas of service –
     to jobs we would rather not do,
     to issues we would rather not face,
     to messages we would rather not deliver.
 Yet once again you promise that you will give us
     the necessary resources to meet the task.
 Give us, then, the courage *we* need to hear your voice
     and respond to your call,
     through Jesus Christ our Lord.
 Amen.

Silence or Hymn *Jesus Christ is waiting*
Lord, as we rise to leave this shell of worship

Blessing

15
First things first

Introduction How many of us would build a house without first laying the foundations, or change a plug without first switching off the power, or get behind the wheel of a car without first learning to drive? In each case the very idea is unthinkable; there is a correct order to do things which we ignore at our peril. But how about when it comes to God – do we get our priorities right there? 'You shall love the Lord your God with all your heart, and with all your soul, and with all your strength, and with all your mind; and your neighbour as yourself.' These, according to Jesus, are the two greatest commandments, the concerns which should come first in our lives: love God, love one another. Is that true of us? Are these the things to which we give first importance? Or does self, for all our talk, still take centre stage – *our* hopes, *our* success, *our* pleasure, *our* comfort all that really matters to us? 'Do not worry,' said Jesus, 'saying, "What will we eat?" or "What will we drink?" or "What will we wear?" For it is the Gentiles who strive for all these things; and indeed your heavenly Father knows that you need all these things. But strive first for the kingdom of God and his righteousness, and all these things will be given to you as well.' Words which remind us of the upside-down values of the kingdom and the true secret of happiness. Are we ready to put first things first?

Silence or Hymn *Be thou my vision, O Lord of my heart*
Give to me, Lord, a thankful heart

Prayer Gracious God,
   we thank you for this opportunity to worship you,
   these few moments set aside to listen,
   to reflect,
   to respond.
Forgive us that we find all too few such moments,

allowing our time with you to be crowded out
by other demands on our time.
There is always something else that needs doing –
another letter to write,
another meal to prepare,
another job to finish,
another meeting to attend –
and so it goes on,
one thing after another calling for our attention
and forcing you to the back of the queue.
Gracious God, there *is* much that needs to be done,
but help us to understand
there is nothing as important
as spending time in your presence,
for without your strength, your peace
and your renewing touch
we lose our perspective on everything,
depriving ourselves of the resources we most need.
Help us, then, not simply to find *some* place for you,
but to give you *pride of place*,
for only then will we experience
the fullness of life you so long to give us,
through Jesus Christ our Lord.
Amen.

Comment   From hero one minute to villain the next – that, in a nutshell, is the story of Saul. Anointed by God as the first king of Israel, his reign began full of promise only to end in humiliation and disgrace. So what went wrong? What was it that led to such a spectacular fall from favour? The biblical explanation leaves as many questions as answers: Saul's crime apparently being that he plundered the spoils of battle rather than destroy them as commanded. Thus far, no problem, but the suggestion that the wholesale slaughter of innocent men, women and children was not only accepted by God but ordered by him is hard if not impossible to accept. This, though, is to miss the point. The actions of Saul typified the sort of person he had become, a man motivated entirely by greed and self-interest, putting God's glory second to his own. He had lost his sense of priorities, failing to understand what must come first in life. It was a weakness that was to prove his undoing.

Reading 1 Samuel 24:1-10, 16-20

Meditation 31 *He could have killed me, had he wanted to* – Saul

Comment There's an old story about a tree and a reed suddenly hit by a storm. The tree, tall and stately, defiantly believes nothing can shake it, but the reed, well aware of its limitations, allows itself to sway wherever the wind wishes. Apparent strength turns out to be weakness as the roots of the tree are torn from the soil and it falls crashing to the ground. By contrast, the reed slowly picks itself up after the storm passes, bruised perhaps, but not broken. The moral of the story is clear: it is better to give a little rather than risk losing everything. Yet what does that mean in practice? How far should we be willing to bend, and when does compromise go beyond what is acceptable? Surely there comes a point when convictions can be so diluted as to become meaningless? The story of Hezekiah illustrates the quandary well. Faced by the all-conquering Assyrian army drawing ever closer, he took what looks like the perfectly natural political decision of entering into an alliance with neighbouring Egypt, the other super-power of his time. The result, however, was not only to risk concessions to Egyptian faith and culture, but also to bring the wrath of Assyria crashing down on his head. Where could he turn next? Should he deepen his links with Egypt, never mind the consequences? Should he sue for peace with the Assyrians, despite the compromises this would inevitably entail? Or would he dare to take the risk of faith, putting his trust in God and staying true to him, come what may?

Reading 2 Kings 18:1, 3, 5-7, 13, 17a, 28-32a; 19:15-19

Meditation 38 *What grounds did I have for confidence?* – Hezekiah

Comment Reading the Bible today is something we take for granted, all too literally. We have all kinds of translations to choose from, and a host of material designed to help us better understand whatever passage we are reading. Most of us will have at least one Bible in our homes and in all probability several more. Yet how often do we make time to read them? In all too many households they are left to gather dust, serving more as a talisman than good news for all. If that is true for us, we do well to consider the reaction of Josiah when, early in his reign, the book of the Law was unexpectedly discovered in the temple, where it had been stored away and forgotten for many years. A regrettable oversight, some might have called it, but not Josiah. For him it was a calamity which needed addressing immediately, for in his eyes this neglect of God's word was tantamount to throwing one of his most precious gifts back in his face. What should have been given pride of place had been relegated to the background. Are we guilty of doing the same today? A Bible sitting on the shelf helps no one; it's reading it that counts!

Reading 2 Chronicles 34:14-21

Meditation 39 *Do you know what we found today? –* Josiah

Silence or Hymn *Take my life, and let it be*
Take this moment, sign and space

Comment We live today, so we are told, in an age of rampant materialism; an era in which everyone is always grasping after the newest gadget, the latest fashion, the most up-to-date model. It is difficult to argue with such an assessment of modern society, but is the phenomenon as new as we sometimes tend to make out? The book of Haggai suggests not. As we read through its pages, we could well be reading a socio-economic analysis of Britain today, such are the similarities in tone. The technology and resources at our disposal may be far greater than those in Haggai's time, but the underlying cravings are no different. Greed, materialism, call it what you will, is an age-old and probably universal characteristic, yet the irony is that it rarely seems to bring happiness, all too often indeed the reverse. Creature comforts have their place, as Haggai would probably have been the first to accept, but if we put these before our spiritual needs, the result is a never-ending striving for an inner fulfilment which will for ever remain tantalisingly out of reach.

Reading   Haggai 1:1-9

Meditation 75   *I could hardly believe what I was seeing* – Haggai

Prayer   Sovereign God,
     you could have washed your hands of us,
     abandoned us to our fate,
     left us to struggle on in all our weakness,
     folly and failure.
But you didn't.
You spoke time and again
     through teachers, preachers, prophets,
     offering your word of life,
     and you spoke again,
     most powerfully, most wonderfully,
     through your Son, Jesus Christ.
You put words into action,
     love into practice,
     living and dying among us,
     bearing our sins,
     enduring our sorrow,
     dying our death so that we, in you, might live.
Sovereign God,
     you could so easily have put us second.
But you didn't –
     you put us first.
Teach us to put *you* first too.
Amen.

Silence or Hymn   *Seek ye first the kingdom of God*
Christ of the upward way

Blessing

16
GRAPPLING WITH GOD

Introduction There is a brief passage in Paul's letter to the Philippians which tells us, 'work out your own salvation with fear and trembling; for it is God who is at work in you, enabling you both to will and to work his good pleasure' (Philippians 2:12b-13). Exactly what these words mean is open to debate, but within them there is the suggestion at least of a formative encounter with God; an ongoing process – even, you might say, a struggle – through which his blessing is finally secured. We have to work out our *own* salvation; nobody else can do it for us. Why? Because we all experience God in different ways and come to faith through pathways that are uniquely ours. For some that involves a life-changing conversion, for others an almost imperceptible coming to commitment; for some it means painful sacrifice, for others unrivalled blessing; but, whoever we are, the journey will bring its fair share of ups and downs. True faith doesn't always come easily, still less cheaply. But, then again, the best things in life rarely do.

Silence or Hymn *Who would true valour see?*
Our God, our help in ages past

Prayer Almighty God,
  we come to you today
  not because we have to,
  but because we want to.
We want to know you better,
  receive your guidance,
  respond to your will.
We want to glimpse your glory,
  understand your greatness,
  witness your majesty.
We want to secure your blessing,
  taste your goodness,
  rejoice in your love.

We want to obtain your mercy,
   accept your grace,
   and experience your renewing power.
So we come,
   hungry,
   thirsty,
   longing to be filled,
   resolved to take hold
   of the new life you have promised.
Respond to us, we pray,
   and, as we have come to you,
   so come to us,
   through Jesus Christ our Lord.
Amen.

Comment   A physical wrestling match with God – it's a strange idea, isn't it? Very different from the more traditional picture of humble and obedient acceptance. Yet that is what we find in surely one of the most dramatic if enigmatic incidents recorded anywhere in the Bible. The imagery is crude, if not to say shocking – a mysterious stranger who accosts Jacob by the ford at Jabbok turning out to be none other than God himself. More puzzling still, so tenaciously does Jacob cling hold during the ensuing test of strength that God is unable to extricate himself without first granting a blessing. It all gets, as Alice might have said, 'curiouser and curiouser'. Yet it is the very primitiveness of this encounter which makes it so compelling. There is no false piety here, no alabaster saint far removed from our human condition. Here is an individual coming, warts and all, before God and struggling to come to terms with the complex realities of life and faith. Who knows quite what Jacob wrestled with in the darkness of that night? Doubt, fear, pride, guilt – you name it and it was probably there! Symbolic the whole story may be – its power remains undiminished, giving hope and encouragement to all those who grapple with God in turn.

Reading   Genesis 32:9-12, 22-31

Meditation 10   *There was no way I deserved it* – Jacob

Comment   We move now to the Psalms, and to one of the best-known and best-loved of them all: Psalm 139. Its verses resonate with a sense of awe as David strives to give expression to his experience of God; an experience which quite clearly had been constantly evolving over many years, culminating in this spontaneous outpouring of praise. It is hard to imagine any testimony which could more eloquently sum up the wonder of God, yet, according to David, his words are woefully inadequate, the realities they attempt to describe ultimately beyond understanding, too wonderful for words! Do we feel a similar sense of awe before God? We may have done once, but familiarity can make us complacent, the flames which fired our faith losing something of their intensity as the years pass. David calls us to meet again with the living God whose love surrounds us, whose goodness sustains us, whose mercy astounds us and whose greatness is beyond all expression.

Reading   Psalm 139:1-18

Meditation 51   *It's no good, Lord* – David

Silence or Hymn   *O God of Bethel, by whose hand*
In heavenly love abiding

Comment   There is much in the story of Hannah which is difficult to accept. That she was one of two wives is hard enough; that God could be responsible for her being childless is harder still; and that a child was finally given to her only on condition she dedicated him to service in the temple seems positively abhorrent. The gulf between past and present, both in culture and faith, is massive. Yet in one sense there is no gulf at all, for human nature, it seems, doesn't change. The insecurity of Hannah, the spitefulness of Peninnah, and the vain attempts of Elkanah to keep the peace have all the ingredients of a modern-day soap opera. As in so many human relationships, when you look beneath the surface there is a complex world of intrigue and misunderstanding – a world in which what we say and do bears little resemblance to what we actually feel and think. From the biblical account of events it would seem that Hannah felt no pangs whatsoever at giving up her son shortly after his birth; her mood on the contrary seems to be one of total exultation. Yet were there no regrets at all? It is pure speculation to suggest it but it is impossible not to wonder if, at some point later in life, there were a few tears shed as the full realisation of what she had sacrificed hit home.

Reading   1 Samuel 1:1-11

Meditation 26   *Did I ever regret that vow? – Hannah*

Comment   There is something hugely refreshing about the honesty with which the prophet Habakkuk tackles the enigmas of life. No pious acceptance here that all that happens must somehow be God's will. No tortuous attempt to find a spiritual explanation for everything. For Habakkuk the world presents deep puzzles, puzzles for which he seeks some answers. Those who find his questions disturbing may prefer to gloss over them, turning instead to the less controversial passages which follow, but to do that is to bury one's head in the sand. Avoiding the issues helps no one, for the challenge does not go away. Simplistic answers are equally unhelpful, in the long run doing more harm than good. We need to admit the limitations of our understanding, for God prefers an honest cry of confusion to a faith which deals with life's riddles by sweeping them under the carpet.

Reading   Habakkuk 1:2-4

Meditation 69   *What's going on? – Habakkuk*

Reading   Habakkuk 3:17-19

Prayer   Eternal God,
         there are times when we find life a puzzle,

your purpose a mystery,
    our experiences seeming to contradict our beliefs.
We try and make sense of it all, but without success,
    the answer always seeming to elude us.
Teach us at such moments to trust in you,
    recognising that what the world counts as folly
    is often true wisdom.
Help us to live with riddles
    and accept apparent paradox,
    confident that in the fullness of time
    all will be made plain.
In the name of Christ we ask it.
Amen.

Silence or Hymn   *Lord, for the years your love has kept and guided*
God moves in a mysterious way

Blessing

17

BREAKING DOWN THE BARRIERS

Introduction Recent decades have seen some remarkable transformations in international affairs: the end of apartheid, the conclusion of the Cold War, the dismantling of the Berlin Wall and an attempt at least to establish peace in Northern Ireland. Momentous events, welcomed with scenes of unprecedented joy. So has our world finally discovered the secret of unity? Are our divisions at last at an end? If only that were true. Sadly, though the structures have changed, the underlying reality is no different; mistrust, intolerance, prejudice, bigotry are as deeply rooted in the human psyche today as they have ever been. We need look no further than the tragic events of Bosnia and Kosovo for proof of that fact; an ugly reminder that the barriers which divide us are still all too real. Can they be broken? Unsurprisingly, many would say not. Yet at the heart of our faith is the conviction that God is able to overcome all the differences that keep us apart. One day, we believe, there will be harmony between the nations, peace on earth. We may not see it in our lifetime, but that does not excuse us from doing all in our power to bring that day a little closer.

Silence or Hymn *Yesu, Yesu, fill us with your love*
Let there be peace on earth and let it begin with me

Prayer Lord Jesus Christ,
you were broken on the cross,
you are broken still today.
Wherever there is division, hatred and pain,
you are there, sharing in the suffering,
your body broken again.
You died to make us one,
to break down the dividing wall of hostility,
to reconcile all things to yourself,
yet still so many are estranged

from you and one another.
Forgive us, we pray.
In your love, have mercy
  on our foolish, faithless world.
  and, by your grace, tend our wounds.
Come again to all who are bleeding and hurting.
Come,
  as the King of kings,
  the Lord of lords,
  the Prince of peace,
  and through your Spirit make us whole,
  for your name's sake.
Amen.

Comment   There have been many atrocities committed against humanity over the centuries, none more so than the Jewish holocaust in Nazi Germany. The appalling suffering inflicted at places like Auschwitz and Belsen leaves us sickened, forcing a constant reappraisal of life and faith, for how can we ever begin to reconcile such unadulterated evil with a God of love? There are no easy answers, only the humbling knowledge that many Jews continue today, despite all they have been through, to believe passionately in the enduring purpose of God for their nation. Faith somehow lives with mystery, even contradiction, refusing to be snuffed out. Some may like to imagine that the holocaust was a one-off aberration, a never to be repeated act of lunacy. History warns otherwise – its pages littered with xenophobia, ethnic cleansing and mass genocide. None of us can afford to forget the terrible consequences to which prejudice can lead; prejudice which lurks deep in every one of us. Of all people, the Jewish nation understands what the awful human cost can be.

Reading   Exodus 1:8-16

Meditation 14   *They hated us* – A Hebrew slave

Comment   'Forgive and forget.' It's a lovely thought, isn't it? What would we give to be able to let go of the past, wipe the slate clean and start again? But instead we allow our lives to be poisoned by the gradual build-up of petty grievances and festering resentments. To forgive is hard enough, to forget can seem well-nigh impossible. Yet as long as we allow past mistakes to come between us there can be no prospect of true and lasting unity. In the story of Joseph we see someone who had every reason to nurse a grudge, yet a man who had the grace and courage to offer another chance to those who had wronged him. Have we the same courage to be peacemakers today?

Reading   Genesis 42:6-9, 15-16a, 21, 23-24a; 45:1-3, 14-15

Meditation 13   *It couldn't be, I told myself* – Joseph

Silence or Hymn   *O Lord, all the world belongs to you*
Father of glory, whose heavenly plan

Comment   We would all, given the chance, wish to enjoy harmony in our relationships, not least with our immediate family and friends, but sadly life isn't always like that. It is all too common to see families divided among themselves, husbands no longer speaking to wives, children having fallen out with their parents; brothers, sisters, cousins, nephews, aunts and uncles disowning the other and refusing to have any further dealings with them. As if that is not sad enough, invariably the cause of such bad feeling proves to be something trivial, blown up out of all proportion over the years because of an unwillingness to meet and resolve the issue. Unchecked, the poison is allowed to fester, feeding on itself rather than the original incident and destroying the lives of all concerned. Whether it was a dispute such as this or something more complex that lies behind Psalm 133 we do not know. But the reminder this simple Psalm gives of the importance of living together in harmony is one we would all do well to consider, whether at the level of our immediate family or the family of the Church. The relationships we are intended to enjoy here are special; can we afford to waste them?

Reading   Psalm 133

Meditation 50   *It was over at last* – Psalmist

Comment   How would we feel if a politician or world leader were to promise a new and better world in which people everywhere will live in harmony; hatred, warfare and oppression a thing of the past; justice and freedom accorded to all? Would we believe it? Most likely not. We'd like to think it were true, of course we would, but most of us would probably take such claims with a strong pinch of salt. Life, we tell ourselves, is just not like that. Realism rather than the idealism invariably wins the day. Such an attitude is understandable given the lamentable record of human history and the continuing divisions in our world today, yet it cannot finally be acceptable. *We* may abandon the world to its fate – *God* never will. He refuses to rest until that day when his will shall be done and his kingdom has come, on earth as it is in heaven. It may seem light years away from the world as we know it today, but we must never lose that vision of what life can become, nor stop working towards it.

Reading   Isaiah 11:1-9

Meditation 65   *Does this sound daft to you?* – Isaiah

Prayer   Lord of all,
    we speak of peace,
    harmony between the nations,
    an end to discord and division,
    and we long for that day to come,
    but we know, deep down, that *we* need to change
    as much as anyone else,
    before it can ever begin to happen.
We look inside
    and we see so much that separates us
    from those around us –
    pride,
    fear,

envy,
suspicion,
an unwillingness to accept new ideas,
a refusal to countenance we could be wrong.
Forgive us our share in the brokenness of this world,
our contribution to its wounds,
its scars,
its continuing pain.
Open our hearts to others through being open to you,
and so may we pursue all that makes for peace
until that day when you come in Christ
to establish your kingdom
and make all things new.
In his name we pray.
Amen.

Silence or Hymn   *There's a light upon the mountains*
Bind us together, Lord

Blessing

18

DECISIONS, DECISIONS

Introduction Decisions are never easy, are they? We want to be bold, to grasp the nettle, but the issues involved invariably turn out to be more complicated than we first imagined. 'What if this were to happen?' we ask ourselves. 'What if that . . . ?' And so it goes on – the more we think about it, the more bogged down with uncertainty we become. Afraid of making the wrong decision, we end up making no decision at all. Perhaps at times we can get away with that, but not always – some decisions just won't go away, and potentially they can determine the rest of our lives. So how do we choose? Is it merely a question of asking God for guidance and then doing his will? It may be that simple on the odd occasion, but life is rarely quite so straightforward. God has given us intelligence and free will, and he expects us to use them both. Certainly he will help point us in the right direction, but the ultimate responsibility for our decisions rests with us, and us alone.

Silence or Hymn *To him we come*
Jesus calls us here to meet him

Prayer Sovereign God,
    we thank you for all those over the centuries
    who have had the courage
    to take difficult decisions.
We think of the call of Abram,
    to venture into the unknown,
    of Moses, to confront the tyranny of Pharaoh,
    of David, to take on the might of Goliath,
    of the prophets,
    to declare your word despite hostility,
    of the disciples, to leave all and follow Jesus,
    of Saul, to turn from persecutor
    to ambassador of the Church.
We thank you for the determination

and the courage these showed,
their willingness to trust in you,
coupled with their readiness to step out in faith,
despite no guarantees of what the future might
   hold.
Speak to us through their example
and through your word,
so that when decisions must be made
we will be ready to make them,
equipped to choose the right path
through Jesus Christ our Lord,
Amen.

Comment   There are times when decisions can be avoided and there are times when they can't. On some occasions we can put them off to another day, on others we must deal with them on the spot. In our first story today, the story of Rahab, we see very much the latter. One moment life is much as it always was, the next there comes a knock at the door and she is confronted by Hebrew spies seeking shelter. What is she to do? If she takes them in she is guilty of treachery against her own people, putting *their* future as well as her *own* at risk. But if she turns them away she is rejecting not only them but their God, a God who, she recognises, is greater than any she has encountered before. It is an unenviable dilemma to be in – a 'Catch-22' situation if ever there was one – and we can only begin to imagine the inner turmoil it must have caused her. There are some who might dismiss the decision she took as nothing more than cynical self-preservation, but ask yourself this: what would you have done in her place? Given the God she was dealing with, was there any other choice she could make?

Reading   Joshua 2:1-14

Meditation 21   *You know what they'd have called me* – Rahab

Comment   Few things are more difficult than living by faith. The idea sounds wonderful, but when it comes to the moment of decision most of us prefer certainties to promise. And if that's true in our human relationships, it's equally so in our dealings with God. Which of us at some time or other hasn't asked for a sign; some clear, unmistakable indication that we have understood his will correctly and taken the right path? Such an attitude is perfectly natural – but it is not faith. It betrays, ultimately, a lack of assurance in God's sovereign purpose – a purpose which, for our own well-being, we must learn to take on trust.

Reading Judges 6:36-40

Meditation 23 *I wasn't sure even then! –* Gideon

Silence or Hymn *When we walk with the Lord*
How firm a foundation, O saints of the Lord

Comment Some years ago a national newspaper ran an advertising campaign based on the slogan 'one million readers can't be wrong'. The implication, of course, was that if enough people subscribe to something it must be right. You might imagine the end result of this campaign would have been to quash such a naïve assumption once and for all, but sadly not. It is part of human nature to want to follow the crowd. Those who dare to question the established norms of our society are branded fanatics, eccentrics, or even revolutionaries, the challenge they bring conveniently side-stepped through the use of such dismissive labels. Questions may, of course, be misplaced, but equally they may be necessary. Time and again in the Scriptures, authentic faith involved taking a critical look at the values which the world takes for granted. So it was for Samuel, sent by God to the house of Jesse to anoint a new ruler over Israel. What he experienced there was to turn his understanding of life on its head, teaching him as words never could that God's ways are not our ways, nor his thoughts our thoughts.

Reading 1 Samuel 16:1, 4a, 5b-13

Meditation 28 *Was it a fool's errand? –* Samuel

Comment   Decisions are never easy, for there is invariably more to any issue than first meets the eye. Take, for example, the celebrated judgement of Solomon concerning two women each claiming to be the mother of a single child. The simple but effective way in which Solomon reached straight to the heart of the matter has gone down in history as an example of his legendary wisdom. Thus far, at least, the decision was relatively straightforward. But what then? The true mother rejoiced in having her son restored to her, but what of the other woman, the impostor who had attempted to pass the child off as her own? Her actions were undeniably wrong, causing untold distress, but when we consider the trauma she had gone through herself it helps us to understand why she acted as she did, even if we can't condone it. So what was to become of her? Should she have been punished for her actions or allowed to walk away scot free? Did she need correction or help? What would we have done in Solomon's shoes? Decisions are never easy.

Reading   1 Kings 3:16-22, 24-28

Meditation 34   *Did she imagine I'd go through with it? – Solomon*

Prayer   Living God,
     you do not compel us to serve you;
     rather, you invite us to respond to your love.
And so it is in all of life.
You do not impose your will upon us,
     dictating the course we should take.
Instead, you offer your guidance,
     giving us signposts to walk by,
     but ultimately leaving the decisions
     we must make in our hands.
We thank you for this wonderful expression of trust,
     this freedom to choose and discover for ourselves,
     and we ask that you will help us to use it wisely,
     trusting you, in return,
     and seeking, so far as we understand it,
     to honour your will.
Give us wisdom and courage

> to make the right decisions,
> at the right time
> and in the right place,
> to the glory of your name.
> Amen.

Silence or Hymn *Will you come and follow me?*
I have decided to follow Jesus

Blessing

19
THE COURAGE OF OUR CONVICTIONS

Introduction We live today in a world full of extravagant claims. On every side we are bombarded by advertisements telling us that a particular product is the biggest, the best, the most reliable you could possibly find, streets ahead of all other competitors. So how do we find out the truth? The only way, of course, is to test such claims for ourselves; to see if the performance matches the hype. It's much the same when it comes to people. Most of us profess certain values and standards as being important in our lives, but what finally counts is not what we say but what we do. And if that's true of everyone, it's true most of all for the Christian, simply because of the nature of the claims we make. We do not maintain we are perfect or even good, but we *do* talk about loving one another, showing mercy, refusing to judge, turning the other cheek, going the extra mile and, above all, following Jesus. It's a lot to live up to, and there is a world out there waiting eagerly for us to trip up. Like it or not, the Christian faith will be measured by how far we live up to the gospel. Are we all talk, or do we have the ability to put our money where our mouth is and demonstrate the sincerity of our words through the transparency of our actions? Have we the courage of our convictions?

Silence or Hymn *Stand up, stand up for Jesus!*
O loving Lord, you are for ever seeking

Prayer Gracious God,
    we praise you for your great love towards us,
    for the mercy,
    the blessings
    and the goodness you show us each day.
You do not simply say you love us,
    you prove it through all you are and all you do.
We claim to love you in return,
    but all too often our actions belie our words.

We speak of serving you but serve ourselves.
We talk of showing mercy but are swift to judge.
We extol humility yet exhibit pride.
We call for truth yet indulge in falsehood.
In so many ways we fail to practise what we preach,
    letting ourselves down as well as you.
Renew us, we pray,
    draw us closer to you,
    and put a right spirit within us.
Teach us not just to accept the gospel with our minds
    but to embrace it in our hearts,
    so that through word and deed
    we may bring glory to you,
    through Jesus Christ our Lord.
Amen.

Comment   Temptation comes in many shapes and forms. For some it is sex, for others money; for some drugs, for others power. All of us have our Achilles' heel – a vulnerable spot where temptation unerringly strikes – and though we may resist for a time it is hard not to succumb faced by temptation's repeated assaults. The same must have been true for Joseph, faced by the flirtatious advances of Potiphar's wife – he would have been less than human had he felt no stirring within him. Yet however attracted he may have been, he did not succumb, because he believed to do so would be to compromise everything he believed. Sold into slavery he may have been, rejected by his own brothers, and faced with an uncertain future in a foreign land; it didn't matter – the principles which underpinned his life and the faith which sustained these still held good. For Joseph, the all important factor was not what *he* desired but what *God* required. And here, for us all, is the key to facing temptation and holding fast to our convictions.

Reading   Genesis 39:6b-20

Meditation 12   *Was I tempted? You bet I was!* – Joseph

Comment   For the unsuspecting reader, the book of Esther may

382 THE UNFOLDING STORY

come as something of a surprise. Why? Because throughout the story mention of God is conspicuous by its absence. On one level we are dealing here with a classic tale of good triumphing over evil – the stuff of legends and fairy stories. Yet to this day Esther is revered within Judaism, not simply as a model of courage but above all as an example of faith. Hers was an example of selfless devotion, freely putting the safety of others before her own, never mind the consequences. We should not be deceived by the absence of religious terminology from the narrative. Esther, as much as any other in the Old Testament, was called to grapple with God. It is the very fact that she saw this not as some great act of piety but as simple expression of solidarity with her people which accounts for the respect accorded to her. Faith and life went hand in hand, each indissolubly linked, the one a natural outworking of the other. Can the same be said of us?

Reading Esther 3:8-10; 4:1, 5, 9-16

Meditation 40 *Could I honestly make a difference? – Esther*

Hymn *One more step along the world I go!*
O happy band of pilgrims

Comment The story of Shadrach, Meshach and Abednego is one of the great biblical classics, an unforgettable tale of integrity and courage which has captured the hearts of countless generations. But, as with all classics, there is a danger that familiarity may inure us to the underlying message. We can read the story knowing the final outcome of events – for Shadrach, Meshach and Abednego there was no such luxury. They staked all in the faith that God would deliver them. They risked death itself rather than compromise their convictions. They had no doubt God could save them if he wished; whether he would choose to do so was another matter.

Reading Daniel 3:1, 3-6, 8-9, 12-14, 16-18

Meditation 58   *Did we know God would save us?* – Shadrach, Meshach and Abednego

Comment   If the story of Shadrach, Meshach and Abednego is a classic, that of Daniel in the lions' den is even more so, surely one of the best known in the whole of the Old Testament. It is a tale which has been told and retold across the centuries, delighting countless generations; another classic example of good conquering evil, a victory against all the odds. But, of course, it needed the faith and courage of Daniel for that triumph to happen, his willingness to make a stand for the things he believed in. Today, thankfully, times are very different; there is little chance of us being fed to the lions, not literally anyway! But we need people of Daniel's stature as much as ever; people ready to risk all in the cause of truth, ready to hold on to their principles despite every attempt to undermine them. Have we even a fraction of that courage and commitment?

Reading   Daniel 6:6-11

Meditation 60   *I knew it was a trap, the moment they anounced it* – Daniel

Prayer   Lord Jesus Christ,
   you faced temptation in the wilderness,
   enticement to put yourself first,
   to seek worldly glory,
   to compromise your calling,
   and steadfastly you refused.
You faced pressure throughout your ministry,
   hostility,
   ridicule,
   threats,
   rejection,
   yet you carried on regardless,
   true to your message,
   true to your mission.
You faced the greatest test of all in Gethsemane,
   as you wrestled there with the prospect
   of betrayal, denial, suffering and death,

but once again you held firm,
    putting God's will before your own.
What you said and what you did were always one,
    each testifying to the other.
Lord Jesus Christ,
    we fall so short of that goal,
    words coming easily,
    deeds to match rarely coming at all.
Forgive us,
    and help us to show in our lives
    the things we proclaim with our lips,
    for your name's sake.
Amen.

Silence or Hymn   *O thou who camest from above*
                      Fight the good fight

Blessing

20
DARING TO HOPE

Introduction Hope, we are told, springs eternal. But does it? Certainly it may show amazing resilience in its ability to bounce back after disappointment, but is there a point of no return, a certain threshold after which hope is finally extinguished? Certainly most of us, as life goes by, become a little less idealistic, a little more cynical. We don't lose hope altogether – God forbid! – but our capacity to dream dreams takes a slow but steady hammering. We make the best of such disillusionment, dressing it up through fine-sounding words like 'experience' and 'realism', but deep within we know a spark has gone out which we yearn to recapture. Is such a downward spiral inevitable? In purely human terms, probably yes, for, despite all its beauty, the world can undeniably shatter our illusions. But to say that is to reckon without God. Time and again he has brought new beginnings out of what seemed hopeless – joy out of sorrow, light out of darkness, life out of death. And he has promised that he will go on doing that until the end of time. In the unforgettable words of Paul to the Romans, 'I am convinced that neither death, nor life, nor angels, nor rulers, nor things present, nor things to come, nor powers, nor height, nor depth, nor anything else in all creation, will be able to separate us from the love of God in Christ Jesus our Lord' (Romans 8:38-39). With a promise like that to hold on to, can we do anything else but hope?

Silence or Hymn *Come and see the shining hope*
All my hope on God is founded

Prayer Lord,
    it is hard sometimes
    not to lose faith in your purpose.
When hopes are dashed,

when dreams are shattered,
when one disappointment piles up on another,
it's difficult not to lose heart completely,
not to retreat into a shell of despair.
We want to believe we can change,
but there seems little evidence to support it.
We want to believe the world can be different,
but experience appears to prove otherwise.
Our hearts tell us one thing,
our heads say another,
and it is the latter that finally win the day.
Yet you have promised
that nothing in heaven or on earth
shall finally overcome your purpose,
and throughout history
you have shown that to be true,
constantly overturning human expectations,
hope rising like a phoenix from the ashes.
Speak to us now through the faith and vision
of those who have gone before us,
so that, however dark the world may seem,
we too may dare to hope in turn,
through Jesus Christ our Lord.
Amen.

Comment   How would we feel if a politician or world leader
were to promise a new and better world in which
hatred, warfare and oppression will be a thing of the
past, and justice and freedom be accorded to all?
Would we believe it? Most likely not. We'd like to
think it possible, of course we would, but most of us
would probably take such claims with a strong pinch
of salt. Life, we tell ourselves, in just not like that.
Realism rather than the idealism invariably wins the
day. Such an attitude is understandable given the
lamentable record of human history and the continuing divisions in our world today, yet it cannot
finally be acceptable. *We* may abandon the world to
its fate – *God* never will. He refuses to rest until that
day when his will shall be done and his kingdom has
come, on earth as it is in heaven. It may seem light
years away from the world as we know it today, but

we must never lose that vision of what life can become, nor stop working towards it.

Reading Isaiah 11:1-9

Meditation 65 *Does this sound daft to you? –* Isaiah

Comment Perhaps one of the greatest dangers we can face in the Christian life is cynicism. We start off on the road of discipleship full of enthusiasm, believing life has really changed and that from then on it will be different, but as the years pass, and time and again we find the old self rearing its ugly head, so we begin to wonder if the transformation effected by Christ is as real as we thought. No matter how hard we try, we cannot seem to rid ourselves of our basic human failings, despite God's promise to make us new. Such frustrations would probably have sounded a chord with the prophet Jeremiah, called as he was to preach repentance and subsequent renewal to the people of Judah. How many shrugged their shoulders indifferently when they heard his message? It sounded good, but experience had taught them that they would go on making the same mistakes in the future just as they had in the past. Jeremiah believed different, looking forward to the day when God would establish a new covenant with his people, transforming them from within. That covenant, of course, has been made through the death and resurrection of Christ, but, though that work of renewal has begun, its fulfilment awaits that day when he shall return in glory to draw all things to himself. We should never lose sight of that promise; of what he has done and what he has yet to do.

Reading Jeremiah 31:31-34

Meditation 71 *You're wasting your time, they tell me –* Jeremiah

Silence or Hymn *Behold the mountain of the Lord*
God of freedom, God of justice

Comment   The words of Joel 2:26-32 must be some of the most often quoted in the whole of Scripture. Yet how many of us have ever actually read this little book tucked away towards the end of the Old Testament? Probably very few, and that's a pity, for the context in which these verses are set makes both the promise within them and its ultimate fulfilment all the more wonderful. Joel spoke to a nation which was both physically and spiritually emaciated. A plague of locusts had brought widespread devastation and consequent famine, yet for the prophet this was just a symbol of a much deeper emptiness – a barrenness of soul. The people of Judah had turned their backs on God, no longer believing he had any relevance to their daily lives, no longer expecting him to speak or act in human history. Think again, said Joel. God is able to fill not only body but spirit, meeting our innermost needs and touching every part of our lives. For us today the fulfilment of those words is seen in the coming of the Holy Spirit at Pentecost, the gift of power from on high. That Spirit is at work in the lives of all, recognised or unrecognised. Are we ready to open our lives and let God shape and fill us as he will?

Reading   Joel 2:12-14, 26-32

Meditation 79   *It had been a hard time by anyone's standards* – Joel

Comment   To have our hopes raised only to see them dashed again is a cruel experience. The result can be to plunge us into a deeper sense of despair than anything we faced previously. So it was for the people of Israel after they returned to Judah following their time of exile in Babylon. An initial mood of jubilation soon gave way to an overwhelming sense of anticlimax, as the Utopia which people had expected failed to materialise. It wasn't just hope which took a battering in consequence; for many it was their faith. Where was the glorious new kingdom God had promised his people? Today the kingdom *we* expect may be different, but the question can seem equally valid. We look forward to the day when God's purpose will be fulfilled, when his will shall be done and his kingdom come on earth. But when will that be? Do we have the courage to keep on hoping, even when everything around us seems to undermine belief?

Reading   Zechariah 14:1, 6-9

Meditation 76   *Was it worth continuing? – Zechariah*

Prayer   Lord Jesus Christ,
    you were cut down from a cross,
    laid in a tomb,
    your body dead and buried,
    and it looked as though everything you stood for
    had been buried with you.
Life, which had overflowed with joy,
    was drowned in sorrow.
The future, which had sparkled with promise,
    was suddenly empty of meaning.
The past, which had offered so much,
    now offered so little.
Yet, all at once, you were there again,
    laughter after tears,
    hope after despair,
    triumph after tragedy;
    the world once again bathed in sunshine,
    dreams coming alive once more!
Death could not hold you,
    good could not be destroyed,
    love had the final word.
Lord Jesus Christ,
    teach us to live this and every day
    in the light of that victory,
    daring to hope, come what may,
    trusting in your eternal purpose,
    for your name's sake.
Amen.

Silence or Hymn   *'I have a dream,' a man once said*
God is working his purpose out

Blessing

INDEXES

Index of Bible Passages

References are to meditation rather than page numbers

Index of Principal Characters

References are to meditation rather than page numbers

Index of Principal Themes

References are to meditation rather than page numbers